Metamorphyx

Embracing Life Experience,
Life Change, and Life Purpose

Thomas M. Schuler

ISBN 978-1-64458-450-7 (paperback)
ISBN 978-1-64458-452-1 (hardcover)
ISBN 978-1-64458-451-4 (digital)

Christian Faith Publishing, Inc.
832 Park Avenue
Meadville, PA 16335
www.christianfaithpublishing.com

Cover Design inspired by Bryan Schuler

Printed in the United States of America

Endorsements

Schuler writes like the aggressive, sometimes ornery collegiate All-American wrestler he was at the Naval Academy. His focus and commitment to make a difference in everything he does in life will engage you. And how Tom finds solace in life can help all of us find new purpose in ours. You will discover *Metamorphyx* to be the ultimate "life coach" directory.

—*Tom Jones, USNA teammate and former*
President of MDL Information Systems, Inc.

Tom's wisdom and life experience overflows with vulnerability and humility. Tom has wrestled through "hard" to find the heart of God—and in turn allowed God to use the "hard" to shape his heart and life. Tom and I have built an enduring friendship on the foundation of our common experience, the loss of a child. Tom shares his story of life change with a refreshing rawness. *Metamorphyx* invites you to join that sometimes painful journey with the Author of our faith. This book will give you a glimpse of glory you won't soon forget—and it propels you toward a deeper pursuit of divine purpose and intentional legacy.

—*Suzanne Phillips, Cofounder,*
Legacy Community Academy

Tom's faith journey has truly been an inspiration for me over the past forty years. *Metamorphyx* is that story. Guided by biblical principles, the book captures the struggles and joys of discovering one's life's purpose in a way you have never experienced. Written with clarity, directness, and humor, *Metamorphyx* is deeply thought-provoking and spiritually challenging. A must-read for anyone navigating the challenges of life with the intent to live a life that honors God and family.

—*Dick Ducoté, Cofounder SDF International, Inc., and Founder of Ultra Performance... A challenge worth taking*™

Even before the end of *Metamorphyx*, I had already changed my perception on some difficult challenges in my life. God wants to teach us something in life, so he forces us out of our comfort zone. This is the way we learn! I've known Tom for over twenty years. He's been my coach, supporter, counselor, and sometimes just a listener. But always with a rich perspective to learn from personal choices and circumstances and with intention to chart a new path forward. The Bible became Tom's "safety belt" in life, but as you will see, that's not where he started.

—*Rejean Fontaine, former Director of Technology Transfer, Johnson & Johnson, Inc.*

Courageous, meaningful, and gripping! Tom has given us a visceral narrative of personal experience and biblical wisdom. *Metamorphyx* will capture you, as it did me, on the common ground of one's personal struggles and pivot points in life. Breathe in the ties to meaningful and insightful scripture. They've enlightened me and will give you hope on your faith journey.

—*Joel Sharratt, Head Wrestling Coach, US Naval Academy*

I've given my life to planting churches and training pastors. These young men often seek my counsel to align their gifts with their calling and life purpose. These vital life-on-life discussions demand a thoughtful biblical framework. *Metamorphyx* provides exactly that—and much more—but not just for pastors in training! The book is highly thought provoking, challenging, and compelling for everyone. You will find Tom's life experiences gripping as they give way to meaningful life change that only God could produce. Put this book in your curriculum of life; it will find a home in ours.

—*Kent C. Shaw, Executive Director, BRAVE Global*

I met Tom in the wrestling room at the US Naval Academy in 1969. We've been close friends ever since. At that time, he was a tenacious ask-no-quarter, give-no-quarter athlete with an attitude, living out a championship lifestyle. Very short on patience, he did not suffer fools or their trivial ways lightly. But as I've journeyed with him in life, I've watched Tom "morph." He's become a life learner and a quintessential mentor. *Metamorphyx* is replete with life lessons that will have an impact on all who read it... including this old combat-hardened US Marine.

—*John F. Sattler, Lieutenant General,*
USMC (Ret.), USNA 1971

For the past twenty-six years, I have had a front-row seat watching God's love, truth, and grace unfold and move in the lives of the Schuler family. Tom writes with authentic passion and raw transparency. He brilliantly uses his brokenness-to-redemption life story to pave the way of hope, healing, and life purpose for any reader who is willing to surrender their life to God. Tom's life story illustrates that God wastes nothing in life but weaves everything together for His glory and our good.

—*Debbie McGoldrick, friend and Founder of*
Neighborhood Bible Study 2 GO, a ministry of CRU

I've known Tom and his family for decades. We've both faced life-altering adversities on this journey called life. Tom and his family faced—and ultimately in faith—prevailed over some of life's monumental challenges. Tom's still-growing relationship with God humbles and inspires me. Don't miss the opportunity to share the *Metamorphyx* journey with him. It's an emotional roller coaster ride where crushing setbacks, great challenges, and even greater victories will test your own faith and resolve. You won't be disappointed.

—*Cathy Tolk,*
Author of the Wisdom Left Behind

We have been blessed by Tom's friendship, wisdom, and investment in our lives. With rare authenticity, Tom shares his fascinating life story in an encouraging and eye-opening way. His experiences drew him to faith in God and directs the reader to the "Caller whose passion is to steer you into meaningful life purpose." This relevant, compelling book will bless all who read it!

—*William A. Rodgers Jr.,*
President and CEO, Four 12 Solutions
—*Evelyn G. Rodgers,*
Board of Trustees, Georgia Center for Opportunity

Tom has written about what he's lived. For over two decades, I've watched my friend grow, change, and flourish from the inside out as only God's Spirit could produce. Take *Metamorphyx* with you on your personal life journey. It will serve you well through trials, tragedies, and pivot points in life where a new road must be taken.

—*Jay Street, former pastor and Founder, Great Oak Enterprises*

To the loving memory of Vanessa Elaine Schuler
(August 31, 1986–June 16, 1992)

"Jesus said to her, 'I am the resurrection and the life. He who believes in me will live, even though he dies: and whoever lives and believes in me will never die. Do you believe this?'" (John 11:25–26).

Contents

Acknowledgments

The inspiration to write *Metamorphyx* came directly from God and his Word. "My Presence will go with you, and I will give you rest" (Exod. 33:14). I have called on God's promise every step of the writing journey.

I'm deeply indebted to my wife, Jan, for her amazing grace and favor. Every word in *Metamorphyx* passed under her eyes... and some brought tears, anguish, and recollections of painfully difficult chapters of life. The encouragement, too, of my wonderful children, Greg, Erica, Bryan, their spouses and their remarkable sister, Caroline, has put bounce in my step.

Mary Beth Bishop is a freelance editor. Without her book writing wisdom, *Metamorphyx* would have meandered into a ditch. Thanks for telling me what I needed to know much more than what I wanted to hear. What a gift!

A boatload of thanks goes out to faithful friends who signed up to be my informal editing team. Their encouragement was instrumental in finishing the work. These fantastically helpful men and women include Dick Ducote (my former business partner) and the likes of Bill and Evelyn Rodgers, Suzanne Phillips, Mark and Susan Spina, Jay Street, and Cathy Tolk—who each invested their valuable time in my writing endeavor.

Debbie and Mark McGoldrick will always have a special legacy in my family. Thank you for showing up on my doorstep twenty-six years ago. Jan and I have walked the trials and joys of life with you.

Kent Shaw, you continue to be a great source of biblical wisdom and encouragement. Thanks for Psalm 92; it has served me well.

Rejean Fontaine is my French-Canadian friend. We're two hard-headed guys who together have engaged in the battle of life. Thanks for your loyal friendship and encouragement.

Gary Franklin is my life coach and a model of unconditional acceptance. What's important to me has always been important to you. Thanks, Gary, for helping me survive myself.

In honoring his memory, I'm also thankful for my indomitable USNA wrestling coach, Ed Peery. Coach, you've left important markers in my life; I'll see you at heaven's gates. Today, I'm thankful that another man of faith carries that torch, USNA wrestling coach Joel Sharratt. Beat Army!

Enduring friendships at this stage of life give greater meaning to life. Some go back more than a half century... and all have factored into my story. They include my lifelong Babylon friends Ken Torrey, John Hemendinger, and Jimmy Van Bourgondien as well as my USNA wrestling colleagues Tom Jones, Andy Tolk, and Lt. Gen. John Sattler, USMC (Ret.)

And finally, I thank God for my parents. Not everything on the home front has been easy, but it's all been ordained by God in his wisdom and sovereignty. I love you, Mom and Dad.

In grace, thanksgiving, and humility,

Tom

Foreword

There are people who make an enduring impression upon our lives. Whether it be their life experience, their sense of humor, their wisdom, their simplicity, or even their peculiarity, they mark our lives in a never-to-be-forgotten way. Tom is one of those people in my life. Tom is one of the most intentional people I've ever met. He brings a passionate and relentless desire for learning to every dimension and detail of his life.

We became friends almost twenty years ago. Over these two decades, a special friendship emerged. We've talked, taught, and traveled together. We've experienced life-shaping learning experiences together. We've walked through painful seasons in each of our lives together. And in the process, we've shared our lives as honestly as we know how. We're better men because of our friendship. The Old Testament author Solomon wrote, "As iron sharpens iron, so a friend sharpens a friend" (Prov. 27:17). That's been the story of our friendship. Friendships like ours are gifts from God and for that reason are enduring.

The most enriching dimension of our friendship, however, is to have witnessed, through Tom's story, the beauty, the mystery, and the purpose that emerges when an intentional pursuit of God intersects with God's intentional design for our lives. That's been my privilege as one of Tom's friends.

That's the story you'll read in the pages of *Metamorphyx*. Tom will share defining life experiences that have shaped him in God's image and toward God's design. And he will do so with compelling honesty, his unique sense of humor, and a humility that invites us to see with more clarity God's intentional design, not only in his story but in ours as well.

> God calls and leads us into various stages of life throughout our journeys. Some of those align with our passions and giftings; others don't. But our God is not a God of chaos—there's Divine intentionality and order in our journeys of life if we're listening to his call and building up skills and knowledge on the pathways of life. (*Metamorphyx*)

When Tom told me a couple of years ago he intended to write *Metamorphyx*, I remember driving away thinking, *Well, of course!*

As you read these pages, I trust you will experience the exhilarating intersection of your intentional pursuit of God... with his intentional design for your life.

Gary Franklin
A friend of Tom's for life

Introduction

The *Metamorphyx* Journey

Do not conform any longer to the pattern of this
world, but be transformed by the renewing of your
mind. Then you will be able to test and approve what
God's will is–his good, pleasing and perfect will.

—Romans 12:2

Every Parent's Nightmare

It was Sunday, December 9, 2007, a cold and dreary winter day. I didn't know the couple I was about to meet, but I knew their desperation. Just the day before, Mark and Susan had tragically lost their eleven-year-old daughter to a rare brain hemorrhage. Before she passed away, news of Gabrielle's critical condition had spread quickly through the crowd at a wedding celebration. Although the family was relatively new to the North Atlanta suburbs, many guests skipped the reception to visit Mark and Susan and offer their prayers and encouragement.

"They were ICU angels," Mark recalls. "They just kept coming, three by three, despite the strict visitation guidelines."

As I headed up their front walkway, my heart pounded, and my breathing quickened. I tried to clear my throat as my mind flashed back to a strangely similar encounter many years earlier. On that day,

Debbie McGoldrick had made her way up the steps to my home with her two young children. Debbie introduced herself and said to Jan, my wife, "I know you recently lost your daughter, Vanessa. We live in the neighborhood and just wanted to stop by and see if we can help with anything."

Not long after that, another neighbor stopped by. "I don't know what to do or say," said George, extending his hand, "so I brought you some bagels."

With me that December afternoon was Executive Pastor Monty Watson. We served together at Fellowship Bible Church. Earlier that day, Monty, Senior Pastor Crawford Loritts, and I had talked through this tragic episode in the life of our church. As I prepared to leave for my visit, Crawford pulled me aside.

"I'm glad you're going to see Mark and Susan," he said. "They will trust your advice and spiritual counsel. Your own experience with loss will help them immeasurably."

My daughter Vanessa had died of injuries sustained in a frightful car crash just a few weeks short of her sixth birthday. Jan and I were heading home with our children after a joy-packed day at Disney World. Mickey's gang and Vanessa's favorite princess, Snow White, were fresh in our minds when a routine lane change on Florida's Interstate 75 went catastrophically awry and hurled us into every parent's unspoken nightmare. Emergency vehicle sirens filled the air that stifling summer afternoon as Vanessa was rushed to Gainesville's Children's Hospital. Four days later, with Jan and me at her bedside, she took her last breath. Just a few weeks earlier, Vanessa had danced as a winged angel in a recital; now she joined heaven's ranks. Disney World and a child's death—who would have ever connected those thoughts?

After Gabrielle's death, Mark and Susan struggled to survive as a couple. Fifteen years earlier, it had been no different for Jan and me. Today our families are bonded not only by the tragedies we hold in common but also in our resolve to survive the kind of life-shattering event that often dissolves marriages. *Nothing* in life prepares a parent for the death of their child. It hammers a sharp and sudden spike into the heart. But today, in a new chapter of life, Mark and Susan's nine-year-old adopted daughter, Isabelle, lights up their home. And in ours, Vanessa's death opened pathways we'd never imagined.

Such is the *Metamorphyx* journey. It's the story of life, but more so, it's the story of overcoming the seemingly preposterous notion that our relationship with God sometimes pivots on his willingness to wound us deeply because he loves us so intensely.

Metamorphyx—Its Origin and Message

"Consider the lowly [caterpillar] worm," says Charles Spurgeon, the phenomenally popular nineteenth century preacher, "for it is only the *beginning* of the matter."[1] Living in a dark and unsightly cocoon for a season, a butterfly defies death and bursts forth in radiant beauty, freedom, and new life purpose. In stark contrast to her beginning, she now gloriously reflects the end of the matter. Life is all about beginnings and endings… and embracing the realities of life experience, life change, and, ultimately, discovering fulfillment and freedom in life purpose.

In early 2010, I grabbed some time with my former ministry partner and friend Jay Street. "I need help finding a name and an Internet domain for a new ministry I'm launching," I told him. "I'd like it to be rooted in the mystery and power of the word *metamorphosis* but firmly anchored to what Romans 12:2 says about life change, "Do not conform any longer to the patterns of this world, but be transformed by the renewing of your mind."

"Here's an idea," said Jay as we hammered out some thoughts in a local coffee shop. "What about Metamor*phyx*? I think it captures your vision, passion, and ideals, and since the word doesn't really exist, you retain the power of definition." His fingers flew across the keyboard on his laptop. "It also looks like the Internet domain is available," he said.

"Grab it!" I told Jay, and there on the spot we locked down the Web domain. In short order, I copyrighted the name, developed

---

1 Reimann, *Morning by Morning*, Day 365 (italics added).

a logo, and planned the launch of *Metamorphyx*. I envisioned my new venture as a "house for ministry" with the tagline *Embracing the Dynamics of Change*. Under the umbrella of *Metamorphyx*, I'd write a blog, support church-planting initiatives, take on life-coaching roles, and help ministry organizations develop their visions and strategies. *Metamorphyx* prospered from its launch, benefitting from a rich array of personal, leadership, business, and ministry experiences that had shaped me over the decades.

"Yeah, I know a thing or two about beginnings and endings," I told my ministry friend Bob over a sushi lunch a few years later. "Life experience, life change, and life purpose are signature interests of mine. Life experience is always the beginning, and it's often uninvited in our lives. Life change is our response to life experience, but many fight it. Life change, however, is never the end of the matter. It only points to the end. The ending is life purpose, which is what gives meaning and outward expression to life experience and life change. That's a key message of *Metamorphyx*."

"I like it," said Bob as he absorbed the message I dangled in front of him. "Have you ever thought about developing those ideas into a blog or a book?"

"I have," I said as I traded my useless chopsticks for a fork. "Metamorphyx the ministry has, in fact, morphed into *Metamorphyx* the book. I'm fleshing it out as we speak. It's all about how life experience, life change, and life purpose penetrated the life of a pugnacious kid from Long Island who found his way into Annapolis, the US Marine Corps, the desperation of divorce, the death of a young daughter, and a ministry calling in Africa, just to name a few pivot points. The book tells the story of how all those dots in life connect. It's about my fight to distance myself from my past and discover meaningful life purpose. There's a lot in *Metamorphyx* that will surprise you, Bob. I'm afraid that some of the things you'll read about my journey through life will shock your pastoral sensitivity, but it's all truth and real life."

You will discover that the name *Metamorphyx* has a deep connection to beginnings and endings in my own life. Thirty years ago—well before a single page of *Metamorphyx* had been written, Jan and I chose Vanessa's name from a book that linked her name to a butterfly. Our choice proved delightfully predictive. Vanessa fluttered around the house like the *Vanessa atalanta* butterfly would dance in the lavender that filled our garden. Vanessa in her short life was a stunningly radiant child, a fair-skinned pixie with a flowing mane of golden hair that was always in her face. Much about our daughter's features stood in stark contrast to Jan's Lebanese heritage and complexion. The *Vanessa atalanta* now inspires the cover of *Metamorphyx*. Who knew then how her short life would forever imprint ours?

The message of *Metamorphyx* centers on one of life's most perplexing questions: "How does one embrace life experience and life change and fulfill life purpose with all the confounding mysteries, tragedies, and challenges that make up the journey? That baffling question opens the door to many others. What does it mean to *embrace* life experience? Why must we experience life change at all? Is it necessary? What exactly *is* life purpose anyway, and who defines it? Do we each have a unique life purpose or calling? If so, how do we discover what it is? When does life purpose kick in? Is it a mysterious, predestined focus that only blooms in a single stage of life? Does it require any spiritual awareness? We will wrestle with all these questions in the chapters that follow. But first, it's helpful to look at snapshots of life change and redeeming life purpose.

Historically, we could look to John Newton; he wrote the ever-popular song "Amazing Grace." Newton in his time was a slave ship captain, harboring all the shame of that despicable profession. Nearly perishing at sea in 1748, he called out to God for deliverance. His rescue was his life-change reveille call… and his legacy was changed in a radical way. In embracing his life purpose, Newton became a passionate abolitionist and worked alongside William Wilberforce to abolish Britain's slave trade.

In a biblical context, there's the apostle Paul, who spent the early part of his life "breathing out murderous threats to the Lord's disciples" (Acts 9:1). Known first as Saul, the Jewish leader and Pharisee was a feared hunter and persecutor of first-century Christians. Jesus got his attention with a well-targeted lightning bolt on Paul's ill-intentioned sortie to Damascus to find and arrest new Christians. Saul thereafter was renamed Paul and took on the mantle of an apostle with divine authority to preach God's Word to nonbelieving Gentiles. On his life-purpose journey, Paul wrote one-third of the New Testament.

In my adopted hometown of Atlanta, the Reverend Martin Luther King Jr. looms large as an American icon of life purpose. MLK's perseverance and unyielding grip on nonviolent societal change forever altered the landscape of racial relations in America. In the process, he brought life change into the hearts and minds of millions of Americans. King forfeited his life in pursuit of his calling and life purpose.

But make no mistake. *Metamorphyx* is not about life change or life purpose as it relates to others. It's about you and me. The goal is a homegrown, deeply personal life change at the core of our very souls, nothing less than God's retooling of our life scripts. I'll confess that some of the bone-jarring events described in *Metamorphyx* were triggered by my own hand. But others were not my doing; they came about instead by the sovereign hand of God, who uses Isaiah's "furnace of affliction" (Isa. 48:10) for life change and compels us to answer the perplexing question I posed to you earlier. It's hard-hitting theology, the idea that God loves his children so fervently that he's willing to hurt us in powerful ways, but it's integral to the journey outlined in this book.

Life experience reconfigures the landscape of life like the pounding waves of an approaching hurricane. My adolescence was troublesome and conflicted, heavily seasoned with violence, fear, and intimidation in the inner circles of my family, community, and church. My fierce independence proved to be an asset in the Naval Academy and US Marine Corps, but it wreaked havoc in my business and personal relationships well into my adulthood, sunk my first marriage, and fractured my young family. An overly harsh and legalistic interpretation of theology fenced me out of any notion or understanding of God's grace for decades. A new marriage granted me a second chance, but everything new I learned—and everything old I unlearned—was tested in the white-hot anguish of Vanessa's death. Thirty months later, Caroline Grace was born, but our miracle child immediately faced daunting odds of survival. Why did God appoint these things in my life and what did he expect from me (and Jan)? Apparently, quite a lot!

He wanted life experience to give way to life change. He wanted me to release the tightly coiled spring of adolescent anger, to subdue the need for approval and acceptance that permeated my adult relationships, to abandon my old notions of a bruising theology, and to redirect my energy from athletics into people. He wanted me to discover his grace and strength in a way that would allow me to survive Vanessa's death. His plans called for me to cling to my newfound faith amid Caroline's uncertain future, to trust him as the Divine Author of my circumstances, and to surrender my will to his purposes for my life. That's what you'll see unfold in my own *Metamorphyx* journey. Beyond that, the world was my oyster.

Learning to Be a Life Learner

A life learner is a person who uses life experience and trials as teaching tools. If your life-learning aspirations are lukewarm, I fear you've chosen the wrong book. The *Metamorphyx* journey will take you into the storms of life experience and pummel you with life-change decisions. Says Oswald Chambers in his devotional classic *My Utmost for His Highest*, "It is a dangerous thing to refuse to continue learning and knowing more. If you don't cut the lines that tie you to the dock, God will use a storm to sever them and send you out to sea. Put everything in your life on the great swelling tide of His purpose, and your eyes [and mind] will be opened."[2]

Life learners aspiring to flourish in life purpose are acutely aware that they must *process* life experience, discern life-change implications, and chart a course where they can proudly but humbly declare to God in the wisdom of reflection, "It was good for me to be afflicted so that I may learn your decrees" (Ps. 119:71).

---

2 Chambers, *My Utmost for His Highest*, June 8.

Initially, I did not make that high-minded declaration when rogue waves threatened my very existence and my ship of life was sinking. In fact, it was quite the opposite. But I learned that affliction and trials can generate a *learned* response that can guide every step of one's future pathway and heighten spiritual vigilance in every stage of life. I've also witnessed the opposite truth, as you will discover in the narrative ahead. Unbridled success, an imbued pugnaciousness, and an unhealthy dose of self-reliance contribute nothing to life change and meaningful life purpose.

Regardless of your current pathway, *Metamorphyx* will nudge you to open your eyes and mind to new possibilities. This book may help you work toward those goals, but ultimately only the Spirit of God can lead you to any true breakthrough. If your circumstances have hardened you and made you bitter or if you can't find meaning or redeeming purpose in life's storms, then I enthusiastically encourage you to read on. Who knows? The words on these pages may lead you to a pivot point in life, a new encounter with God, and a life purpose narrative you never imagined possible.

A final life-learning caution: there is no linear equation to embracing life experience and life change and thriving in life purpose, and *Metamorphyx* does not offer one. Life change will always be a highly personalized process and almost never an overnight event. I wish the truth were different.

The Mandate for Life Change

Romans 12:2, with which this chapter opens, has a lot to say about embracing life experience, life change, and life purpose. It was written by the apostle Paul and can be read as a biblical mandate with a built-in promise. Let's confess, there are many complex elements to life change, but the *mandate* for life change isn't one of them. Whether you are a Bible scholar, Bible scanner, or reading the verses for the first time, Romans 12:2 points you to life change and a new future.

"Do not conform any longer to the pattern of this world," is a jarring biblical imperative. It plainly highlights a collision of values in the apostle's day... and in ours. Just glance at the evening news. Gross injustice and conflict abound in the patterns of this world; many oppose God's timeless standards, debase human life, and validate the selfishness embedded in the hearts of men and women.

"But be transformed," says Paul. The words he chooses affirm the progressive nature of life change. Paul isn't speaking of the one-time "come to faith" decision we all need to make. Instead, he is talking about how we live out our faith. That may involve a radical retooling of your heart and soul, as it did for former slave trader John Newton. It's not unlike crawling into a dark cocoon as something bizarrely nasty... and emerging as something beautifully alive with a new identity and purpose.

Life change, Paul says, is accomplished "by the renewing of your mind." Our minds are the control centers for the spiritual and intellectual rebooting of our life-experience software. The mind constantly craves new calibration and updates, without which it turns rigid and biased. Paul then adds a deeply personal promise to the command for a reboot. "Then you will be able to test and approve what God's will is—his good, pleasing, and perfect will."

I believe that with all my heart now, but on the *Metamorphyx* journey, there were episodes of life when I thought Paul's writing (yes, God's Word!) was sheer folly and a mockery of my circumstances. But I learned God's "good, pleasing, and perfect will" leads to new beginnings in life, even when he takes our children home before he does their parents. That's more hard theology, but I assure you, *Metamorphyx* will validate its truth.

Romans 12:2 tells us we can become something we're not, something new we were divinely created to be. The apostle Paul preached this principle to Timothy, his younger ministry pal. He called it training in the "battle of life" (1 Tim. 1:18), and he encouraged Timothy to help others avoid a "shipwreck of their faith" (1 Tim. 1:19) on life's journey.

The apostle Paul was no dummy. He knew the battle of life and a shipwreck of faith were two different things. The battle of life occurs every day within the patterns of the world. If we live on planet Earth, we're in the battle. Shipwrecks of faith, however, are another kettle of fish. They lead to a cynical view of God and a victim mentality. The *Metamorphyx* journey will help equip you for the battle of life and keep you off the shoals of discouragement and cynicism.

The Rearview Mirror of Life

Søren Kierkegaard was a highly respected nineteenth-century Danish theologian and philosopher. He also knew a thing or two about life experience, life change, and life purpose. My first encounter with Kierkegaard came in 1998, and he deeply influenced my thinking. "Life can only be understood backwards; but it must be lived forwards,"[3] he says. I'm no match for Kierkegaard, so I use simpler language; I call his discovery the rearview mirror of life. I use that expression often through the pages of *Metamorphyx*. Here's a first-hand application of the principle.

Not long after Vanessa's passing, my good friend and neighbor Jim Hawks and I decided to take a week off, fly to Alaska, and backpack through Denali National Park. We intended to scale North America's highest peak. Denali rises to 20,310 feet above sea level, no doubt a monumental challenge for two novice hikers. The Alaskan park ranger wasn't impressed; he refused to issue the required hiking permit, citing our lack of common sense.

Not discouraged, we redirected our planning and aspirations to the Continental Divide in the Colorado Rockies. That shaved off about seven thousand feet of challenge. At the base camp, we plotted our ascent.

Day one's trek left us utterly exhausted. Day two was no walk in the park either. Day three, however, was even more brutal. Our novice map-reading skills led us straight up a huge rock field as we approached the continental summit. At times, I even found myself

---

3 Guinness, *The Call*, 53. Note: Guinness paraphrases Kierkegaard's original quote.

crawling up the steep escarpment to prevent tumbling over backward. We pondered admitting defeat but persevered.

The most discouraging dynamic of the climb was perspective. As each rock field was conquered, it gave way to a larger one. But when we finally reached the summit, all discouragement melted into late-afternoon victory. The magnificent vistas to the east and west were breathtaking. We took refreshing breaths of the brisk mountaintop air before contemplating our descent—which we needed to hasten before darkness set in.

And then we saw it. There in plain view from the mountaintop was a well-groomed trail that snaked its way up alongside the vicious rock fields that had taken us all day to conquer. We had completely missed it on the way up. That, my fellow travelers, is the battle of life. A tough ascent up… and then a new perspective after reflection.

From today's rearview mirror of life, some fifty years up the mountain of life experience, my perspective on *everything* that has gone before and shaped my life is vastly different. Rearview-mirror clarity is a source of wisdom and change. Jim and I hiked down the Rockies on a different path than we had chosen on the way up. That's the value of understanding life backward and living it forward. It's also the signature of a life learner aiming to embrace life experience, life change, and fulfilling life purpose along the steep climb of life.

Cheshire Cat Wisdom and the Metamorphyx Journey

Think about this as you plow ahead through *Metamorphyx*: if you have no sense that you're being guided in the battle of life by the Divine Author of the Universe, you are no better off than Alice in Wonderland.

Alice, you may recall, was traveling down the road in Lewis Carroll's iconic novel when she paused to ask directions of the Cheshire Cat. The Cheshire Cat answered with a question of its own. "Where are you going?" asked the cat. Alice didn't know! So Mr. Smart-Aleck Cat shrewdly advised her, "Well, my dear, then any road will get you there!"

Reader friends, don't travel like Alice. Any road will *not* lead you to fulfilling life purpose; there are too many off-ramps to nowhere.

Here's your roadmap to *Metamorphyx*.

Introduction: The Metamorphyx Journey. Carry with you the foundational premise of Romans 12:2. That's God's personal invitation to a life transformation journey. The wider you open the door to personal life change, the wider God will open doors to you for fulfilling life purpose.

Part I: Understanding Life Backward. This section will take you on the trail of life experience with all the pivot points, trials, and challenges that marked my own life purpose journey. Each chapter illuminates a stage of life and ends with a look back that captures critical lessons, insights, and changes.

Part II: Living Life Forward. This section captures vital life purpose principles and wisdom, which can be applied to your personal *Metamorphyx* journey.

Epilogue: House on Fire. Here you will encounter the most important life purpose decision you will ever make.

Your Life Purpose Legacy

As you prepare to embark from the trailhead of the *Metamorphyx* journey, I want to unashamedly poke you with some edgy wisdom from John Piper, a noted theologian, pastor, and writer of more than fifty books. Speaking to life purpose, Piper cautions, "Let none say in the end, 'I've wasted it.'"[4]

What's behind his warning? How boldly and purposefully you live the "dash" in your life—that future etching on your gravestone that will come between your birthday and the date of your death. Your dash is your life legacy. It will be the prevailing theme of your eulogy and characterize you as a life learner, a faith warrior, a lover of people, a lover of God, a man or woman who embraced life change and lived for a high calling… or it will not.

---

4 Piper, *Don't Waste Your Life*, 183.

INTRODUCTION

Have you pondered God's call on your life? Are you at risk of wasting the gift of life? Are you willing to embrace life experience, life change, and a life purpose that honors God? Your personal *Metamorphyx* journey awaits you.

—Tom Schuler

PART I

Understanding
Life Backward

Survival

"For I know the plans I have for you," declares the LORD.
—Jeremiah 29:11

A Priestly Encounter

I guessed from Father Ulrich's cold stare and brusque demeanor that our meeting might not have the redemptive outcome I'd hoped for. Even the simplest courtesy was lacking. Father Ulrich (not his real name) was a rotund man and sported a bushy beard, which made him look even more intimidating and resolute. I sat opposite the Catholic priest in one of two naked chairs facing his box-like oak desk. He made no move to come out from behind the desk and take a chair alongside me. I saw the battle lines forming. Father Ulrich, in his priestly collar, held the spiritual high ground; I was in the valley.

As a young thirty-something, life in South Georgia had short-circuited. My marriage had failed; friendships had dissolved. I was living like a drifter in a ramshackle studio apartment and facing an inopportune job transfer. Looking across his desk and through the lens of time, I pondered how life had gone so far off the rails.

I interrupted the awkward silence and pitched my question. "Father Ulrich," I said, "I've attended a lot of churches in this season of life. No matter where I go, it seems I find myself in the back of the church where no one talks to me. I find no peace in the sermon messages, and I always feel like a leper in the church community. But I don't know where else to go. Yes, I've made some dreadful life decisions, but how do I get back into good standing with the church?"

For too long my question hung in holy space as the eyes of the priest surveyed mine. Then he said, "I know *of* you." (Not a great opening, I thought!) "For *you*, there is no way back. You're going to hell."

To say I was shocked or rattled by the priest's pronouncement would be… well, not at all the case. Why? What Father Ulrich barked at me was completely consistent with the fear-based religious messaging I'd grown up with. But before turning back the clock to the theology of my adolescence, here's the rest of the story and how God's grace later interjected itself into the equation of my life.

Knowing *of* me apparently meant that Father Ulrich had been handed my dossier. In recent months, I had begun dating a high-profile personality while attempting to find a church that would have me. *Everyone* south of Georgia's gnat line—that imaginary geographic anomaly where scads of those annoying critters ruin picnics—knew Jan. She was the nightly news anchor on the local NBC affiliate. Every evening at 6:00 p.m., you could tune in Jan and get the local and national news. I did so regularly. Like me, she was recently divorced. Jan is now my wife of thirty-five years, but back then, we were a troublesome topic in the church circles of the Deep South… and apparently, Father Ulrich wanted nothing to do with us.

The words of Father Ulrich's trumpet blast abruptly ended our conversation. I waited momentarily for a "But…" or "You should do this…" but no help was forthcoming. Just silence. So I stood up (he did not), and I walked out of his office. Exiting through the sanctuary, I glanced at the crucifix towering over the altar and walked past the iconic stations of the cross which commemorate Christ's pathway to his crucifixion. Pausing in pensive reflection for a moment, I then made my way to the parking lot.

There, I took a deep breath and contemplated what had just gone down. In that instant, a message thundered through my mind and stopped me cold. I shuddered as it reached its full crescendo. "You have just heard the wrong answer. Now go find the right one."

In reflection, I have no doubt Jesus tossed me a life ring that day. Quite literally, that's exactly what he did for all of us two thousand years ago. But on this day, I had no context for my rescue; the Jesus I'd grown up with had been no friend to people like me.

Years later, on a Medical Missions Ministry trip to the mountains of Guatemala, I encountered a young woman whose despair mirrored the way I'd felt that day after I left the priest. "In your situation," I told her in my barely passable Spanish, "Jesus is your only hope and rescue." Her body tensed, and she quivered in fear and shame. Raising her eyes, she said to me, "If Jesus knew my life, he would kill me."

"I know that feeling," I told her. Then I asked her if I could read her a Bible verse. She agreed. "It's Romans 5:1," I said. "Justificado, pues, por la fe, tenemos paz para con Dios por medio de nuestro Senor Jesucristo." (Therefore, since we have been justified through faith, we have peace with God through our Lord Jesus Christ.) The pivotal words? *Justified through faith* and *peace with God*—not by what we have done or not done—but *through* what Christ has done.

She motioned for my Spanish Bible, and when she read the passage herself, she broke into sobs. She had been trapped in her human culpability for many years. As I reminiscence on the emotions of that day, I find it difficult to hit another keystroke. God rescued her from guilt and despair that summer day, and life took her in a new direction.

Fear and Uncertainty

From about age ten or eleven until I graduated from Long Island's Babylon High School in 1967, fear and uncertainty dominated my life narrative. That will greatly distress (but may not surprise!) some members of my family and close friends, but it's the raw, gut-wrenching truth. When you live in fear, uncertainty is your bunkmate.

That does *not* mean, however, that there were not joyous family events and delightful episodes with friends, but the overarching theme was fear—fear in my school and community, fear in my church, and, most distressingly, fear in what I called the "home front."

Let's face it—fear is a relative entity. I write today as unparalleled fear and uncertainty reign in Syria. While in Israel in the spring of 2017, I saw the bombed-out shells of homes with my own eyes from the Golan Heights. Few of us have faced that level of paralyzing, life-altering fear... or the fear and uncertainty forced on the young girls taken hostage by the Nigerian thug Boko Haram. I have been spared their level of pain and suffering for no reason I deserve or can explain. That said, as a young lad, I had my own brand of fear and uncertainty that God had uniquely scripted for me in his unwavering sovereignty.

As any child psychologist will confirm, circumstances and events in youth leave indelible imprints; behavioral crystals begin to form in adolescence, and soon one has stalactites in the caves of his or her mind. However, our future lots in life and choices are *never* frozen in time. If they were, personal change would be impossible (and the Bible would be lying to us). There comes a time in life when a young adult takes command of his or her life and makes important decisions: which habits and patterns of life are healthy and should be replicated and which should be rejected. It's a threshold of life we all must cross.

Don't be alarmed by the notion of taking command of one's life in adulthood. In no way does that notion stand crossways with a life surrendered to God's purposes. Simply put, you're taking responsibility for the decisions that you make and rejecting a victim mentality that assigns blame to your troubled background.

Since I spilled the beans earlier about my divorce, I can tell you that my first marriage was done in by dysfunctional habits and patterns which crystallized in early adulthood. But I alone am to blame for that, not anyone else in my topsy-turvy background. Later in life, through God's grace—and Jan's patience—I was able to subdue my marriage-killing attitudes and behaviors. But I had much to learn (and unlearn) on the path of life.

But first, travel with me to Babylon on Long Island, New York.

Babylon on Great South Bay

Originally called Sumpawan, Babylon was purchased from Native Americans in 1670. Considering our nation's history with Native Americans, I suspect the "purchase" might have been made at the muzzle of a musket, but that's another story.

As legend has it, Sumpawan became Babylon in 1802 when a then-famous socialite and staunch Bible advocate likened its rowdy lifestyle to that of the more famous Babylon. The name stuck. Even today, the town draws countless thousands from New York City to its nearby beaches and smartly renovated downtown restaurants.

Fire Island is Babylon's not-so-distant cousin. It's another thirty minutes across Great South Bay, via the Robert Moses Causeway. Still trendy and rowdy, Fire Island boasts of great beaches, bars, fishing, and restaurants, which populate the bay and ocean-side communities. I won't go into detail about my youthful exploits there, but when I was growing up, the legal drinking age in New York was eighteen.

Babylon sits on Great South Bay, which in the late fifties and sixties when I was growing up was a haven for fishing and sailing competitions. It also supported a robust clamming industry, providing high-quality shellfish to the best restaurants in the greater New York region. Early every morning between April and October, dozens of clam boats would head into the bay and "dig" for clams with eleven-foot hinged forks that we called tongs. Clam digging was phenomenally healthy and grueling work for a young Babylonian. For my height-challenged brothers and me, it was even more so; we stood half the height of the towering and weighty tongs.

But our hard work was richly rewarded. We diggers of clams were paid in cash every day at the Babylon Pier. As a teenager in the mid-sixties, I could earn thirty-five to sixty dollars per day when I grew strong enough to work full days. On days when I hit a mother lode of clams, I could haul in eighty to ninety dollars for a day's work. On summer break from the US Naval Academy in 1971, I earned enough cash in ten days to pay for my girlfriend's engagement ring. To this day, I connect my strong work ethic to my days shell fishing on Great South

Bay. If my brothers and I worked hard, we were handsomely paid. If we goofed off, drank beer, and went water skiing for most of the day, we'd make pennies and go home with a bad-day-on-the-bay story.

My family moved to Babylon in 1954. The $9,999 mortgage on the new home was a heavy burden on my dad. His insurance sales were growing, but to glean extra cash, before hopping the Long Island Railroad into Manhattan each day, he would deliver morning newspapers to our neighboring community. On weekends, my younger brother, Bob, and I would help hand deliver the rolled-up *New York Times* or *Herald Tribune* exactly where customers demanded—or we'd get complaints.

I later asked dad what he paid us on those early Saturday and Sunday workdays. Not hesitating a beat, he said, "Why do you ask? Do you think I still owe you guys a few bucks?" There were many things my dad was not, but he took seriously our family's financial wherewithal. It's a high standard that burrowed deeply into my own family values.

Our family grew in our Babylon enclave. My brother, Paul and sister, Kathy joined the litter in the mid-fifties, and then John Peter showed up twenty years after me—proof, I took it, that my quarreling parents didn't fight all the time.

Some of the great blessings to come from Babylon on the bay are the lifelong friendships forged there. To this day, more than fifty years after graduating from high school, four of us Babylon amigos still make time to see each other regularly. Some of us go back to our kindergarten years. Kenny Torrey was our star high school quarterback; Jimmy Van Bourgondien, a top-notch high school basketball player; and John Hemendinger was a first-class... well, I can't fill in that blank! John lives close by in Atlanta and may be the only guy at Babylon High School who spent more time in the high school principal's office than I did. We're all great friends, and for more than five decades, we've weathered life's toughest storms shoulder to shoulder. There are also enough antics, girlfriend pursuits, crashed yacht club parties, reckless boating exploits, police encounters, and Fire Island nonsense to fill a separate book. Annual embellishment, however, has reduced our stories to a shred of their original truth.

The Prophet Jeremiah's Babylon

"'For I know the plans I have for you,' declares the LORD." Here's the rest of that prophetic and highly personal Bible passage: "Plans to prosper you and not to harm you, plans to give you hope and a future" (Jer. 29:11).

I get antsy when people ceremoniously pitch this verse into a conversation without any understanding of its context. It's a verse that requires a deeper dive to fully understand what's going on. Sure, it's true as it stands, but it is often quoted as a single verse and is frequently misapplied when extracted from its larger narrative.

In chapter 29, the prophet Jeremiah is speaking to Jewish exiles in the biblical Babylon, a real, historic place assumed to be what is now Iraq. About 600 BC, King Nebuchadnezzar, Babylon's ruler, brutally besieged the city of Jerusalem. When it fell, he force-marched the surviving Jewish remnant across the Middle Eastern desert to Babylon. Against their will and most likely as slave labor, Nebuchadnezzar planted them in a foreign city in a culture they abhorred.

"For I know the plans I have for you" was no campfire melody sung roasting marshmallows around a desert oasis. It was spoken to a defeated people who were being disciplined by God for losing their way with him, the same God who'd led them out of Egyptian slavery centuries earlier. Over time, the nation of Israel had decided to abandon God's precepts and go their own way. They didn't have much use for the Ten Commandments. God had other ideas.

Jeremiah chapter 29 offers encouragement to the Jewish exiles to flourish in a land they don't know, don't like, and don't want to be in. They were to endure the painful challenges of living in a warring nation that was infamously identified with brutality and apostate practices. *The plans I have for you* would be revealed indeed, but not before seventy years would pass, encompassing the lives of two generations of Israel's refugees.

I can't, of course, equate the culture and norms of ancient Babylon and its exiled Jewish community to my boyhood home. That would be reckless exaggeration. But on a deeply personal level, there are common themes and parallels connecting the two Babylons that profoundly shaped my life story.

Jerusalem's people in 586 BC were carted off to Nebuchadnezzar's kingdom. Jeremiah's own words in chapter 29, verses 1 through 10, tell us why. They were exiled to Babylon for three overriding purposes: to *survive* (not die as an exiled group), to *thrive* (seek peace and prosperity), and to *be delivered* (in fulfillment of the promise they would return to their homeland, where they would once again enjoy their relationship with God on their own turf).

It's in those clearly stated purposes—to *survive, thrive,* and *be delivered*—that I extract my ancient-to-modern-day Babylon parallels. Ultimately, I am a victor, not a victim, of my Babylon experience. That's the story that lies ahead. Modern-day Babylon was the setting for my adolescent battle of life. It would play out in my school and community environments, my church experience, and on the home front.

"'For I know the plans I have for you,' declares the LORD, 'plans to prosper you and not to harm you.'" That was *not* apparent to me as a young adolescent buck. Everything I learned reinforced the idea that to survive, I needed to be cunning, tough, and resourceful when facing uncertainty and conflict. In reflection, I see God's sovereign hand in my life at an early age. I *survived* a very challenging environment, *thrived* in an extraordinarily unique context, which you will read about, and was *delivered* out of Babylon to new chapters of life.

My Babylon: School and Community Testing

For thirty years after I left home, I was ignorant of any link between the place I'd left behind and ancient Babylon. I've since learned a lot. In the book of Revelation, the biblical Babylon is singled out as "the mother of harlots and abominations" (Rev. 17:5). At social gatherings, hometowns are frequently an introductory topic. Among church friends, I wait for the inevitable jokester to weigh in. "You're from Babylon? Well [ha-ha], that explains a lot!"

"*Yes, it does,*" is always my unspoken reply. "*More than you will ever know.*"

I attended Babylon High School (BHS), where about 165 students graduated in 1967, a very turbulent time in our country. The Vietnam War was raging, and the military draft was radically altering the lives of young men across America. My die, however, was cast. I had a ten-year commitment ahead of me: one year in prep school, four at the US Naval Academy, and five more years of military service after graduation.

For reasons I've never understood, BHS had a pervasive "fight" culture. Or maybe it was that as one of the shortest guys in the class, I had the tallest chip on my shoulder. Or both! Before I entered high school, the junior high wrestling coach, Bob Harris, cornered me one day. "Schuler," he said, "I understand you like to fight."

"Not so, Mr. Harris," I said, "but around here that's what it takes to survive."

"How would you like to fight someone your own size—with rules?" he asked.

"Sign me up," I told the coach.

And that's how I got into the game of wrestling. I excelled at wrestling in high school, and it opened many doors for me in future years. Through my dad's promotional work, one of those doors led to Coach Ed Peery's office at the US Naval Academy. Coach Peery would become a pivotal figure in my life.

Recently, while thumbing through an old scrapbook, I found a letter he had written to my parents in 1971. "I didn't think Tom had much potential at first, but now he is poised to win a national championship." (I didn't. I lost by one point in the NCAA finals.)

"Tom is the most competitive athlete I've ever coached," continued Coach Peery, and that's no small potatoes coming from him. Peery won three successive NCAA titles in his day and was at the helm of Navy's wrestling program. In the years ahead, I discovered that there's a subtle dark side to competitive tenacity. On the wrestling mat, fierce competitiveness is an asset, but unbridled in everyday life, I learned it crushes people and breeds self-reliance and arrogance.

Coach Harris's invitation to fair fights with rules played out powerfully in my adolescence. His offer was prompted by a school episode he had refereed… intervened would be more accurate. At the time of the incident, I didn't know my foe from Adam's house cat, but that would change. One day, unprovoked, my non-friend Doug spilled my armful of books and made me look exceedingly foolish in front of friends—which no doubt included a gathering of girls. Doug was cocky and reveled in my embarrassment—for about two seconds—until I rocked him with a punch that sent him crashing into the school's athletic trophy case, shattering the glass enclosure, and scattering its contents. By the grace of God, he was not impaled by shards of glass and seriously injured.

Harris marched me to the principal's office (again!), where another phone call home was made. Mr. Stack, the principal, dispensed his discipline, and a payment plan was worked out to replace the glass. No joke. It was fifty cents a week until the debt was paid.

At home, I knew I'd face the inevitable questions from Dad: "Who started it?" and "Who finished it?" In each case, only one answer would do: "He did" and "I did." In those situations, that was usually the end of it.

The fight culture at school, however, always demanded more. In another who-knows-why confrontation, a young hooligan named Phil was determined to test my wrestling notoriety and "called me out" off the school grounds. As was the norm, a dozen or more friends from each side would gather as the combatants squared off. Phil never really had a chance. What he didn't know was that I had been well trained at home in pugilistic skills.

Boxing gloves had been Christmas gifts to me and my brother Bob when we were young. We would fight ferocious battles in our backyard. Dad would give instructions on how to square off, lead with a left jab, stay on our toes, and tuck our chins behind our left fists. There were always scuffles at BHS; they came and went like the wind. But the news quickly spread: don't mess with the little guy who fights like a caged wolverine.

In my sophomore year, however, an unusual spark of conflict from a neighboring community ignited a firestorm in my life. It was to occupy my heart, mind, and soul for many months to come.

Babylon, like many small towns in that era, had a local movie theater. Saturday afternoons at the theatre took on a circus-like atmosphere. Before the days of security checks, youthful pranksters would smuggle pigeons into the theater and release them halfway through a John Wayne flick. The terrified birds shadowed their erratic flight patterns on the big screen while everyone hooted and hollered their displeasure. Other jokesters on occasion would set off small bottle rockets during the movie to the delight and fright of fellow movie-goers. Still others, when the flick reached its most suspenseful point, would release a flood of marbles down the inclined wooden floor. The marbles would bang and clang off every chair as they rolled to the screen. All in good Babylon fun!

On this Saturday, neighbor and good buddy Pat Napolitano and I chose seats in the balcony. There were three guys behind us making a lot of noise and wisecracking throughout the movie. Pat made our complaint known. As he stood up and turned to face them, he was met with a vicious kick that nearly catapulted him over the balcony rail. A scuffle broke out, of course, but was quelled for a moment by an agreement to settle the score in the men's room. While Pat left to do battle, I stayed glued to my seat with two of the loudmouth punks behind me. But in short order, I turned and noticed their seats were empty.

Racing to the restroom, I found a three-on-one battle in full swing. Two of the guys were attempting to subdue Pat while the third (whose name I later learned was JP) was pummeling my friend. I joined in the fray until the police arrived. The police officers separated us, lectured us, and escorted us out of the theater, but not before contingency plans were finalized to finish the fight. We would reengage behind the municipal courthouse in downtown Babylon.

JP was the gang leader. Behind the courthouse, he pointed to Pat and angrily shouted, "It's me and you!" Then he motioned to me. "You will fight Dugan," he ordered, matching me with the smaller of the remaining rivals, a kid with a silver crown on his right front tooth; I would see that tooth again. On cue, JP and Pat closed in and Dugan circled me. The number-three hoodlum (on the premise of a fair fight, I guess) stayed out of the fray.

Dugan, I judged quickly, lacked both fighting skills and authority. I took my backyard crouch and launched the attack. In short order, he was bloodied and beaten. Pat also had the upper hand over JP but in a more vicious encounter. Finally, the hostilities ceased, and we parted ways, swearing and cursing at each other. Pat and I celebrated our victory on the walk home, but the conflict wasn't over, I was to later learn.

It was weeks later at my obligatory Tuesday evening CCD class—that is, Confraternity of Christian Doctrine—that I realized I was being hunted. JP and a companion (who turned out to be his older brother, Bazile) were scanning the faces pouring into the St. Joseph's Catholic School entrance. I knew in an instant they were looking for me (and for Pat, who didn't attend CCD). I was terrified. I was no match for JP or his larger brother. I knew the St. Joe's turf well, so I slipped into a side entrance unseen. How JP and his brother ever determined I attended CCD remains a mystery. But if they knew that, I reckoned, they also knew I attended the nearby Babylon High School. The cat-and-mouse game had begun.

Over the next year, vigilance and escape became my two best friends. I charted new routes home from school, nothing less than a jigsaw puzzle of turns and misdirection. One of my new ways home was a circuitous route through the wooded state park near my house. The route took me over a bridge and an elevated spillway we called the "falls," where I liked to fish for eels. What to do with the wriggly critters when I caught them was always a challenge.

At home I began manufacturing stories about why I couldn't attend CCD. Excuses were generally characterized as whining by my dad. But fear of being caught by JP and his bunch on the way home from school (or anywhere else for that matter!) was my daytime nightmare, and on CCD nights, my fears rose to a terrifying level.

Then one random Tuesday evening, it happened. After taking a seat in my CCD classroom, Bazile causally walked in, locked his eyes on mine, and sat down at the desk behind me. Bazile was more powerfully built than JP. He had a hawk-like nose underneath his tousled, sandy-colored hair as well as razor-thin lips, and menacing eyes. He was a frightfully mean-looking package. For the next hour, Bazile taunted me and made his purpose very clear; he would avenge Dugan's beating. I had no doubt that if Bazile caught me, he would make good on his promise to cut me to ribbons and watch me bleed to death.

Let me hit the pause button for a second. I told Jan that reliving this episode of life still knots my stomach. I can still sense Bazile's finger poking me in the back and feel his hot breath on my neck. "Why," she marveled, "did you not tell your dad what was going on?" I don't have a good answer for that, other than it just wasn't the family norm. In retrospect, I should have. But Dad, in time, would enter the cat-and-mouse game at a critical junction.

The split second the clock struck nine and CCD ended, I bolted like a cat on fire out the classroom door, raced down three flights of stairs like Jason Bourne, and hit the first-floor landing at full tilt. Zipping out the front door of the church school, I aimed for the "safety" of two-way traffic. There, I hoped to brush-off Bazile with the threat of an oncoming car. A "brush-off" was a well-honed defensive practice. You run against the traffic flow and then abruptly dart into the center lane—in front of an approaching vehicle—with a timing your pursuer can't match, or he'll risk getting hit by the oncoming vehicle! One or two brush-off maneuvers is normally sufficient to shake an antagonist, but Bazile didn't miss a beat, and he was closing in fast as I sprinted away from the church.

I had no choice. As abruptly as I'd bolted, I reversed gears and turned and faced my adversary. "It was a fair fight!" I screamed, "I beat Dugan in a fair fight!" Bazile stopped dead in his tracks, winded like I was.

"Tell me *exactly* what happened," he demanded. And I recounted the movie theater incident in out-of-breath, begging-for-my-life technicolor, just as it had unfolded that day. To my utter shock and amazement, Bazile extended his hand for a handshake and said, "Okay, we don't have a problem." He turned and walked away. I never saw him again.

I took that Tuesday evening as closure and liberation from the daily fears that had stalked my school week and Tuesday nights. I shared a Cliffs-Notes version of the episode with my dad who regularly picked me up at CCD. That proved to be a wise decision, though woefully late. But it created a latent sense of urgency for him that was to play out later in a showdown that would follow. Bazile's declaration established peace between me and him, but apparently the terms of the truce did not extend to JP and Mr. Silver Tooth.

With the CCD confrontation in the past, it seemed safe to now take more direct and shorter routes home from school each day. One of those routes was a shortcut near the state park. Some months later, my brother Bob and I were taking that route home from school. We exited the wooded trail that ends about six hundred yards from home. There, blocking our safe passage, stood JP, Dugan, and a third member of his squad, each wielding a club.

"Bob, get help!" is all I could breathe out, and I sprinted toward the bridge where I did my eel fishing. The three hooligans took chase as Bob raced homeward in the opposite direction.

At the bridge, the mystery ruffian tackled me, and we rolled toward the water's edge in a tangle of arms and legs. That provided time for slowpoke Dugan to catch up. Standing over me, he raised his club and cracked it across my shoulder. JP now entered the game. He and Dugan proceeded to punch, kick, and drag me back up the hill to the bridge. I soon got the gist of the drill; they were going to throw me off the bridge into the rocky waters where I fished for eels!

In the next instant, however, a wild flurry of activity exploded on the bridge. With police sirens blaring in the background, all 220 pounds of Dad plowed into JP. He then hoisted JP off the ground by his lapels and dangled him perilously over the bridge. Dugan and the other ruffian tried to escape but were snagged by the police. Dad surrendered JP to a police officer's grasp, and things calmed down as quickly as they had escalated. Initial questioning was concluded, and Dad, Bob, and I walked home.

I don't recall a single word spoken on that ten-minute walk home. But a painfully long and chilling episode in the life of a young Babylonian had finally found an ending.

My Babylon: The Church Experience

"By the fear of God, I am what I am, and His fear towards me was not without effect." No, wait. That's not what it says. Let's try this:

"By the *grace* of God, I am what I am, and His *grace* towards me was not without effect" (1 Cor. 15:10; emphasis added). Now, we have it right. That's the apostle Paul talking about the power of grace in his life—God's amazing, unmerited favor. Fear did not alter Paul's nature a speck, but grace changed the man.

Paul was a former Jewish Pharisee, Christian hater, and all-around bad dude in his time, until he was stopped dead in his tracks by the blinding light of Christ's truth on a foray to Damascus. In an instant, Paul embraced the reality of Christ's resurrection and became a changed man and devoted Christ follower. In that moment, *grace* became Paul's password in life.

Doesn't the Bible say, "Fear God?" (1 Pet. 2:17, Eccles. 5:17) you may ask?

It does, but never in the context of God as some vicious pit bull waiting to tear you to pieces for venturing onto his turf. No, the fear of God, in a biblical context, is an awe-inspired, holy reverence in the presence of the Divine Creator who spoke the world into existence. It's the profound humility brought on by one's imperfectness laid bare in the presence of a holy, powerful, and sovereign God. "Woe is me," said Isaiah in God's presence. "I am a man of unclean lips" (Isa. 6:5).

As an adolescent, I attended St. Joseph's Catholic Church in Babylon. More accurately put, I was regularly delivered there Saturday afternoons and Sunday mornings, much like the morning newspaper. I learned *nothing* about God's grace at St. Joseph's. On rare occasions, we'd attend St. Joe's as a family. But woe was us on the three-mile drive across town. Inevitably, Dad would scold one of us about something, and tears would ensue. That would in turn signal more brotherly provocation in the back seat until everyone was in trouble. Not much different, I'm sure, than most families. But the excitement would build until the inevitable shouting match in the parking lot between Dad and any other New York driver seeking a parking spot near the church.

Then all hyped and angered-up, we'd head into the sanctuary or school auditorium for what was supposed to be a solemn worship experience. If we happened into a service officiated by Father

McCarthy, all the better. He could rip through the liturgy and sermon in about twenty-five minutes.

St. Joe's added little spiritual calming to Babylon's storm of life. I don't recall any of the messages from the sermons, of course, but much of the Sunday school drum beat brought to us by the Franciscan brothers and nuns still echoes in my mind. They pounded into us a take-no-prisoners, performance-based, mortal-sin-encumbered, guilt-oriented, you-might-go-to-hell-if-you-drop your-prayerbook... and by the way, when was your last confession? Other than that, it was a warm and nurturing setting for a Sunday visit.

The clergy at St. Joseph's prepared me well for the encounter with Father Ulrich that was to come many years later. The message was the same. Thankfully, the Catholic Church and its messaging have changed greatly over the last thirty years, to our Savior's glory. But in some church settings, grace can still be a commodity hard to find.

The Saturday confession and Sunday Holy Communion routine at St. Joe's added more intrigue, drama, and fear to the mix. Typically, Dad would somehow determine the extent of my spiritual deficit and decide when to deliver me to the church for confession, but he never accompanied me into the confessional arena. I'd venture in through the towering double doors of St. Joseph's, sometimes accompanied by my younger brother, with my own brand of fear and trembling. Once inside, I'd join the line with others waiting to reveal their grievous misdeeds of the prior week.

"Bless me, Father, for I have sinned," I'd pronounce in the confessional. Then, afterward, my brother, Bob, and I would compare the penitential prayers we were assigned to say. "Whoa! He gave you ten Our Fathers'?" Bob would say. "I only got five!"

In proper context, the Lord's Prayer (the "Our Father" of my youth) is a deeply personal and sacred prayer, coming directly from the mouth of Jesus when he was asked by his disciples, "Lord, teach us to pray" (Luke 11:1). Back then, I confess, I knew none of that and could knock-out ten less than heartfelt Our Fathers in about forty-five seconds.

Saturday afternoon confession, of course, was the prelude to Sunday morning Holy Communion—but at enormous risk for a brazen Catholic sinner like me. Why? Because grievous deeds committed between Saturday afternoon confession and Sunday morning communion were new on the sin ledger. The list could include a spat with my brother, not eating my lima beans at dinner, or paging through one of Dad's *Playboy* magazines that I'd squirreled away in a closet. Today, the idea of a sin ledger seems like a cruel joke, but in the reality of that time, it was an alarming, fear-based dilemma. I had two choices: fear God or fear man.

On the fearing God side was my overnight unworthiness to receive Holy Communion. "Don't *dare* go to the altar rail and receive Holy Communion with unconfessed sin." That was the eleventh commandment I'd learned in Sunday school, and I took the Franciscan warning *very* seriously.

On the fear-man side was Dad. He knew the drop-off protocol for confession had been executed the day before. If I didn't go to the altar rail and receive Holy Communion, he would want to know why and there would be a father's wrath to contend with. Many a Sunday I hung in that spiritual imbalance and sweated out my options during the first fifteen minutes of the church service. Fear God or fear man? What was a young Babylonian to do?

At that stage of life, I confess, it was no contest. Fear of man ruled the day; the immediate consequences were more predictable. I'd take my chances with the eleventh-commandment consequences and make my way to the altar rail. I was no faith warrior like Daniel of the Bible, who rejected Nebuchadnezzar's demand to cease his daily prayers. Daniel's faith was rewarded. After being thrown in the lions' den, God subdued the big cats and rescued him without any evidence of a single nip. I did not share his confidence or courage.

The fear-God-or-fear-man conflict tore at the spiritual fiber of my soul. For many years, its tension wound my theological spring tighter. No one ever pointed me to the apostle Paul's grace or Daniel's courage. Ultimately, however, God's grace to me was never in vain. Recognition of it, however, just came much later in life.

I have joked with friends that the solution to my spiritual conundrum as a young Catholic would have been a policy change at the Vatican. Why not just exit the confessional, recite one's penance, and beat feet to Holy Communion? That would eradicate any time to dilly-dally in sin!

In writing about this, I know I am making light of the situation. It helps take the sharp edge off a deeply troubling and conflicting chapter in the life of a young man trying to sort out his relationship with his church and his God. To be clear, I'd *never* poke fun at the sacred rites of confession, Holy Communion, or the Catholic Church, only my mixed-up perception of them. Today, with a more robust and grace-oriented faith, I'd like to believe I would never again elevate fear of man (or woman) over fear of God in any life choice.

But full detox from adolescent, fear-based theology took a long time; that kind of spiritual poison is purged slowly from one's veins. But I'm forever grateful for the journey and not bitter. My Babylon church experience gave me a keen nose for bad theology—any fear or performance-based premise that trumps God's grace for mankind. That grace is manifested in the person of Christ and a relationship with him. More on that later.

My Babylon: Life on the Home Front

Ninety-nine Pilcher Street, Babylon, New York, was my boyhood address. We didn't have zip codes back then. It stood as one of about sixty modestly built two-story homes in a densely wooded section of suburban Long Island. In the fifties and sixties, Long Island was noted for its sprawling vegetable and duck farms. The latter were a source of ire for Long Island's clam-digging community, who blamed duck farmers for the rising pollution of Great South Bay and the resulting lesser hauls.

Home, as anyone will attest, is much more than an address or piece of real estate. It is the melting pot of life experience. Everything converges there. For the most part, what goes on inside the front door remains shielded from neighbors. Home is the nexus of family comfort, collisions, harmony, discord, routines, lessons taught, discipline administered, and encouragement offered as children are raised and parental values passed on. It's the place we leave when we go out to play, attend school, or go to work, and it's where we return from those endeavors to find safe ground and rest. Or so it should be.

The name *home front,* however, takes on a larger significance. In wartime, it's the informal term for the civilian support systems and services that bolster military forces in combat. That definition still carries a lot of weight. Ask any soldier, marine, sailor, or police officer about the significance of support they receive on the home front, and you will never doubt its importance. It's the same with any teenager struggling to make life work. Ask him or her about life on the home front, and you'll likely get an earful.

Dad was the dominant force on the home front. Mom faithfully labored as the traditional Mrs. Cleaver, overwhelmed no doubt by the monumental challenges of raising three young boys and their sister, all born within a six-year window. You don't see many family clans like that today. Mom kept us all fed, clothed, safe, and off to school on time. How? It must have been divine intervention. Mom was also our steadfast advocate and protector. For her, it was an uninvited and unsettling role, filled with unfathomable angst thrust upon her by Dad's explosive temper and fearsome discipline.

Boys will be boys, of course, which often resulted in collisions with Dad's rigid mentality. He was a former New York City cop. On family visits and outings, we boys always marched to the gold standard of obedience. Fearsome repercussions awaited anyone brash enough to break ranks with the unwritten family code of compliance. Family peace always teetered on the unpredictable ledge of Dad's temperament. We boys would frequently huddle when the temperamental winds shifted and assess our options. How would we make ourselves scarce if a sudden firestorm of wrath were to erupt? Pervasive fear on the home front was an everyday reality.

Arthur Gerard Schuler, the family patriarch, was born in Greenpoint, a small enclave in the Brooklyn borough of New York City. Dad's boyhood home, Jackson Heights, was another small community in Queens County, just a stone's throw from NYC. I have fond memories of Jackson Heights. My dad's father remained there well into my teenage years. A visit to Grandpa's always included a train ride to Coney Island's amusement park on Brooklyn's south boundary. That was boyhood city fun, unlike anything in Babylon's rural setting.

Grandpa's apartment was a welcome refuge from the storm of life in Babylon. His calming demeanor is such a powerful memory in my life that my second son, Bryan, carries Grandpa's first name, Martin, in his signature. Bryan *Martin* Schuler is Grandpa's legacy in the modern version of my family.

Six years ago, upon the birth of my first granddaughter, my daughter Erica asked me, "What do you want Bethany to call you, Daddy?"

"Grandpa," I answered in a New York second. "Just have her call me Grandpa."

Dad's mother tragically died of colon cancer at age forty-three. Dad also lived through the hardships of the Great Depression, which no doubt cauterized his outlook on life. I can't fathom sharing one banana for a family dinner as he once related to me, choking back the tears he'd stored away for nearly eighty years.

Dad directed the family's religious focus to Catholicism. On his mother's side were staunch Irish Catholics, the Magee clan. Dad's uncle, Father Tom (my namesake), served his priestly duties at a Catholic Church in Flushing, New York. Flushing Meadows is still the home of Shea Stadium and those amazing NY Mets who spectacularly won the 1986 World Series.

Dad was fifteen at the outbreak of World War II. At nineteen, in the concluding chapter of the war, he joined the newly formed Army Air Corps. Two years later, in 1947, New York City was backfilling the ranks of its police force, which had been depleted by the war effort. Dad signed up, serving as one of New York's finest for the next seven years. His beat? The flashy and racy streets around Times Square.

Dad's formidable six-foot, one-inch frame and a badge were all he needed. "It was the best job with the best men I've ever worked with," he proudly told me. But over the years to come, promotion opportunities on the police force slackened and our family numbers grew, necessitating a change of career and location. After a hop to Flushing and a skip to West Hempstead, Long Island the final jump landed our young family in rural Babylon.

I recall little of family life in our interim homesteads around NYC, but life focus for me sharpens acutely with the transition to Babylon, which at that time NYC dwellers might have likened to a wilderness adventure. There were two factors for that heightened focus.

The first is the natural progression in a home in which rules and compliance (mostly for a child's own protection) give way to an adolescent stage of exploring and maturing. With that comes bids for more independence and the inherent challenges for kids and parents alike. Rule-based compliance is simple parental math. It's pretty much a binary do-or-don't-do formula. The adolescent stage that follows is not so formulaic. It requires a much higher level of parental math.

The second reason that my Babylon days are so clearly etched in my mind was an ever-growing awareness of a home atmosphere abundantly laced with fear and violence. While I have truly forgiven Dad for this raw and painful stage of life, and we have weathered the relational challenges in its aftermath, I nonetheless view these years as a trial by fire experience. But I also see them as a God-appointed catalyst for personal reflection and change.

Young minds are extraordinarily impressionable; they capture in cinematic clarity significant people, incidents, and relationships. I can tell you what meals I enjoyed as a youngster; every enduring detail about my collie, Laddie, who lived sixteen years; the names of my elementary school teachers; how many injured ducks I rescued from the lake; and so on. I can also relate to you in excruciating detail memories of the shock-and-awe atmosphere that often filled the home front. A young mind's cache stores much of what it would like to forget.

Dad had little empathy and regard for higher parental math. Therefore, episodes of raw fear and terror were the natural consequences of juvenile misbehavior. The reality of those early years in Babylon is stark; the NYC cop, now dressed in a business suit, came home to mete out street justice to family offenders. That authority model, coupled with a penchant for harsh physical discipline, seriously strained the threads of our family fabric. Fear and unpredictability frequently held court at the dinner table. The focus could be school performance, homework problems, brother-on-brother squabbles that leaked out during the dinner hour, or failure to produce a clean plate (lima beans again being the culprit). At bedtime, brother-to-brother conversation from the upper to lower bunk was met with severe consequences. Why, I'll never know.

The disciplinary kiss of death, however, was any rumor or evidence of disrespectful behavior toward Mom. I still hold to that principle today but loathed the double standard on the home front. It was crystal clear for us boys; Dad lived to his own standard.

It's important to note that my memories of family life are filtered through my personal frame of reference. I speak only for myself in this narrative, not for my three siblings who also lived at home at that time. For me, Dad's discipline, backed by his massive two-hundred-pound frame, was akin to adolescent terror. These violent childhood episodes upset my emotional apple cart well into adulthood. To the degree my siblings internalized their trials differently, God bless them, but our family equilibrium was forever altered.

Sometimes boyhood discipline and physical punishment escalated dangerously. In those cases, my mother's protective shouts would reach a fever-pitch crescendo until calm was restored. But not before deep wounds and resentment were etched into my heart and mind. That turmoil would beg to be purged in later years. In contrast, this was the same Dad who sprinted to the bridge to rescue me from gang thugs, worked tirelessly to network me into the Naval Academy, drove hours on short notice to College Park, Pennsylvania, to watch me win the Eastern Intercollegiate Wrestling Championship, and knitted together a band of young brothers who would fight to the death to protect one another and their sister. In hindsight, those adolescent years were dreadfully fearful and uncertain but always held promise for a better future. They were also confusing years, a dichotomy of over-the-top discipline and veiled affirmation. They kept me off-balance but somehow—miraculously—always moving forward.

This is an exceedingly difficult chapter to write; I'd prefer to leave it out. But it's an integral part of my life's journey and inseparable from all that comes after Babylon's timeline. We each make choices about which behaviors we replicate in life, and I never learned the true source of Dad's volatile legacy. For years to follow, I remained angry to the core of my soul over his punitive behavior on the home front and treatment of my mom and siblings. It took hundreds of hours of mental retooling and counseling to overcome the scars of adolescence. Restoration of our relationship seemed hopelessly blocked by my bitterness and the questions that I had about his parental math. Ultimately, the breakthrough that eased my rage would come decades later, ushered in under the enormous weight of my daughter Vanessa's death. But that's a story for a later chapter. Here's why I mention it here.

As I write this chapter, Dad just celebrated his ninety-second birthday. I hope he makes ninety-three—and many more. "Honor your father and mother" (Exod. 20:12) is *not* a conditional, criteria-driven commandment. There's no third tablet from Mt. Sinai with small print disclaimers for painful parent-child relationships. Neither does the fifth commandment sit outside the boundaries of forgiveness and grace. That's been a tough go for me, but I can't pick and choose which of God's commands I want to follow. As I've been offered grace, I need to extend it. That's much of the endgame of life. Absent that, I'm a hypocrite.

My intent is not to punish Dad with my writer's voice, but to this day, he and I still ascribe to vastly different models of family math. Recently he admonished me, "I wouldn't complain too much, Tom. Things for you didn't turn out too badly."

"I'm not complaining," I replied, ready to spar once again, "but how things turned out for me is not the acid test of your methods or means. Only God in his perfect wisdom chooses the best method and means to achieve his goals. Only he has the whole chessboard of life on his lap."

Dad and I have made our relationship work. It's not been easy. He's a tough old dude and there's still a lot of NYC cop in his DNA. Our relationship has endured many new trials. Sometimes still, we hang on to a precipitous relational ledge, but so far, we've survived the grueling test of life as father and son. That's important to know as you turn the pages of this book. Dad is not a kicked-to-the-curb dismal chapter of failure. Our relationship is not on the dust heap of life. Many years after I left home, we worked hard to get our relationship on a positive track. Ultimately, that took some fearsome toe-to-toe confrontations.

Metamorphyx will be another test of my relationship with my dad. There is not a single detail I have shared that we have not talked through, sometimes at great and painful lengths. But it has never been in print. So, to some degree, what went on in the home front behind closed doors is now out on the front lawn.

"What will you say in your book about us?" Dad asked one day.

"Nothing we haven't fought through," I said. "I love you as my God-given dad. God's in control of everything we endured together—for he knew the plans he had for us."

Survival—Looking Back

At a recent church gathering of new members, the group leader opened with an icebreaker question. "As a young high schooler, what was your ambition in life?"

I hate that question. I twitched with anticipation as it made its rounds. Each age forty-something adult offered up their youthful dreams, and there were a lot of laughs around the table as almost no one had hit the bull's-eye of their childhood vision.

My turn. I should have manufactured a crowd-pleasing response, but instead I just spoke the truth. "My ambition in high school was to survive and see where life would take me. I never had a burning ambition."

"Too bad," said Joe Engineer, a man who had made good on his youthful aspiration. "Sounds like you had a rough upbringing?"

"It had its challenges," I agreed, "but I'm no victim. Who hasn't had tough trials in their life? God had a plan for me. It just took a while to develop."

I still have a visceral reaction to the notion of victimhood. I've been through enough of life to know that wearing that title is a choice—or, worse, a self-imposed proclamation about one's life.

Victimhood calls out to the lessons of life experience and says, "No. I'll stay wounded, thank you!" It doesn't embrace change. It's a death knell to life purpose, poisoning the mind, contributing to learned helplessness, and scuttling initiative. There will *always* be catastrophic events and challenges in life; only the unscathed reject that truth.

Do I have regrets about my adolescence? Yes, two.

Firstly, I had no spiritual frame of reference for fighting life's battles. Everything boiled down to self-reliance, tenaciousness, and a survival-strategy mind game. Secondly, I had no role model to point the way to positive change. Releasing the tension in the tightly coiled springs of my life would take decades.

Our circumstances, of course, need not define us or cast us into victimhood. That's the dirty work of despair and hopelessness. For twenty-three years, I've carried a small devotional book with me in the side pocket of my car. It's opened to January 2, 1994. The page is dog-eared, coffee stained, and ragged, but the message is timeless: "The wise people of today are those whose journey is determined by what they believe instead of having what they believe determined by their journey."[5]

Faith and hope are the antidotes of despair. After seventy years in captivity, the Jews still left in Babylon, about fifty thousand men and their families, returned to Jerusalem. Jeremiah's prophecy proved accurate. Exile and hardship are not all bad. They reconstitute the soul and produce a keen awareness that life purpose is best understood in affliction. Take note that the returning Jewish exiles are never once depicted as victims in the Hebrew scriptures. They learned discipline in the trials that God's sovereignly inserted in their lives. Life is never to be lived haphazardly. Ultimately, they *survived* their Babylon experience, *thrived* in a renewed faith, and were *delivered* to their homeland, Jerusalem.

In many ways, I claim a similar legacy. "'For I know the plans I have for you,' declares the LORD, 'plans to prosper you and not to harm you, plans to give you hope and a future.'"

---

5 Charles H. Long, *Forward Day by Day*, January 2, 64.

Embracing life experience, not victimhood, leads to life change. And ultimately, life change leads to discovery of life purpose. But Paul McCartney, Ringo Star, and the boys had it right. It can be a long and winding road.

Failure to Launch

Being confident of this, that He who began a good work in you
will carry it on to completion until the day of Christ Jesus.
—Philippians. 1:6

Navy Grace

"Tell me, Midshipman Schuler, what you were thinking! Tell me how your actions reflect military discipline and your role of authority. Tell me how this stunt honors the reputation you earned within the brigade of Midshipmen." Captain P. J. Ryan got all that out in one animated breath.

Ryan was the deputy commandant of midshipmen, the third-ranking officer at the United States Naval Academy (USNA). His role was much like that of an executive officer on a ship—to set leadership standards, maintain combat readiness, and execute discipline. But it was the rapid pace of his words, the harsh lines in his face, and the crescendo of his voice that exposed my tenuous position. My graduation in June, as well as my commission in the United States Marine Corps, was at risk; I was walking the plank of dismissal.

Captain's Mast is a disciplinary process hailing from the sailing days of old. In the era of iron men and wooden ships, it would be at the foot of the main mast where the captain would publicly sentence a crew member for a breach of the ship's disciplinary code. Captain's Mast was conducted in full view of the ship's company to discourage further infractions, which would compromise the ship's operational readiness. From the time of John Paul Jones to present day, navy commanders know their crew's readiness to fight effectively at sea is always a reflection of tight ship discipline.

Here's what had preceded my high-level meeting. Every day during the fall and spring semesters at the Naval Academy then and now, all four thousand midshipmen assemble outside in their assigned areas for noon formation. In the main courtyard, Tecumseh Court, there's always a lot of pomp and circumstance to wow tourists and guests. Then on signal, the entire brigade of midshipmen—from all corners of the assembly—march off in formation to King Hall, where lunch is served family style. Some days, however, there are surprise inspections by brigade officers, visiting dignitaries who love the pageantry of the scene, and VIPs who unrepentantly hold up the whole show. Lunch for hungry midshipmen, then, must wait until the guests' agendas will allow.

One balmy spring day, I decided unilaterally to speed things up. As a midshipman platoon commander, I asked my forty ravenous men if they were ready for lunch. Taking a few nods as consensus, I called the platoon to attention and marched my fearless cadre off to the noon meal. Once inside King Hall, there was a lot of raucous high fiving, but the bravado of the event paled measurably with every passing second. My rebellious band of brothers filled just four tables in a remote corner of the cavernous dining hall. The remaining 3,960 seats remained empty for another ten *very* long minutes, lots of time to contemplate my impetuous decision. As the celebration waned, I sensed storm clouds on the horizon.

Not long after that, a rumor of "flagrant disregard for authority" with my name attached to it began circulating among the senior class officers. Those are deeply threatening words at the Naval Academy. Leading the disciplinary howl was a classmate who wrote up the charges and launched the disciplinary process.

Standing humbly before the deputy commandant, I took full ownership of my bonehead decision. His eyes drilled deep into my soul, acknowledging that I had put him in a very awkward position. Captain Ryan was a die-hard wrestling fan; he never missed a home match and I had met him several times over the years. Now my graduation fate lay in his hands. He could throw me out of Annapolis or delay graduation on disciplinary grounds. Instead, he offered me unmerited Navy grace—restriction for the next six weeks to the academy's campus with all its aggravating and petty demands. But I'd graduate in June and receive my commission as a second lieutenant in the United States Marine Corps.

Size Waivers Matter

My brush with Captain Ryan centered on USNA graduation standards. Ironically, a few years earlier, the issue for me had been entrance standards. I didn't measure up! As a high school senior, I was one inch below the minimum height requirement and woefully short on my English SAT scores.

"I can offer you a temporary height waiver and an appointment to the Naval Academy Preparatory School [NAPS] in Bainbridge, Maryland," said the admissions director. "Surely, you'll grow, but more importantly, you'll boost your academic credentials."

To comply with that, I'd need to enlist in the US Navy, attend boot camp at the Great Lakes Naval Training Center in Michigan, and sign up for a nine-month intensive academic curriculum at NAPS. If I successfully leaped through those hoops over the next year, I'd get an appointment.

Academically and athletically, I excelled at NAPS. With no thugs chasing me around town, my English SAT score improved 150 points and my math and chemistry scores clawed at the threshold of 700. Apparently, I had some smarts; they'd just never bloomed in high school. As a NAPS wrestler, I defeated my Naval Academy counterpart, justifying Coach Peery's confidence that I had some upside potential. All that said, with my NAPS year behind me, I remained at the towering height of five-feet three-inches tall—still one inch short of the minimum entrance requirement.

Another waiver was granted, and in my freshman (plebe) year at the academy, I would grow nearly four inches and add twenty-five pounds of good wrestling mass the year I turned nineteen. That weight has settled a bit today, but I can still squeeze my 150-pound frame into my US Marine Corps uniform. My son Bryan won't mess with me. He says that what I have is a combination of old-man strength and twenty years of experience flipping man-turtles on their backs on a wrestling mat.

Life marched on, literally and figuratively. With a height waiver and solid SAT scores, I entered the US Naval Academy, destined to graduate in 1972. Babylon was a distant blur in my rearview mirror though its trying legacy remained. Some of that testing proved helpful in meeting the rigorous physical and mental demands at the academy. The rest I shoved underwater for a season of life.

What Worked There… Works Here

The rigor of my first year at USNA was set against the backdrop of the Vietnam Tet Offensive in 1968. That sobering punch in the mouth to America was a dreadfully painful chapter in the widely unpopular war. Naval Academy graduates, particularly men choosing US Marine Corps assignments, were heading off to war after initial combat training at the Marine Basic School in Quantico, Virginia.

In that year, my class numbered 1,371 young men (women would be granted admission in 1976). Nine hundred and five would make it to the June 1972 finish line. Attrition math, which revealed that 34 percent of my incoming class had washed out, stoked the fires of a congressional inquiry. Something must have been dreadfully wrong with—or within—a system that pushed 466 of my classmates out the gate. In fact, there was fault on both sides of the equation. Then as now, there are candidates who master the admissions process but should never lead men or women into battle. One departing classmate said he came to the Naval Academy to "learn how to sail." Hmmm. What was he smoking his senior year of high school?

Plebe year at the Naval Academy always holds unique challenges. That shouldn't surprise anyone; plebe year is designed to challenge and re-program high schoolers and turn them into future naval officers. But for some head scratcher of a reason, some senior midshipmen who controlled much of the plebe indoctrination process latched on to a bizarre mantra: *Attrition is the mission.* Many seniors raised that refrain to a punishing art form of physical and mental hazing. "Gentlemen, look to your right and left," was their heralded warning. "One of those men won't be with you next June."

Although some myopic seniors torched the career aspirations of my classmates, their effect on me was just the opposite. Their cockiness just served to harden the gritty self-reliance, perseverance, and determination that I'd come in with. At that juncture of life, I was not overly committed to a career in the naval service (although many classmates were), but I sure wasn't going to cave in to some senior's bias to run me out of the academy because he didn't believe athletes made good naval officers. Today, attrition rates are down to 10 to 12 percent, the result of a much-improved admissions process and a healthier leadership culture.

The mission of the Naval Academy hasn't changed in a hundred years. "To develop Midshipmen, morally, mentally, and physically and imbue them with the highest ideals of duty, honor, and loyalty… to prepare them for a career of naval service." Today, plebe year remains physically, mentally, and academically challenging. It must! Graduating midshipmen serve on battleships, not cruise ships.

Festivities that first summer concluded with plebe leadership evaluations, followed by August's parents' weekend. By then, a sizable contingent of plebes had made their go/no-go decisions and would be returning home. For those that remained, the first academic year loomed ahead—nineteen to twenty-two credit hours each semester—and obligatory Saturday classes.

Midshipman Savage, Second Class, a Naval Academy junior, called me in for my evaluation.

"Midshipman Schuler, Fourth Class, reporting as ordered, sir."

Savage, of course, knew I was a "NAPSter" and that my military immersion had begun a year before my peer group had joined the brigade. That experience had served me well. I could easily follow a marching cadence and wasn't surprised whatsoever that someone with stripes on their sleeve would call me a maggot.

"You had better stand at attention, mister," said Savage. "You came out of NAPS thinking plebe summer would be a cakewalk. Is that right, Mr. Schuler?"

"No, sir. I don't think it's a cakewalk, sir."

"If you have that attitude when the first classmen return in September, you won't make it to Christmas. Do you understand?"

"Yes, sir. I understand, sir!"

"You'd better," continued Savage. "Now, here's how your classmates rated you, Mr. Confidence. Are you ready to hear that?"

"Yes, sir. I'm ready, sir!"

"They ranked you *first* in leadership, physical aptitude, and military discipline. That means you will assume a leadership position among your fellow plebes in the year ahead. Congratulations, Mr. Schuler, but don't let that go to your head, or the seniors will draw a bead on you. They feed on proud plebes like you. Is that clear?"

"Yes, sir. That's clear, sir!"

"At ease, Mr. Schuler," said Savage, and he offered a handshake. All that had preceded his gesture was just good ol' plebe summer encouragement.

"You're dismissed. I'll announce this to your classmates at evening formation," said Savage. "You're a gifted leader, Schuler. Use those skills wisely."

"Aye, aye, sir.

My encounter with Savage validated the skills I'd developed earlier in my life. What worked for me *there* (in Babylon) was working for me *here* (the USNA). I was putting to use my resourcefulness, tenacity, athleticism, self-reliance, and ability to find the right performance buttons to push. There wasn't much reason to recalibrate or change much of anything—except, perhaps, when to go to lunch.

Officially Pugnacious

Synonyms for *pugnacious* are not warm and fuzzy. They include *aggressiveness, fierceness, intensity, forcefulness,* and *confrontation-oriented.* Today I wince when I read the *Washington Post* article snatched from my scrapbook archives. The headline "Pugnacious Types Prevail in College Wrestling."[6] There's certainly nothing wrong with a strong competitive ethic, but what the newspaper feature indicates about my younger self is something deeper and troublesome. It's an identity built on attributes which are useful in wrestling but bruising in life. Pugnaciousness is not easily pigeonholed into one compartment of life; like a caged animal, it chews itself into other facets of life.

The *Washington Post* article ran on February 22, 1971—just a few short weeks before my final NCAA tournament. Staff Writer Kenneth Turan centered the piece around my competitive ethic. "Lean and angry is college wrestling," says Turan, "a sport where mental toughness, even pugnacity, is demanded, success going to the man who has his mind under the tightest control. Schuler wrestles for Navy, where for obvious reasons, he's been its most successful competitor."[7]

I can no more isolate wrestling from my life narrative than I can separate blood from life itself. Wrestling gave me an identity, value, a sense of accomplishment, and the lifelong habit of strict discipline. For six months every year at the academy, I'd work feverishly to shed twenty pounds by Thanksgiving to compete at my assigned weight. To accomplish that, I'd forfeit Turkey Day festivities as an annual training norm, going instead with a six-ounce serving of scrumptious StarKist tuna right from the can! Why that insanity? Because in that era of college wrestling, it was the norm of the sport. In those days, everyone "cut" to a weight where they were dehydrated and as mean as a junkyard dog. That would change in later years as the NCAA

---

6 Turan, Kenneth. "Pugnacious Types Prevail in College Wrestling." *The Washington Post*, April 22, 1971.

7 Ibid.

weight-loss rules changed and favored more common sense than any of us athletes could muster.

A wrestler's meager menu changes his demeanor, as my USNA classmates will testify. Each fall, I was at risk of being the last man chosen in the roommate lottery. No one wanted to spend a semester with a Tasmanian devil in need of a meal. I'm grateful for roommates Gregg Hamelin and Lenny Cooper, who apparently lost the final coin toss and got stuck with me. They were both gracious, supportive, and somehow resistant to the ill effects of my hunger and pugnacity.

I may be one of Navy's top ten wrestlers over the last fifty years. Who knows? I've never researched it. But for the forgettable record, I won the Eastern Intercollegiate Wrestling Association Championship three successive years, became a two-time NCAA All-American, medaled annually at the US armed forces tournaments, and won a berth as an alternate on the 1976 US Olympic Greco-Roman wrestling team. Greco-Roman wrestling is related to its freestyle cousin but prohibits attacks on your opponent's legs. Instead, Greco ops for judo-like throws to score points.

Upon qualifying in the Olympic trials held in Cleveland in 1976, Marine Corps headquarters issued me temporary orders to train and travel with the Olympic team through the Montreal Games. My former USNA teammate and Marine Corps colleague Lloyd "Butch" Keaser was the number-one man on the USA freestyle team and won a silver medal in Montreal.

I mention Keaser because his legacy is unique. He was a fierce competitor *and* a gracious guy. That's a rare counterbalance that escapes many wrestlers. Even today I tilt too easily to confrontation when poked. Apparently, the apostle Paul also needed a reminder to keep his mind fixed on his power source. Scripture doesn't specify his malady, but it kept Paul humble and boasting about his weaknesses, not his strengths. Paul prayed for release from his "thorn" but Jesus wisely nixed his request. "My *grace* is sufficient for you, for my power is made perfect in [your] weakness," he told Paul (2 Cor. 12:9; emphasis added). That's great counsel for me too. An aggressive nature has deep roots in my DNA. To overcome it, I need a bushel basket of grace.

Wrestling also introduced me to an icon in my life, Coach Ed Peery. Peery took a lukewarm but authentic interest in my athletic abilities when I was in high school. But as I matured as an athlete and young man at the academy, his involvement in my life went much deeper.

The title "coach" holds special significance to any athlete. A coach *prepares* an athlete for competition in wrestling, soccer, or gymnastics. But when the competition begins, coaches are prohibited—usually under penalty—from stepping onto the mat or playing field. Therefore, a coach is only effective to the degree he or she *transfers* skills, capacity, and motivation to their athlete. Everyone acquainted with Coach Peery knew him not only as an incredibly demanding and competitive athlete himself but also a true coach. Most of us loathed his Monday-through-Friday training regimen, but come Saturday's competition, we were well equipped for battle.

On a personal level, Peery was much more than a wrestling coach; he was a *life* coach to me, something I became aware of many years later in a life-mapping workshop. "Now think about role models, heroes, mentors, and life coaches you've had in your formative years," said the workshop facilitator, "and tell us their impact on your life."

At first, I was dumbfounded by the facilitator's question and then a bit testy. *What are we talking about? What is a mentor or life coach? I'm the captain of my ship. I alone make my life work!* But after deep and intimate reflection (and some embarrassing tears), I recognized Coach Peery's influence in my life. Peery, I realized, taught me much more than wrestling skills; he took on the bigger landscape of my young life. A few years after graduation, Peery would lose a young daughter to cancer. I watched him graciously, in faith, navigate those turbulent waters. Pugnaciousness, as I would later learn, is no ally in that storm.

Coach Peery was always "Coach." I never once addressed him by any other name. In 2010, he died of pancreatic cancer, a vicious, life-sapping disease. I flew up to Annapolis to see him shortly before his death. We reminisced and prayed together. The service a few weeks later at the US Naval Academy chapel was packed with men like me who had Peery's imprint on their life. Many told their favorite story. Here's mine.

In 1971, the NCAA National Wrestling Tournament was held at Auburn University, more a venue for football than wrestling. I defeated my Oklahoma foe in the semi-final match and advanced to the NCAA finals. My opponent was Greg Johnson (Michigan State), who had won the title the year before. We fought a pitched battle for eight minutes. In the final seconds of the match, it could be argued that I was due a point that would have evened the match and sent us into overtime. The referee saw it differently; no point was awarded, and I lost the match.

Exiting the mat with the crushing realization that I had just lost the national title, I leveled swift and severe judgment upon the referee. Coach Peery's response to me was equally swift. Looking at me eyeball to eyeball that Saturday night in Auburn, he said, "You should never have let the match get to the point where the referee's call would carry the day." There would be no victims in Coach Peery's corner. It was a life lesson I've never forgotten.

In early 2005, I received a letter from the Eastern Intercollegiate Wrestling Association (EIWA), inviting me into its Hall of Fame. The ceremony would be conducted on my home turf at the Naval Academy; the EIWA tournament that year would be in Annapolis.

"I'm not going," I told Jan. "It's a prideful celebration of one's past accomplishments." I'm not a big fan of Halls of Anything, excepting perhaps the Bible's Hall of Faith in Hebrews chapter 11. There you will find the likes of Abraham, Isaac, Jacob, and Moses. Jan, who could make her own run at the Hall of Faith, graciously disagreed.

"It's actually not about you, Mr. Humility," she said. "It's about an athletic gift God gave you—one that opened many doors for you in life. Why would you not share that with the next generation of wrestlers at the hall of fame ceremony and honor God in the process?"

I can't say I deliberated long and hard on Jan's counsel. Instead, I just booked the flights. My parents, along with many wrestling colleagues and Coach Peery, attended. I did exactly what Jan suggested. I told the story of how wrestling and a healthy dose of God-given talent had helped push me through life, given me an incentive to build needed discipline, and opened doors for a pugnacious lad from Babylon to prosper in life.

There's much the sport has given me. It was good to give something back and encourage younger men to pursue excellence in a worthy contest in life.

Semper Fidelis

I'm routinely asked how, after graduating from the Naval Academy, I ended up in the US Marine Corps. The simple answer is that the marine corps is also part of the Department of the Navy, which has big ships and planes to get marines where they need to go.

A less flippant answer encompasses factors that burrowed much deeper into my decision-making process. First, there was the powerful influence of two Marine Corps officers at the naval academy. Major "Skip" Sweetser was always a man of reason and professional poise. He stood alongside me at Captain's Mast and when it was over, never hounded me about it. Also important was Captain Charles Krulak. Krulak was the officer representative of the Navy wrestling team. He was always a mountain of exuberance and encouragement during his tenure with the team. He's also a man of high standards and impeccable values. Krulak advanced to the rank of lieutenant general and became commandant of the US Marine Corps. He served on the joint chiefs of staff under President Bill Clinton.

Future wrestling competition was certainly another incentive. "Don't forget," Krulak said, "you might have a shot at the Olympic team with the marine corps. That's a lot tougher to pull off when you're on a ship in the Pacific Ocean." What Krulak said was true, but my competitive spirit had bottomed out as I neared graduation, a casualty of the grueling weight loss routines and too much StarKist tuna. I passed, therefore, on the 1972 Olympic trials, a decision I'd regret four years later. Krulak's prophecy, nonetheless, was fulfilled. The spark of Olympic competition ignited again for me in 1976.

The third factor played no small part in my decision. The marine corps has a very proud tradition, which is embodied in its *Semper Fidelis* (Always Faithful) mantra. I embraced the marine corps' exclusivity, elitism, and inherent spirit of feisty nonconformity. That two-hundred-year heritage is built on the backs of men who fought and died courageously defending our nation. The marine corps' legacy also fueled my growing penchant to distance myself from earlier chapters of life and join a company of men I could trust with my life. I longed to build a new future.

Admittedly, my service selection decision in 1972 was emotionally charged and to a degree, wrapped in defiance. My family took a deep, fear-based breath; the Vietnam war was going badly, and no one quite knew where things were headed. That said, God's plans are never thwarted by one's defiance. We can think we're headed off on some mutinous, self-guided venture, but he steers those initiatives to his purposes. In Proverbs 16:9, God says to us, "Sure, I know you have a plan, but don't forget who's directing your steps." In the rearview mirror of life, it's clear that the US Marine Corps was the best decision for me after graduation for all the *right* reasons. God dismissed my defiance and advanced his own agenda in my life.

The legacy and fellowship of my fellow marines remain strong to this day. On November tenth every year, all my USMC buddies celebrate our service and the USMC birthday with email high-fives and greetings of *Semper Fidelis*. The 242nd anniversary just passed, but I remember the 200th like it was yesterday.

On that historic day, fellow Navy wrestler Tom Jones and I executed a brilliant tactical maneuver at the Marine Corps Birthday Ball in Okinawa, Japan. After one too many Dr. Peppers, Lt. Jones and I angled a firecracker into the right rear pocket of our executive officer as he concluded his commemorative comments. Seconds later, it ignited and blew off his pocket and scorched his skivvies to the raucous delight of every marine in attendance. Only on the two hundredth USMC anniversary would junior officer felons like us go unpunished for such bravado. November tenth each year covers many junior officer sins.

I resigned my commission as a captain in June of 1977. If anything, my esteem for the US Marine Corps, its time-tested values, its outstanding men and women, and its enduring legacy has multiplied over the decades. I proudly fly my USMC flag on national holidays—and, of course, every November tenth.

Loose Threads: Life Unravels

My marine corps career and exit to the civilian sector was not a solo journey. Ten days after graduation from the Naval Academy, I married my high school girlfriend. We tied the knot in June of 1972. Believe it or not, we married at St. Joseph's Catholic Church in Babylon, despite my desire to distance myself from that chapter of my life. Go figure.

Andrea had graduated from Babylon High School a year behind me. Her class voted her best-looking senior girl. We dated through my senior year in high school and then weathered plebe year's challenges. For two additional years, we maintained a long-distance relationship with letters (email hadn't yet been invented), phone calls, and holiday visits. In my senior year at the academy, Andrea moved to Annapolis but spent most of the spring alone due to the penalty imposed by Captain Ryan for my early lunch gathering.

Greg, my oldest son, was born almost one year to the day after our summer wedding. June 16 is Greg's birthday. It's also the anniversary of Vanessa's death, and every few years the calendar produces a trifecta: Greg's birthday, Vanessa's anniversary, and Father's Day all fall on the same Sunday. It's always a blessed but conflicted day.

Life in the US Marine Corps would take my young family to the marine officers training school in Quantico, Virginia, where I learned infantry tactics; the sweltering desert heat of 29 Palms, California, where I honed air defense practices; Camp Pendleton (north of San Diego) where my team repeatedly practiced air-to-air combat drills with US Marine, Navy, and Air Force fighter squadrons; and then Okinawa, Japan, where my family set up roost despite opposition from the local USMC authority.

Okinawa was designated as an "unaccompanied tour" due to short-notice deployments, but I found no regulations *prohibiting* bringing family if one could find suitable housing, which I did shortly after my arrival. Andrea and two-year-old Greg then joined me in a small flat just outside the gates of the Futenma Marine Air Station. I was the married envy of my unaccompanied friends. Plus, I had a good excuse to pass on the Officer Club drinking games and the rowdy bars in Naha, Okinawa. Instead, I'd head home to my family.

After Okinawa, I was technically assigned to the Cherry Point Naval Air Station in North Carolina, but it was from there that I "deployed" to the US Olympic training camp for the first seven months of 1976. Andrea and Greg tagged along for most of that venture as well. We were a very resourceful, flexible, and adaptable family.

When I returned to Cherry Point after the Montreal Games, my unit set sail almost immediately to a NATO assignment in Norway. On this truly unaccompanied assignment, I camped in the Norwegian mountains overlooking the North Atlantic Ocean with a small contingent of sardine-eating Norwegian rangers. Our interest was the Russian navy.

After listening in on the Russians for a few long months, I returned to Cherry Point and made plans to leave the Marine Corps in June of 1977. At a junior-officer career fair, I was connected to a job with consumer products giant Procter & Gamble. P&G was expanding its manufacturing operations in South Georgia and hiring men and women with leadership experience. My career focus instantly shifted from spying on the Russians and directing vertical take-off Harrier jets to making paper—Charmin toilet paper. Yup, go figure!

P&G proved to be a hand-in-glove assignment for me. My career took off on a fast track. My job was technically challenging, teamwork oriented, highly competitive, and demanded strong problem-solving and leadership skills. In one assignment, I led a team piloting an innovative work system that shattered existing labor and managerial norms. We knocked the project out of the park and kicked off a new era of self-directed work teams, which transformed the manufacturing landscape at P&G. But behind the mirage of professional success, my marriage was disintegrating. What had happened to that relationship that began in high school and endured the rigors of military deployments? I'm not proud of the backstory.

In short, I loosened the straps of marital discipline and established my own boundaries. Some of that craziness came from an upwelling of the rebellious, high-risk nature that had served me well through high school, the Naval Academy, the marine corps, and now the business sector. Deep inside, I knew my compass heading was wrong, but it was easy to pin blame on my contentious adolescence and ignore the consequences of risky behaviors. God, whom I hardly had time for, gave me ample warnings, but I chose to ignore them.

Every marriage has its challenges, but for the liberated, free-wheeling, non-military community of thirty-somethings in the late seventies, it was very easy to wander. When a guy chooses to have more female friends than male—in the work setting or community—an inner alarm should sound, but I squelched it. My wife Jan, the TV personality at that time, was one of these friends but not the only one. In retrospect, I should have been talking to a counselor to help me unwind the tight spring of my discontent, which had much more to do with my inner personal conflict than anything related to Andrea.

Officially, Andrea and I were married for ten years, but we were separated on and off for the last two. We made several attempts at reconciliation. Andrea approached each of those in good faith with forgiveness and humility; I did not. I played by my own rules in the rough seas of our separations. In that tumultuous zone, God's grace nevertheless prevailed with the blessing of our daughter Erica, the awesome and beloved mom of my first two grandchildren. Ultimately, however, Andrea decided that she'd had enough of my noncommittal nonsense and rightfully divorced me.

The divorce was particularly traumatic for my son Greg. In the years that followed, I attempted to rebuild my relationship with him, but with limited success. It was a discouraging and painful season of life for us both. One afternoon in his early high school years, I took a new tact. "What's the *one* thing I can do to improve our relationship?" I asked Greg over lunch.

Greg is a brilliant, Georgia-Tech-educated, computer science engineer, but it can take him ten minutes to decide if he wants cheese on his hamburger. But on this afternoon, there was no hesitation in his response. "Apologize to my mom," Greg said. "That's the single biggest thing you could do."

So I did, and I invited grace and humility to subdue my pride and pugnacity. In my letter to Andrea, I took ownership of the events precipitating our divorce and apologized for a chapter of life that had knocked us both off our horses. It took some time, but when Andrea recognized my apology was authentic, she accepted it and planted a peace offering in our blended families that has served us well for twenty-five years.

Our two families are comprised of people of all ages who have learned to come together to celebrate weddings as well as some of our holidays and birthdays. There have been a few funerals too. At our last Christmas gathering, I told Andrea, "You deserved better than I gave you, and I admire the character of your husband, Brad." She simply nodded.

Exiting my divorce, a new word became lodged in my personal history—failure. Until now, I had always triumphed over adversity. But at this juncture of life, for the first time, cunning, resourcefulness, and tenacity yielded no victory. God was attempting to teach me something important in life, but I kept him at arm's length. Says the prophet Isaiah about the mysterious work of God, "I reveal myself to those who did not ask for me; I am found by those who do not seek me" (Isa. 65:1).

It was my divorce and the weight of its consequences—relationally, spiritually, and professionally—that finally tilted me to meet with a church priest. No, I didn't get much encouragement from him, but God used him nonetheless. Failure does that; it redirects our focus and opens our minds to hard truths and pivot points in life. Ultimately, my P&G boss would pound the final nail into the coffin of my tenure in the Peach State.

Tom, you're an outstanding complement to our team, a bold and innovative thinker," he said. "But your relationship with Jan is a poke in the eye to our plant culture. I can't promote you to the next level. Jan's former husband is on that team, but you're well suited to a role on P&G's corporate staff in Cincinnati. I'd suggest you get a fresh start there. It will be good for your career. You're finished here."

Failure to Launch: Looking Back

"Being confident of this, that He who began a good work in you will carry it on to completion until the day of Jesus Christ" (Phil. 1:6). Yes, God's work in our lives continues until, well… until Jesus hugs us at heaven's gate! But on this side of eternity, God's work in us is often carried out in our failures, trials, and setbacks, and, occasionally, through great victories. Every chapter of life demands meaningful life change and helps point us to greater life purpose. But we need to be enrolled in God's game plan.

In my early thirties, life change was elusive because I savored the role of captain of my ship and zeroed in on my own agenda. But the consequences of self-reliance were high. "The way of a fool seems right to him," says the writer of Proverbs, "but a wise man listens to advice" (Prov. 12:15). If self-reliance has you in its grip, cut loose of it and latch on to the advice in Proverbs. By God's grace, it will help free you from yourself.

I've also learned God uses what he hates (divorce, in my case) to accomplish what he loves. He hates a haughty and proud spirit and stands opposed to it (James 4:6). But he loves the work of running down people who are running away from him… and giving us a new nature. He's the "Hound of Heaven,"[8] and even if you have not invited God into your life, you may sense Someone nipping at your heels.

Grace is difficult to accept and graciousness even harder to live out if you are strong, self-reliant, and accomplished. But when your

---

8 Thompson, *The Hound of Heaven*, 38.

life is ripped apart by self-inflicted failure, your inner compass starts seeking true north. "God speaks in the language you know best," says Oswald Chambers, "not through your ears, but through your circumstances."[9]

I still find it intriguing that God's permissive will allows us to make fantastically foolish choices. But the Bible is full of people who experience colossal failure on the journey to greater purpose. King David, Bathsheba's lover and the murderer of her husband, Uriah, is one. So is the apostle Peter, who denied his association with Jesus to save his own skin. David finds restoration in Psalm 51—it's an amazing read—and Peter is forgiven by the risen Jesus himself after the resurrection (John 21:17). Imagine that turnaround experience!

Life unraveled for me in this chapter of life, though not without hope for a fresh start. The F-word—*failure*—took up residence within me along with its painful consequences. I was on my way to a new job, a new city, and 462 miles would separate me from my two young children.

The apostle Paul tells us that "in all things God works for the good of those who love him" (Rom. 8:28). This can be a hard truth when life turns on you—or when your own behavior creates a crisis. On life's journey, God often gives a pop quiz before the syllabus is completely understood. Life experience with no life change, however, invites more life lessons. We're supposed to learn something on the journey of life!

At this point, among other things, I learned that resilient character rests on the foundation of integrity, wisdom, discipline, humility, and respect for God-given boundaries in life. But the *power* of God made perfect in my weaknesses eluded me. All I had was an inkling of him nipping at my heels.

---

9 Chambers, *My Utmost for His Highest*, January 29.

3

White Hot!

See, I have refined you, though not as silver.
I have tested you in the furnace of affliction.

—Isaiah 48:10

Anguish… and a Cry for Help

From my journal (September 1992, Scunthorpe, England): "It has been three months since the accident. I've returned to a work assignment in the UK and I'm alone and terrified. It's my first business venture out of the country since Vanessa's death. I think I'm emerging from shock and entering the stark reality of unfathomable loss. I'm at frightening level of hopelessness with no one to hold on to."

With my desperation recorded, I ventured out from the Beverly Hotel onto the streets of Scunthorpe, a small and very British village in northeast England, not far from the Scottish border. I'd found a small park near the hotel to vent my pent-up anger. There, I poured out my heart and soul to God and tried to bridge the chasm of perceived betrayal that separated us. I thought of David's groan of anguish, "My God, my God, why have you forsaken me?" (Ps. 22:1). It was the same agonizing cry Jesus poured out before yielding to death on the cross. No one can fully comprehend Christ's physical and spiritual anguish on that day; he was to drink the cup of suffering on the cross.

There was no other way. But neither should we *mis*understand it. It was a dreadful cry of despair! Though my anguish would not touch a Savior's grief, I had my own cup to drink. There was no other way.

In reflection, I can't imagine what passing townspeople may have thought about the despondent Yank in their midst. Emotionally exhausted and contemplating my trek back to the hotel, I sensed something invading my space, but I was alone in the park. From that mysterious presence, however, came a vexing question: "How is your tenacity working for you?" It was an inner voice reminiscent of my priestly encounter several years earlier—nothing audible, just a poignant and disturbing question piercing my soul.

Entering the Beverly Hotel (it's still there!), I moseyed up the stairs to the second floor. On the wall next to my room hung a poem. I stopped for a moment to read it. It spoke of a man's (or woman's) dream where they envisioned themselves casually walking along the seashore with God. They pondered a deep and disturbing mystery.

> Across the sky flashed scenes from my life.
> For each scene, I noticed two sets of foot-
> prints in the sand...
> I noticed that many times along the path of
> my life there was only one set of footprints.
> I also noticed that it happened at the very
> lowest and saddest times in my life.
> This really bothered me and I questioned
> the Lord about it...

"Footprints in the Sand"[10] is the poem's title. I later learned of its wide popularity, with more than one writer over the years claiming authorship. At the time, I'd never heard of it, but its vexing premise taunted me.

> I don't understand why when I need you most
> you would leave me.

---

10 Pearls of Wisdom entry on Footprints in the Sand by Mary Stevenson (1922–1999), accessed on May 9, 2018, www.sapphyr.net/largegems/footprints.htm.

Yes, I thought, I know that sense of loneliness and abandonment. I read on.

> My precious child, I love you and would never leave you.
>   During your times of trial and suffering, when you see only one set of footprints, it was then that I carried you.

Standing alone in the hotel hallway, the last three months of life raced, frame by frame, through my mind. It then halted abruptly at the "tenacity" question posed in the park.

"Not very well, Lord," I answered.

And my inner voice spoke again. "Your walk into the future demands *surrender*. It is a new word you need to learn."

I pondered the source of the message. Was it the Spirit of God, an angel, maybe Jesus himself? There was no harp concerto, no angelic chorus in the hallway, no promises of an easy pathway, and no miraculous balm for the grueling pain of grief and loss. There was just God's presence, which I imagined to be manifested in surrender. In the flood of tears that followed, I tried to envision how this new word might change my future.

For the first time, my journal testifies, I off-loaded the crushing weight of self-reliance, control, and survival to someone else. That September night, the hint of a new beginning was in the air, but no one handed me a get-out-of-jail-free card. I just embraced a new pathway. There were many days following Vanessa's death when there was only one set of footprints in the sand—and they weren't mine!

Rewind: Fresh Start in Cincinnati

My Scunthorpe experience came ten years after my "pep" talk with my P&G boss in Georgia. Here's what came earlier in that pivotal decade of life.

With the tragedy and trauma of our divorces behind us, Jan and I began to look to the future. It was an awkward season for both of us, and my exile north to Cincinnati was on the horizon. One day in late 1982, Jan surprised me with a question: "Would you be willing to meet with the priest at my church?"

Jan knew of my encounter with Father Ulrich, so my hesitation didn't rattle her. "No more priests, thank you," I told her.

But she persisted. "John Jenkins is very different from the priest in your Catholic experience. He's an Episcopal priest. I think you will like him."

Jan prevailed, of course, and I did like her priest, although I knew nothing about Episcopal anything. Jan had been attending St. Paul's Episcopal Church since her divorce, and Jenkins, she said, was a welcome breath of spiritual fresh air. Father Jenkins introduced another new word to my vocabulary—*grace.* I was thirty-three years old and realized instantly I had no context whatsoever for the concept. What was this crazy notion of undeserved merit and favor connected to God's love? Nothing in life had ever been given to me unmerited. It was either earned, taken through hard work, or unattainable.

Father Jenkins and I had long conversations about religion and grace. He helped wean me off my spiritual bitterness and revived my spiritual growth, which for a long time had been stunted. I attribute the launch of my spiritual awakening to Father Jenkins. Even today, I glibly tell friends that St. Paul's Episcopal Church served as a spiritual halfway house for a grace-deprived Catholic. There, my spiritual needle began to creep out of the red zone.

In early 1983, after many get-togethers with Father Jenkins, Jan and I asked him to marry us. He responded by taking us further under his wing for much-needed marriage counseling. He also announced he could not marry us during the church's Lenten season. "But," he added gleefully, "why not April third—Easter Sunday? In addition to being outside the period of Lent, the church would be ornately decorated for Easter services, and we wouldn't need to buy any flowers!"

The timing would be tight, however. My fresh-start date in Cincinnati was Wednesday, April 6. So, early on Monday, April 4, the day after our wedding, Jan and I forfeited any honeymoon adventure, jumped on Interstate 75, and headed north.

Once in Cincinnati, Jan brandished her television and journalism credentials and quickly landed a job with a renowned public relations and marketing firm. Soon thereafter, we joined a small Episcopal Church. It became the center of our social life, but it lacked the robust theological grounding we'd experienced with Father Jenkins at St. Paul's. Perhaps the most notable memory from our Cincinnati church was our friendship with the inventor of the popular card game Uno.

Once in Cincinnati, however, three issues quickly gathered at our front door and began to work against any long-term stay.

Jan is from Jacksonville, Florida. In her mind, we had moved to the frozen tundra. She was not far off the mark. Our first winter in Cincinnati was the coldest one there in fifty years. With the temperature bottoming out at minus twenty-two degrees Fahrenheit one winter day, even the garage door opener called it quits!

Also complicating our new life was time spent making a biweekly excursion to Atlanta to spend time with my children. Every other Friday afternoon like clockwork, we'd make the eight-hour drive, find a hotel, and host ten-year-old Greg and toddler Erica for the weekend. Then on Sunday evening, we'd scramble back to Cincinnati. The hotel setting was never ideal for leisurely visits with the kids, so we searched for a condo in the North Georgia mountains. Big Canoe—about thirty-five miles north of our biweekly destination to pick up the children—offered a perfect solution. But the twice-monthly jaunt to Atlanta tore at the new fiber of our marriage.

One time, in tears laced with exhaustion from too much time on the road, Jan squeezed out a hard message on the drive home. "I, too, love seeing Greg and Erica, but our lives revolve around this eight-hour drive every two weeks. I'm not sure where I fit in." Jan's question had nothing to do with her unqualified love for the children. It was a simply a relational wake-up call in our fledgling marriage.

Thirdly, I found the P&G corporate atmosphere in Cincinnati stuffy and oppressive. In Georgia, innovation and new ideas had been celebrated. In frozen Cincinnati, the culture mirrored the weather.

It rewarded compliance and discouraged originality. That sent me home frustrated and professionally wilted many evenings.

The cold weather, the biweekly scramble, and a stuffy work environment all shouted, "Change!" So in the summer of 1984, we sold our house, gave notice at work, and planned our foray to Atlanta. I, as yet, had no job there. Jan, on the other hand, had floated her résumé down Atlanta's Peachtree Street and grabbed an exciting new job in a week.

Atlanta: Fresh Start, Take Two!

Living temporarily in our mountain condo, I learned that military experience, a feisty leadership profile, and Procter & Gamble on my résumé could generate job opportunities. In the fall of 1984, I seized one. Then, on the strength of Jan's employment with her high-profile PR firm, we managed to purchase a home—just five miles from Greg and Erica.

Jan worked with Coca-Cola during their New Coke fiasco as well as with head football coach Vince Dooley at the University of Georgia. Another client was New York Yankees legend Mickey Mantle, with whom she worked in a real estate endeavor. Her work with baseball's famous number 7 frustrated me to no end. No matter how I played my New York legacy, Jan was unwillingly to wangle an autographed baseball.

"Can't you tell him it's for your New York husband?" I pleaded.

"No, it's unprofessional," was Jan's response.

Mine was, "Gimme a break!"

The private company I joined was headquartered in Canada and had three manufacturing sites in the US, one in England, and one planned for France. As the new thirty-something VP of manufacturing, I had more challenges and headaches than I'd ever hoped for. The biggest issue? As an outcome of a chaotic leadership chapter, the company was swimming in red ink, and the bank creditors were preparing to cross the Rubicon.

Enduring principles, systems, and disciplines, I'd learned at P&G worked their operational wizardry, and in under a year, profitability had turned around nicely. New management in the company's largest US plant proved to be an asset in the financial transformation; I'd hired friend, West Point grad, and P&G alumnus Dick Ducote to run the Philadelphia operation.

The allure of black ink motivated the company owners to invest, but not in the next generation of new products, operational improvements, or new technology. Instead, they were more interested in a sleek new jet with a full-time salaried pilot. I pitched a hissy fit over the misguided use of capital and predicted the company would be bankrupt in a year. I missed the mark by three months; insolvency followed about fifteen months later. But before that, in the months surrounding the aircraft purchase, my over-the-top criticism alienated the management team. They gave me a choice: resign or they would fire me. For prideful reasons, no doubt, I chose the former and resigned.

Battle weary but somewhat relieved, I limped home early that October Tuesday. Vanessa at the time was only six weeks old.

"What are you going to do next?" Jan asked, without a hint of panic in her voice.

"Not sure," I said, "but my severance package will get us to Christmas. Management was generous," I remarked. "They could have stiffed me. We'll figure it out in the weeks ahead."

The next move on the chessboard, however, answered Jan's question. Unknown to me at the time, company management had also cornered my colleague Dick in Philadelphia. "We know you're aligned with that malcontent in Atlanta," they said. "We don't need you either."

Dick called me the next day and related the story above. Then he asked, "Any ideas on what we are going to do next?"

"'Next,' became Schuler-Ducote and shortly thereafter, SDF International, a consulting company we envisioned in my basement in the fall of 1986. Since we had just forfeited our company cars, we leased a snazzy Honda Accord to get around town and swapped it every other week. A fax machine was our first capital purchase—

costing us a whopping $3,500 back then! Over the next twenty-two years, however, SDF International flourished. We worked in over twenty countries around the world, offering breakthrough-inspiring insights to product-development processes, manufacturing operations, and progressive employee work systems.

On the home front, even with a healthy dose of business travel, life assumed a treasured normalcy. Our neighborhood was chock-full of young families with children. Cul-de-sac parties, backyard gatherings, rope swings, monkey bars, and an occasional acorn fight launched great friendships that have lasted to this day.

Predictably, Greg and Erica visited every other weekend. Bryan, Vanessa's younger brother, joined the clan in December 1987. At birth, Bryan weighed in just shy of ten pounds. That's significant given the fact that Jan, if soaking wet and with her pockets full of BBs, would never tilt the scale at more than 118 pounds while pregnant.

Vanessa and Bryan attended a Montessori school and day-school sessions at our church in Roswell, an emerging suburb in north Atlanta. The Episcopal Church we chose there, unfortunately, mirrored our church in Cincinnati. Theologically, it was shallow, often elevating an Atlanta Falcons win over the Exodus led by Moses. But it, too, was full of great people who cared for one another.

About a year later, we sold the condo in the North Georgia mountains and searched for another vacation spot where we could enjoy a getaway for our blended family. St. Augustine, a historic and attractive beachside community in Florida, fit the bill, and we bought a beachside condo there. Three to four times a year—and almost always at Christmas—we'd pack the van with four kids, beach toys, and car seats and make the six-to-seven-hour trip to the beach.

It was there we headed in June 1992 to enjoy a few days in St. Augustine and then drive to Orlando to visit Disney World. Greg had school obligations and couldn't go this time, but Vanessa, Erica, and Bryan were so juiced up to see Cinderella and the Ninja Turtles that we could hardly keep them bridled in the van. With astonishing creative genius, Disney World succeeds in infusing joy and excitement into kids of all ages! Vanessa, with her blond, princess-like, flowing hair and limitless energy, insisted on photo ops with every

Disney character in the park. We obliged until her Disney battery ran dry that Thursday evening.

After spending a few hours the next day at MGM Studios, we opted not to return to St. Augustine for the night as planned. Instead, we'd make the long haul to Atlanta in one shot. The kids could sleep a good part of the trip home.

But about eighty miles into our journey, near Ocala, life would be forever changed.

Every Parent's Nightmare—Revisited!

Cruising home on I-75, I caught a glimpse in my mirror of a driver approaching at an alarming clip. He abruptly veered into the center lane of traffic to avoid a rear-end collision with our van. But it was too late.

The approaching vehicle clipped the right rear fender of the van and spun us into the grassy median separating northbound traffic from vehicles traveling south. In an instant, the tires bit the soft turf, and the Caravan flipped and tumbled across the seventy-foot median—five times, per the police report. It landed upright on its wheels in the *left lane of opposing, southbound traffic.*

The violence of the crash ripped open the hatchback, crushed the front passenger cab, and pitched Bryan and Vanessa out of their car seats. Bryan lay on I-75, to the utter shock of an approaching driver, who miraculously avoided running over him. Exiting through the shattered driver's-side window, I scooped Bryan off the roadway and carried him onto the median. Erica, stunned and in shock, remained pinned to her seat inside the twisted wreckage. Jan, miraculously uninjured, crawled into the back seat and extracted Erica from the van through the severed hatchback. She then ran to Vanessa, who lay motionless in the median, and began to breathe life into Vanessa's lungs. I laid Bryan in the grass near Jan, Erica, and Vanessa and collapsed alongside them. Injured too, I labored desperately for a breath myself.

Two short hours before that, the chills and thrills of an MGM Studio tour and the gleeful shouts of a family on a date with Snow

White had filled the air. Now, we lay huddled together in the median like ship-wrecked refugees, waiting desperately for rescue.

Gracious people on I-75 interrupted their summer drives to help. Emergency-vehicle sirens screamed at a frightening pitch, and police cruisers converged on the scene. EMTs quickly assessed the situation and tended first to Vanessa and then to me. An emergency worker patched up Bryan's cuts and bruises, but miraculously, Bryan was not seriously injured. Erica too, though traumatized, had escaped serious injury.

Jan accompanied Vanessa to a waiting ambulance, which then raced to Ocala General Hospital, followed by a second ambulance with Bryan and Erica. A third took me as I struggled to breathe and maintain any mental awareness of what had just happened—and then the lights went out.

On awakening the next morning, I learned Vanessa's condition was critical; she had been transferred to ICU at Shands Children's Hospital in Gainesville. Jan's brother, a police officer, lived close by in Jacksonville and came to pick up Bryan from the hospital in Ocala. My parents drove in from their home in St. Petersburg, briefly popped in on me, but more importantly, got Erica to an airport and on a flight home. I would spend another agonizing day in Ocala, away from Jan and Vanessa.

On Sunday, I was unable to convince the doctors to release me, but my chest and lung injuries were the least of my worries. Against the doctors' counsel, I checked myself out of the hospital, rented a car, and drove to Shands. I arrived at the ICU disheveled and one flip-flop short of a pair.

Vanessa's condition was still serious; her vital signs kept her prognosis wavering between critical and guarded. She'd made enough progress to prompt a word of encouragement from Miranda, the ICU nurse. It was a moment the nurse would come to regret for years to come. "I think she's out of danger," she said. "When she came here, it was touch and go, but I think she'll be okay."

Vanessa fought for life another day. On Tuesday, the doctor's routines changed noticeably, and we knew Vanessa had entered a new phase of her life-and-death struggle. We pleaded with God to miraculously intervene and touch her failing heart.

He did. He stopped it.

It was June 16, four days after the accident. I held Vanessa's precious tiny hand as the heart monitor went silent and announced her departure. Jan kissed her and whispered, "*Now* you will know everything, Vanessa." It was the answer to a perplexing question Vanessa had asked Jan many times at bedtime: "Mama, when will I know everything?" Jan's answer was always the same: "When you get to heaven, sweet girl. When you meet Jesus."

We would later learn that God's definition of *healing* and *a miracle* is radically different than our own. We live in the moment; God is never constrained by time.

Miranda, too, was devastated and she grieved deeply with us. Her mistaken prognosis of Vanessa's recovery tormented her soul and in part, ultimately drove her to leave the ICU nursing field. Jan bonded deeply with Miranda and they stayed in contact for many years.

That Tuesday evening and for months to come, I would rewind my mental tape of those moments on I-75. Shock had obscured critical details and blurred the boundary between nightmare and reality. Many things were unclear; one was not. The accident could have taken an enormously higher toll on my family; it could have been *much* worse!

The image of a two-thousand-pound missile of a van hurtling across the median into oncoming traffic must have been terrifying to the drivers in its path. If another vacation bound family had slammed head-on into our disabled van, Jan, Erica, and I would have been killed instantly. With vivid acuity, I recall that very thought as I lifted Bryan off the roadway; my son was bruised, bloodied, but alive. Not thirty feet from Bryan, I saw a truck stopped on the roadway and its driver running toward me. If he had traveled *one-half second* longer, Bryan's life would have been snuffed out as well.

It's both mystical and exasperating that certain parts of an experience stay chiseled in the mind. I knew instantly that fateful day that we had been spared greater tragedy; I was sure of that even before the end of Vanessa's story had played out. But dark thoughts had also been awakened: *Why am I going through something so devastating? Am*

I being punished? Why did God let this happen? What did I do wrong? Who's in control of this world… or is everything spinning out of control?

All questions I'd have to answer in the months and years to come.

Crisis of Belief: New Threads in One's Life Tapestry

About a year after Vanessa's death, I read James Dobson's *When God Doesn't Make Sense*—which by our standards is frequently! I still recall a pivotal story that went something like this.

A man is enjoying the thrills and chills of racing his late-model sports car down a mountain road in the Colorado Rockies. Successfully negotiating dangerous hairpin turns, he cranks on a few more RPM's. Suddenly, his high-speed driving skills betray him, and he fails to bend the steering wheel tightly enough into a turn. The car launches sideways off the roadway, pitching the driver into a tree on a near-vertical wooded slope. Snatching hold of a branch, he dangles above the valley, watching in horror as the car crashes and explodes in the valley below. He begins to shout wildly, "Help! Help! Is there anyone out there?"

God hears his plea. "This is the Lord. What do you want me to do?"

"Save me, Lord!" the man shrieks.

"Okay," says the Lord, "let go of the branch. I will catch you as you fall."

The man hesitates and contemplates his options. His reply echoes across the valley. "Is there anyone *else* out there?"[11]

At a recent church service, the pastor asked a very simple question: "When trials or tragedy find their way into your life, will you move toward God or run from him?" Unassumingly, I let my eyes wander to the congregants sitting near me; I wanted to gauge their outward reaction to his question. Based on text-message activity and the number of people thumbing through church bulletins, I sensed

---

11 Dobson, *When God Doesn't Make Sense*, 25.

that the question for many was on par with the weather forecast—easy to ignore when things were going well.

Dobson's reckless mountain driver, however, answered the pastor's question; he was undergoing a crisis of belief. His reaction is not uncommon; it mirrors what most of us do when we face a crisis. Our natural reaction is to run *from* God (or opt for a better alternative). Few of us run *toward* him.

I am an experienced kayaker, and dozens of times, I have tackled the famed Chattooga River in North Georgia (of *Deliverance* notoriety). It's full of highly challenging class 5 rapids that can snuff out a life under a rock shelf or drown you in a keeper hydraulic—an undertow that won't release its catch. No one with any common sense challenges the Chattooga River without proficiency in getting their boat back into a right-side-up position after turbulent waters, paddling mistakes, or underwater boulders have their way with you. One can practice rolling a kayak all day in a swimming pool, but when you flip and are mauled by the raging river, there is always a moment of panic—a crisis of belief—as the frigid water snatches your breath away. Survival, though, depends on calmly executing a well-practiced righting technique, not punching out of the boat.

It's the same with our faith journeys.

Many authors over the decades have attempted to put meaning to the term *crisis of belief.* I like Henry Blackaby's take in *Experiencing God.* A crisis of belief is not a calamity in your life, he says, "But a turning point where you must make a decision. You must decide what you truly believe about God."[12]

In reflection, Jan and I would characterize the first two years after Vanessa's death as an upside-down existence coupled with a crisis of belief. The accident snatched our breath away and laid our faith bare. That meant different things to each of us. For Jan, I came to learn, the struggle had largely to do with trust. Her daily prayers before the accident were always centered on the safety of our children. The loss of Vanessa struck at the heart of the vulnerability of her faith.

---

12 Blackaby, *Experiencing God,* 109.

I pinned my own hopes for survival on some bizarre notion of toughness and tenacity, a ridiculous self-scripted doctrine I had latched onto much earlier in life and now held on to with a death grip. Three weeks after our accident and still recovering from a disabling lung injury, I ran the annual Peachtree Road Race, a 6.2-mile jaunt through downtown Atlanta on the Fourth of July. I'm not sure what I was trying to prove to God, but as I crossed the finish line, I pumped my fist at him.

Shortly after Vanessa's death, a friend invited me to lunch. I remember the restaurant, the booth location, and the conversation—but not a hint about this person's identity. In reflection, I've often wondered if the date was a dream or a hungry angel looking for a meal! Without any accommodating preamble, my angel friend rocked my upside-down world. "Tom," he said, "your marriage is at risk. If you don't take responsibility for the survival of your marriage, it will fail. Half the couples who lose a child don't make it. Believe me, it can happen to you."

Jan and I were already facing challenges in our marriage; they ignited instantly after Vanessa's death. Bridging the new challenges of grief and the resulting questions about faith would be no easy path. For instance, we were finding that our grieving patterns were completely out of sync. When Jan mustered up the energy to talk, I'd prefer to take a long run. She could watch videos of Vanessa; I'd storm out of the room in anger and despair. Jan was reading everything she could get her hands on to bolster her faith; I passed on most of her reading list.

In the crucible of grief, Jan and I switched processing modes. God has wired me as an *external processor*; I like to work things out verbally, but in this season, I went silent. Jan, on the other hand, is an *internal processor*… but now she wanted to talk things out. The problem? I didn't want to listen. In many ways, we answered the pastor's "Will you turn from or to God?" question differently. Jan diligently pursued God's help in finding faith-based answers. I was attempting to make the self-reliance option work.

Four-year-old Bryan faced his own demons and was doing so under our umbrella of watchfulness at home. He was ready for preschool, but no school would accept him. They considered him to have been too recently traumatized and thus at a high risk for having behavioral issues. We took him to a child psychologist to help him work through his post-accident recovery.

Holidays, birthdays, and anniversaries also offered unique tests. Each in its own way takes on a muted celebratory tone when there is an empty place setting at the table. Christmas morning, without the joyous squeals of six-year-old Vanessa, crushed our spirits.

All around us were hard questions that seemed to have no answers. It was agonizingly difficult to walk past Vanessa's empty bedroom every day, but it seemed harder still to sell the house with all its memories. Should we hold onto every toy, favorite book, and teddy bear or pitch the whole lot?

Close friends didn't know what to say and avoided eye contact. More distant friends fumbled over their choice of words. "How's the family?" they might try and then offer an awkward apology for not knowing what to say.

For me, New Year's Eve became an exasperating and emotional tug-of-war. I wrestled with the question of what I should hold onto from the past and what I should release as I moved on to a new future. Burdened by those questions at our first New Year's party after Vanessa's death, I bailed out before midnight and walked home alone in the dark of night.

Seeds of discouragement also sprouted at our church. In our small Episcopal community, the idea of devastating tragedy was conveniently denied, not confronted as reality in a broken world. Many in our church, however, ached to learn more about our faith journey amid our grief and invited Jan and me to small-group gatherings and Bible studies.

The pastor wanted to learn less. "Your story is too painful and uncomfortable for our church members," he told us one day. "I want our church family to be happy."

Be assured, *nowhere* in the Bible are God's people promised happiness in this world. Instead, faith, perseverance, and future hope are more resilient biblical themes. "I should not be debating this point with you," I argued with the rector. "You should be telling me this!"

A year later, we would leave that church community, suffering a slow death from spiritual malnourishment. In explaining our decision, I told our church friends that our refrigerator was full of their kindness and love, but that our hearts and minds craved the spiritual food we needed to survive.

My Scunthorpe experience followed my initial discussion with the rector. That was an important pivot point of life focus. When you meet Jesus, he will tell you quickly, "I am the way, the truth and the life" (John 14:6). I desperately needed that spiritual infusion. But if you have an encounter with the risen Christ like I did, don't expect him to give you a pass to Easy Street. That, he never promised. In fact, he told us just the opposite: "In this world, you will have trouble, but take heart! I have overcome the world" (John 16:33).

Jan and I did *take heart*, but as Jesus said, we had trouble. I teetered still in a crisis of belief, my parachute of surrender nowhere near fully deployed. Yes, I had an encounter with the living God in a park in England, but I had not yet fully reconciled what I believed about him.

"God does not give us overcoming life," says Oswald Chambers. "He gives us life as we overcome."[13] Perseverance, initiative, and hope beyond our circumstances are vitally important biblical themes. I learned there is no winged Uber chariot to transport us to the promised land; we must fight in the strength God gives us to possess it. To be healed, Jesus told the invalid, "*Go...* and wash in the pool of Siloam" (John 9:7; emphasis added). He told the man with the shriveled hand, "*Get up* and stand... stretch out your hand," before he could be fully restored (Luke 6:8–10; emphasis added). When ten lepers called out to Jesus for healing, he said, "*Go,* show yourselves to the priests" (Luke 17:14; emphasis added)... and each was healed as they obeyed.

And so it is in our own trials. We must take some initiative, or we become victims of our circumstances. The trilogy of perseverance, human initiative, and future hope (beyond this broken world!) are vital *new* threads that must be woven into the tapestry of life.

---

13 Chambers, *My Utmost for His Highest*, February 16.

Depression's Clutches

As the calendar rolled deeper into 1993, my despair showed itself in new ways. I sensed my mental acuity waning, and sleep became elusive. "When I wake up, I get up!" I confessed to Jan. Frequently that time of waking was in the wee hours of the morning. Exhaustion set in, and I found it difficult to function at work. Anger boiled just below the surface and gushed out inexplicably.

I also became obsessed with determining *precisely* what God was doing in this wretched chapter of my life. Routinely, I would over-think my way into a cul-de-sac where there were no answers and then weep in frustration. I moved grimly toward a Dr.-Jekyll-and-Mr.-Hyde existence. My accommodating façade at social functions was masking a more threatening and dangerous private reality.

In this debilitating season, I faced a day when the grip of melancholy on my soul escalated to a dangerous level. My inner conflict was incapacitating, and I began to sense evil's hand reaching for me and inviting me into death's inner circle—a place where I could be free from my pain and anguish. It one sense, that option frightened me to the core of my soul, but in another, it drew me closer to a promise of calm and escape. It was an appealing offer—and I forged a plan. But God in his power intervened.

As a fledgling Bible student at the time, I could quote almost nothing in God's Word. But on this day, Romans 12:1 thundered in my head, not unlike the voice I'd heard after my encounter with Father Ulrich. "Therefore, I urge you, brothers, in view of God's mercy, to offer your bodies as living sacrifices, holy and pleasing to God—this is your spiritual act of worship." I stumbled over the word *living*… and let its command rescue me from my own hand. I have no doubt God tossed me another life ring that day—literally. He's always been in the rescue business.

Jan, too, was concerned about my worsening state. Seemingly in passing, she handed me what appeared to be a random magazine questionnaire. In truth, it was a calculated move on her part. The survey pointed to the markers of depression and I scored miserably in every category. Seeking vindication, I subtlety introduced the disturbing results to my office colleagues. Unanimously, they piled on. "Tom, you've lost your way," said one of my associates. "Get some help!" Before that, no one had dared broach the topic of "getting help" with the company leader. I was too distant and bristly when dressed as Mr. Hyde.

In God's grace, "help" had a name. Dr. Shirley Parsons was a gifted and skilled family counselor. She came highly recommended by my new church family, and I had talked with her previously about another topic—forgiveness issues centered on my dad.

Shirley disarmed me immediately. "You're an athlete, right?" she said.

I nodded.

"If I showed you an x-ray of a broken bone, could I convince you it should be reset to heal properly?"

I agreed.

"Here's your psychological x-ray. Then I'll explain how you got here," she said. "You're suffering from clinical depression. It's a medical condition as real as a broken bone, but it often takes longer to heal, and you can't see it on an x-ray. You need an antidepressant, which you will resist because you're a tough-guy athlete. But the antidepressant will help restore your equilibrium and make life going forward a fair fight. Then we'll talk about the loss of your daughter, your family history, and why you're struggling so badly. How does that sound?"

I nodded again. I knew I was losing the most important bout of my adult life.

Shirley was God-sent. If another pair of footprints had mysteriously appeared on the sandy beach that season of life, I'd have measured her feet. She helped me regain my physical, mental, and spiritual footing and moved me toward surrender. There would be no euphoric buzz from the antidepressants, just nourishment to restore my ravaged mind.

Within a month, my mental fog began to lift, and I recognized how much altitude I had lost over the prior year. I was shocked. Jan and my work colleagues were not. After regaining my equilibrium in life some months later, I weaned myself off the antidepressant drugs… and I've never needed them again. That note is for you, my reader friend, if you are anything like I was: proud, self-reliant, and sorely in need of restoration that only a prescribed medicine can provide.

Shirley helped me understand why my body had caved in to stress. She also pointed me to scripture. "The Bible," said Shirley, "can't answer *every* question in life, but it will answer yours." We talked many hours about the stages of grief, the Bible's definition of future hope, clinical depression, and how the death of a child can shred a marriage. "I can help you with all those issues," said Shirley, "but don't forget, there's that one remaining issue only you can put to rest. You alone must forgive your father. I can't do that for you."

Yes, about a year before our tragic loss, I was working with Shirley and an elder at my church to bridge the deep relational divide between my dad and me. R. T. Kendall's *Total Forgiveness* laid out the syllabus and principles. Reconciliation with Dad was an issue I'd pushed deeply underwater for many years. At that time, I was trapped in my own bitterness, but I was working toward resolution as my faith awakening progressed.

My journey toward reconciliation, however, was cruelly interrupted on I-75. With the trauma of losing Vanessa, the challenge of holding my marriage together, and increasing business pressures, my emotional reserves were depleted. In that zone of life, the unresolved issues with my dad began to creep once again into an already punishing chapter of my life.

Much of my resurrected anger centered on the "Tough it out!" philosophy my dad had instilled in me many years earlier in life. I deemed it corrupt and absent of any spiritual wisdom: it was no help to me in this bitter season. Surrender, I was learning, was a much better antidote. In retribution, I lashed out at him with corrosive words which only deepened our relational chasm. "It's not a new issue," I told Shirley. "It's just back on the front burner of life again."

Later that year, with Shirley's guidance, I wrote a letter to my dad, sharing how my bitterness had evolved, beginning in my adolescence. I still have a copy of the letter. It was not an appeal for an apology. Rather, it was a confession of truth made in hopeful anticipation of a more positive future. If measured strictly by the outcome, the letter and ensuing dialogue did little to improve our relationship. Dad would offer no *mea culpa* for the difficult chapters of life we'd endured together. But Shirley helped me understand that unconditional forgiveness has nothing to do with an apology. Rather, it douses the embers of bitterness in the forgiver and opens the jail door to new freedom.

Twenty-five years this side of losing Vanessa, I remain deeply indebted to Dr. Shirley Parsons. Absent her encouragement and clinical skills, there's no telling where I would have ended up. A competent Christian counselor is a unique breed of cat. Clinically trained, these professionals know the science behind their work. But spiritually astute, they also know when to release their patients to the grace of God.

New Hope—and (a) New Life

Father Time pushed one year off the calendar and introduced another. In 1994, I began to measure "progress" in larger increments—days and sometimes weeks versus hours free from the scorching reach of depression. Prayer became more routine, but when that failed, Psalms always gave voice to my pent-up frustration with God (just as it does today). The *peace* that Jesus promised his followers—*his* peace that came from total surrender to his Father's will—gradually became more spiritually tangible for me. But families who have lost loved ones know that feelings can turn on a dime. A child building a sand castle at the beach, a scene in a movie, or even a color-splashed butterfly dancing on a garden flower can send one reeling down memory lane.

My family's tenure at our local Episcopal Church was ending at that time. The decision to cut ties was tough and emotional. There, we had built the Vanessa Memorial Playground, generously funded by our church friends and family. Every year on Vanessa's anniversary and birthday, we go there to spiff up the playground and trim the landscape. On those visits, we frequently encounter Vanessa's Sunday school teachers and share memories—and a few tears.

Invited by neighborhood friends, we attended our first service at Fellowship Bible Church (FBC), where years later, I would serve in a pastoral role. The Sunday sermon topic? God's Sovereignty, taught by Pastor Art Vander Veen, a Dallas Seminary grad who opened the scriptures to us in a way we'd never experienced. Then we moved on to Sunday school, where a gifted young pastor, Tim Kallam, was leading a stirring series on "God's Eternal Reward—Heaven." We had found our new church home.

That's only one of a hundred accounts testifying as to why I have stripped the word *coincidence* from my vocabulary. God is the Divine Author of what people call coincidence; make no mistake about it. Astonishing new chapters of life would spring open for me at Fellowship. But first there was a question for Jan and me to debate.

After diligent and faithful prayer, Jan passionately believed we should have another child. The thought paralyzed me and exposed vulnerabilities and fears I had not worked through: *What should I do with the memories of Vanessa? Would we be replacing her? What if something goes wrong? I can't ever endure that again.* I was opposed to the idea; in truth, I was petrified.

Prayer is a very intimate thing between God and his children. Charles Spurgeon calls it the "struggling speech of an infant, the war cry of the fighting believer... the comfort, the strength, and privilege of a Christian."[14] Jan asked me to pray through her question and my fears. Reluctantly, I obliged. Occasionally, we prayed together, awkwardly at first, but marking a first in our relationship. Prayer ultimately settled my fears and brought forth a blessing.

In mid-1994, dark clouds again hovered over Vanessa's second anniversary, as they did for many years. As the day approached, we made our pilgrimage to the cemetery and memorial playground for reflection and prayer. I know nothing about women's intuition (except that it exists), but Jan, of course, does. She decided that Thursday, June 16, to take a pregnancy test. It confirmed she was! And with a confounding mix of joy and loss, we tried to comprehend the magnitude of God's mystery and grace. On the very date God

---

14 Reimann, *Morning by Morning*, Day 2.

took Vanessa home, he gave us hope for a new life. As I've said, I make no room for coincidences in my theology.

Later that summer, Jan and I sat in another FBC Sunday school class. The topic was Future Hope. The teacher, Dan, somewhat nonchalantly talked about a family's spiritual focus after they had lost a child. We didn't know him; he didn't know us. But after the class, someone apparently reminded Dan that there were parents in the classroom who had lost a young daughter.

Dan called me that afternoon, aghast that he might have said something offensive in the class. I assured him he had not but gently coached him on the depths of grief that a family endures when they lose a child.

"Let's grab a coffee and talk more," Dan suggested. I agreed.

The next week we sat down at a local coffee shop. After a short chat, Dan popped an astounding question. "In November, I'm teaching at a pastors' conference in Kenya," he said. "Kisumu is in the western part of Kenya, alongside Lake Victoria. I see God working in your life. Come with me and share your experience with small-group Bible studies. That idea is catching on in Africa too."

I pondered Dan's invitation for a short New York second. "I'd love to," I told him.

When I arrived home, Jan casually asked, "How was your meeting with Dan?"

"It was wonderful!" I said. "I'm going to Africa!"

From the Classroom to the Slums of Nairobi

As the fall of 1994 approached, I began planning and preparing for the conference. Dan told me it would be at a pastors' retreat center in the African bush. No problem. Privately, I recalibrated my hotel expectations from a Marriott or Hyatt to a Motel 6 experience with no room service.

But I was excited, nonetheless, to make the trip to Kenya and then the two-hundred-mile drive from Nairobi to Kisumu with our host, Pastor David Kitonga and Dan. The drive would take nearly eight hours; we averaged a roaring twenty-five miles per hour over the Kenyan roadways that led westward. Passing over the Great Rift Valley, I was captivated by the brilliant pink landscape—and discovered I was gazing at thousands of flamingoes roosting in the distant salt flats.

The pastors' workshop went well. The settling in to the accommodations went… well, badly. In reflection (no pun intended), a light in my room would have been wonderful, electricity even better. On arrival, I was warned to ensure my bed netting was tight and would not give entrance to malaria-carrying mosquitos. But the real malaria challenge was the bathroom—an unfenced unisex hole in the ground where three hands were required to take care of all functions *and* keep mosquitoes off exposed skin.

Then in the middle of the first night, I was jolted awake when my door nearly burst off its hinges. Apparently, my assigned bunk was trespassing on the turf of *ng'ombe jike's*, a large brown-and-white cow. I snapped a picture of him, thinking no one would believe me. The gracious retreat caretaker had also given me a bucket of water for a refreshing morning soaking. But overnight my water was requisitioned by small frogs. A bucket shower would have to wait.

Returning to Nairobi after two days in Kisumu, we made much better time. We averaged thirty miles per hour on the reverse trek! Bunking that third night in the clean and accommodating Methodist Guest House would set the stage for a day that would forever change life for me and my family—and change the lives of hundreds of Americans and thousands of Kenyans as well.

David promised to come by the Methodist house at 9:00 a.m., which I quickly learned in the Kenyan culture means any time before noon. *Hakuna matata* is a real colloquialism in Swahili (made popular by *The Lion King*). It embraces both *whatever* and *whenever!* That's the spirit that governs one's daily agenda in East Africa.

David would take me to Kawangware (pronounced *cow-when-gwar-eee*) that morning. Kawangware is one of three sprawling slum communities in the city of Nairobi. Locals put the population at about three hundred thousand desperately poor people, but no one knows for sure. Kibera, the neighboring and largest slum dwelling in

Nairobi, has well over one million inhabitants. Passing by dozens of dust-laden roadside merchants and outdoor shops, we turned onto a potholed and muddy dirt road crowded with kids, pigs, and an occasional goat.

"We're entering Kawangware," David said amid shouts of "Mzungu, mzungu!" (White man, foreigner!)

Once inside Kawangware, the sights and smells of wretched poverty assaulted my senses. Some of it emanated from garbage heaps picked at by an occasional goat or chicken, some from piles of boiled cow bones drained of their marrow for the day's nourishment, some from shallow ditches transporting raw sewage to who knows where, and some from the rancid, nose-pinching aroma of homemade liquor stills. Those stills produce a moonshine aptly named *slow death*. Men sip the deadly cocktail through long plastic tubes, much like vapor hookahs, until they pass out or die from overdoses. Apparently to many, slow death is a better alternative than long life in Kawangware.

A short distance inside Kawangware, pursued by dozens of shoeless and runny-nosed children, David stopped the car. As the kids raced to catch up, we exited and stood in a patchy field bordered by a sewage ditch on one side and shanty dwellings (it's hard to call them homes) on the other. As the kids ventured closer, I stiffened, drove my hands deep into my pockets, and just absorbed the hopeless vista of poverty. The kids ignored my aloofness and chuckled as they rubbed the hair on my short-sleeved arms; the men in Kenya have smooth skin and almost no body hair. I guessed I was the first *mzungu* they'd ever touched.

But as the children swarmed around me, they touched my heartstrings as well, and I knelt to greet them. David snapped a photo that remains a treasured possession to this day. He then pitched his vision and the reason for our visit. "God has called me to build a school and a church in Kawangware to transform this community. The church and school will be called *Huduma*, which in Swahili means *hope*. I could be a rich bishop in this country, but that's not my call or life purpose. I need a partner, Tom. Do you think God has brought you to Africa for this?

Kawangware Kids… The First Encounter

I rose very slowly to my feet that November afternoon and surveyed everything in sight. "You can't be serious?" I thought. "Has this man been out in the African sun too long?"

David said nothing more; he just waited patiently for a response. East Africans are good at that. As I pondered his question, my mind's eye flashed back over my two-year-long faith journey—Vanessa's death, my Scunthorpe experience, my bout with depression, the new life developing in Jan, the Sunday school class that led to Dan's invitation to Africa—and the throng of shoeless Kawangware kids in my midst. *Did God script this whole scenario?*

After a few minutes with that backdrop playing in my mind, I simply told David, "Yes, I'm in." But, admittedly, I had no idea what that meant. I'd come to Africa to teach at a pastors' workshop on the shores of Lake Victoria. I was going home with a God-ordained assignment beyond anything I could imagine. I wondered if anyone at home would believe or listen to my story.

Returning to Atlanta, I shared the story with Jan just as I've outlined it to you, and together we pondered its significance in the weeks preceding the turn of the calendar to 1995. Family life nudged ever so slowly to the enviable norm of years past. We readied the nursery for our new arrival. He or she was only six weeks away from making an entrance.

In early January, however, tensions sky-rocketed. Jan went in for her thirty-four-week check-up; it was supposed to be a routine visit, but when she called my office from the clinic, I could hear restrained panic in her voice. There had been an alarming development in her pregnancy. It was urgent that we meet with her doctor, a neonatal specialist, and a geneticist. Our Vanessa-anniversary baby was in grave danger. Jan's team of doctors gave the baby a 25 percent chance of survival at birth.

God had let another arrow fly from his quiver. This time it struck the bull's-eye of the faith vulnerability I had debated with Jan before we decided to have another child. We were heading back into the furnace of affliction.

White Hot: Looking Back

There's a place in Israel called Beer Lahai Roi, meaning the "well of the living One who sees me."[15] It's southwest of Beersheba, deep in the Negev desert. Scripture tells us that there were many visitors to that place, but Abraham's son Isaac, made Beer Lahai Roi his constant source of life-giving water. Spiritually, your own Beer Lahai Roi is not a bad place to hang out while contemplating life's greatest challenges. Not coincidentally, Isaac met his future wife, Rebekah there, and later the Twelve Tribes of Israel sprung forth through Jacob, their son. The One who sees us knows *precisely* where things are headed.

In that respect, the White Hot chapter of my life was no different. It presented mountainous challenges, searing-desert desperation, and miraculous provision. From a fresh start in Cincinnati to the loss of a child, from flirtation with a death wish to a providential Sunday school encounter, from the promise of new life to a pastors' conference in Africa, the living One who sees me knew what lay waiting on my calendar.

---

15 Reimann, *Morning by Morning*, Day 48.

The prophet Elijah had his own desert experience; why shouldn't we? (You can read all about that in 1 Kings 9). Ahab's wicked wife, Jezebel, had him on the run (v 3). Elijah prayed that he would die. *"I have had enough, LORD," said Elijah, "Take my life"* (v 4). But it was in Elijah's searing desert depression and desperation that he felt the touch of God's angel. "Get up and eat!" said the angel (v 7). Twice strengthened with spiritual Cheerios and water, Elijah nonetheless wandered aimlessly for forty days. God poked at him again.

"What are you doing here, Elijah?" (v 9). That was a question for Elijah to ponder, not an inquiry from a puzzled God.

Elijah complained bitterly that life was harsh and unfair. God brushed aside Elijah's monologue and countered with his power in a raging wind that tore apart a mountain, an earthquake, and a furious fire (v 12). He then gave Elijah new marching orders which would come in a gentle and loving whisper. "Get up and go, I have new work for you!" (v 15).

I'm no Elijah, but I know how it feels to suffer in discouragement and entertain a death wish before hearing the gentle whisper of the One who sees me. I can't overspiritualize this crucial phase of life. If not a spiritual journey, I had no journey at all. Only a fool would characterize the White Hot chapter of my life as a testimony to human tenacity or toughness!

Eight hundred years after Elijah, the apostle Paul says this: "I have learned to be content whatever the circumstances" (Phil. 4:11). That's a bold statement from a man who was repeatedly flogged, shipwrecked, jailed, and attacked by Jews and new Christians alike. Paul's declaration gives us three vital life experience and life change insights.

First, are we open to learning something? In Paul's context, contentment represents a new dimension of life. Biblical contentment is *not* a happy-happy exuberance. Inner peace and surrender are much closer to the spiritual mark. And neither is contentment mastered with knowledge alone like a math problem would be. We must embrace contentment in the context that the One who sees us knows what he's doing, even if we don't.

Secondly, contentment is *not* the natural human pursuit. In fact, quite the opposite. Like Elijah, I like to complain! To learn something difficult (like contentment), it takes faith, perseverance, and grace from the One who sees us when we fail to grasp it.

And thirdly, there's new discovery in contentment; it throws open the door after a crisis of belief to life change and fulfillment. There are new opportunities and assignments to be found in contentment and new threads to be woven into tapestry of our lives by the One who see us in our trials.

Fix Your Eyes

But he knows the way that I take; when he has tested me,
I will come forth as gold. My feet have closely followed
his steps. I have kept his way without turning aside.

—Job 23:10

"Pray for Grace"

I call it the trilogy of faith. Think about it. *If* you "fix your eyes on Jesus" (Heb. 12:1) and "fix your eyes on the eternal, not the temporary" (2 Cor. 4:16), you will be blessed with the "assurance of what you hope for, and the certainty of what you cannot see" (Heb. 11:1).

For thirty months, Jan and I had learned to live in those truths. Now, we were being called on to apply them again.

In the opening days of 1995, we didn't know if our unborn child was a boy or a girl. We had always loved the mystery of God's providence and let it play out in the delivery room. This time would be different. As we approached the mid-February due date, we wanted friends and family to pray for the baby by name. We couldn't bear the thought of the child being nameless if the doctor's dire odds played out.

At Jan's follow-up OB/GYN appointment, we learned that the baby was a girl. The doctors reviewed her prognosis. They noted skeletal, cranial, lung, and cardiac abnormalities associated with an unspecified type of dwarfism. The baby's undersized rib cage, they said, was compacting her heart, lungs, and other vital organs in such a way that her diaphragm could not trigger a normal breathing response. Pediatric geneticists were called in to sharpen the diagnosis. That required an amniotic test, which we were warned could prematurely trigger labor, something that would mean certain death for our unborn child. But the test would provide essential information so that the staff in the delivery room and ICU could be properly prepared when the baby was born. Jan submitted to the test; there were no better options.

The avalanche of new information from the genetic testing confirmed that the baby had an exceedingly rare type of dwarfism called Kniest dysplasia. Neonatal specialists gave her a 25 percent chance of survival at birth. The hospital social worker coached us to accept the probability of the child's death after delivery and a compromised life if she survived.

"Yes, the odds and genetic statistics are sobering," I confessed to the social worker, "but we've been on a faith journey these last few years. We know God is in control of our child's life from this very moment forward. He will determine the outcome, and we're at peace with that."

The social worker rocked slowly back in her chair, crossed her arms, studied our faces, wished us well, and said nothing more. I sensed she thought we were foolishly naïve.

Jan and I chose Caroline as the baby's name shortly after the social worker's visit. Then we walked across our backyard to share our decision with our neighbor Carol and her eight-year-old daughter, Jordanne. Carol is a beautiful woman with a giant Memphis heart. As neighbors for the past ten years, we'd seen our kids share backyard picnics, swing sets, and an occasional childhood squabble. Carol's daughter, Jordanne *Caroline*, was Vanessa's closest friend. For five wonderful years, the two of them were inseparable. When Jordanne married later in life, she celebrated her wedding with six groomsmen and five bridesmaids, honoring Vanessa and the role she would have played in the wedding party.

We shared the doctor's prognosis with Carol along with our yearning to name the baby Caroline, forever linking our family legacy with theirs. The uncertain outcome of Jan's pregnancy loomed over our announcement.

Carol, who can go from jubilation to tears in a Southern heartbeat, held tightly to the script. She celebrated our choice of name and then burst into tears at the uncertainty we collectively faced. Eight-year-old Jordanne told us she was happy to lend her middle name, but she was more interested that day in hunting for frogs and salamanders, as she was prone to do.

The next week, we took Caroline's story and prognosis to our Sunday school class. Friend and class leader Jay Street set two chairs up front, invited us to sit, and encouraged class members to join hands around us and pray spontaneously for Caroline. Jay closed the prayer session with an emotional plea that pierced his normal calm. "Pray for God's favor," he pleaded. "Pray for *grace*." And in that instant, Grace became Caroline's middle name.

The 2:10—2/10 Riddle

Early on February 10, while contractions were demanding Jan's full attention, a throng of doctors and nurses assembled for Caroline's delivery. Huddled in the delivery room were a cardiologist, a pulmonologist, a neonatal specialist, a respiratory physician, the pediatric ICU team, and Jan's OB-GYN. Even with that array of medical horsepower, Caroline Grace faced daunting odds of survival. I'd also asked Jay to make a visit to the labor room and pray for Caroline. It wouldn't be the last time we would summon him to the hospital.

At 2:10 p.m. on February 10, Caroline was born. She was unable to breathe on her own and was immediately intubated. Instantly, her heart raced to more than 150 beats a minute, attempting to supply her underdeveloped lungs with life-giving oxygen. The neonatal ICU team quickly went into high gear and connected Caroline to the critical life-monitoring equipment.

Shortly thereafter, the cardiologist took Jan and me aside to hear his forthright prognosis. "We are doing everything we can," he said, pointing to the digital readout on the heart monitor, "but your daughter cannot sustain that heart rate very long." Caroline's heart was now beating three times a second in its attempts to oxygenate her blood supply.

That was Caroline's first challenge; there would be many more. But in the controlled chaos and life-and-death tension of the ICU, there was a moment of joyous levity. At six pounds, Caroline was triple the size of most of her ICU bunkmates and seemed astonishingly out of place. Nothing distinguished her more than her full head of radiant orange hair. One of the ICU nurses put a small hair clip in her carrot top; she was the only baby in ICU with a wisp of a ponytail.

Friends and neighbors joined the faith journey as well and showered us nonstop with encouragement, prayer, and meals to fill our refrigerator. Carol was always at the ready, and another neighbor—the same Debbie who had visited unannounced after Vanessa's death—came to us with a startling discovery.

Debbie had been intrigued by the perfect match of the clock and Caroline's birthdate. February 10 at 2:10 p.m. meant *something* and she was determined to unlock the riddle. Debbie went straight to her Bible and searched it book by book—every chapter 2 and verse 10—intent on finding the answer. After scanning all thirty-nine books of the Old Testament and nine in the New Testament, Debbie landed in the book of Ephesians, the apostle Paul's Gospel message to the church in Ephesus. There in Ephesians 2:10 was the nugget of wisdom she was searching for: "For we are God's workmanship, created in Christ Jesus to do good works, which God prepared in advance for us to do." In that verse, we all saw God's vision for Caroline.

Ephesians 2:10 became our spiritual hope and grounding for the next two months in ICU. More importantly, it has become Caroline's signature verse as she makes her way down the long and difficult road of life she is destined to travel. She continues to live in God's grace, as her life story magnificently testifies.

Perseverance and Keeping the Faith!

Early in the book of Job, the title character is severely afflicted when the devil himself makes a wager with God. Why? The antagonist tells God that Job's faith is rooted in his prosperity and nothing more. In effect, God accepts the wager and says, "Okay, let's find out!" God, of course, already knows the answer to the quiz, but it's withheld from his antagonist. Job, then, is summarily hurled into calamity to discover it himself.

Job lets it rip after his children, livestock, servants, and health are stricken. "Tell me what charges you have against me" (Job 10:2), he bellows out to God in righteous defiance. But not far down the turnpike as his trials progress, Job recalibrates his complaints. He's learning a few things from his experience and the counsel (and accusations) of friends. "Though he slay me, yet will I hope in him," he says (Job 13:15). Some Bible translations rightly equate the word *hope* with *trust* in God. Either way, it's truth, but in Job's case, it's tough theology.

Job's ongoing trials begin to open his spiritual eyes and draw him closer to a sovereign God who doesn't need to explain anything he does. Nonetheless, Job is confused and indignant. "Why is this happening to me?" he complains. "I have kept to his [God's] way without turning aside" (Job 23:11).

In the biblical account, God listens patiently to Job during his meandering faith journey, but then in a pivotal teaching point, God launches his own tirade. It's another tough theology lesson from the God of the universe. "Where were you when I laid the earth's foundation?" (Job 38:4) says the LORD to Job. "Who marked off its dimensions?" (Job 38:5). "Have you ever given orders to the morning or shown dawn its place..." (Job 38:12). Job is adding understanding, surrender, and perseverance to his character and faith journey. Jan and I were on the same road.

If you're struggling with tough circumstances or doubts about God's power in this world, read Job, chapter 38; it will fuel your faith engine. God is *infinitely* more powerful than any human counterpart; his omniscience reigns in the present as it will in the future and has in the past. He's in control of all creation, life and death included. People come to believe that, or they don't. But no other truth really matters, not even a warning from a cardiologist when you're glued to your little girl's heart monitor.

As Caroline's stay in the hospital continued, Jan and I thought back to our time in another ICU, where we lost Vanessa. We were in a very different place now, having learned a lot in the past thirty months. We had come through refining fire and Job-like testing once before. We were committed in faith not to turn aside in despair. But there would be agonizingly difficult days of perseverance and faith testing.

In her first weeks, Caroline and her medical team faced vexing life-and-death challenges. The first was striking the delicate balance between her ultra-high heart rate and her body's demand for oxygenated blood for her lungs. Medicine to slow her heart rate would, within minutes, launch respiratory distress, and Caroline's rosy-pink skin would darken to a bluish tint. It was painfully difficult to witness. Meanwhile, the gifted ICU team labored to wean her off the respirator that was keeping her alive.

For weeks, her life hung in an uneasy balance while doctors struggled to improve her lung efficiency, decrease the assisted breathing, and not overtax her weary heart.

Jan and I alternated "Caroline shifts" to cover as many hours as possible. Many times, I'd leave ICU, drive home, and be met with a phone call. "Caroline is back in the critical zone," an ICU nurse might tell us. "One of you needs to come back!"

Might she suddenly die? Yes, that was always a punishing reality, but it was something else that prompted those calls. The ICU staff had made an astounding discovery. "Caroline knows *exactly* when you're here, and when you're not," they told us. "We can watch it on her heart monitor. When we're out of medical options to slow her heart rate, we call you. When you sit, talk, and pray with her—or play that little music box that Tom brings with him—her heart rate drops twenty to thirty beats per minute. We can't explain it."

We could. It was God's unmistakable hand on Caroline's heart and on our hopes.

Nonetheless, the ICU doctor called us into conference in early March for a sobering talk. We had come to an especially crucial point in Caroline's fight to live.

Praying for Grace—Again!

"You know we can't sustain Caroline's life indefinitely with the respirator," he said. "We're approaching a time when we need to determine if she will ever breathe on her own. Do you have a pastor or priest?"

We did, of course, and I called Pastor Jay—again. The ICU battle plan all along had been to grow Caroline's lung capacity so that she could hopefully breathe on her own. Then the team would systematically wean her off the respirator. We now faced a prickly trial.

Together we prayed for God's intervention to calm and strengthen Caroline's heart and help her to breathe on her own. We then gave the ICU team a thumbs-up to crank down the respirator dial. Almost immediately, Caroline became agitated, and her pinkish tone faded. Then she began to squirm uncomfortably, and her big blue eyes signaled panic. We hastily aborted the trial while the ICU team worked feverishly to rescue Caroline from the brink of respiratory failure. When they succeeded, we all breathed deep sighs of relief. The respirator did the same for Caroline.

We were all disheartened by the outcome. The neonatal team went back to the drawing board and forged a new strategy. After a few days of analysis and consultations, a date for the second trial was set with a warning from the presiding physician. We were approaching forty days in the ICU, and there were very few options left on the table.

With that said, one of the nurses decided some entertainment might help and set up a VCR and TV next to Caroline's bed. Watching Disney features was now in the new protocol. Caroline seemed to like it, so the nurse added a pillow speaker. Caroline now enjoyed full surround-sound entertainment as we labored in prayer and counted down the days to her next trial.

March 24, the second trial date, arrived. With a potpourri of anxiety, hope, fear, faith, and resolve, we gathered around Caroline's ICU nest. It was overloaded with medical contraptions, monitors, IVs, prayer cards from friends—and her music box.

Dr. Saul Adler now added a new wrinkle to the respirator-weaning protocol. Prior to turning Caroline's breathing apparatus off, he would administer a mild sedative to counter her panic attack. His hope was to keep her heart rate below 130 while forcing her lungs to draw life-giving oxygen on their own. It was a high-risk plan; both parts of the equation had to fall in place, but there were no better choices. Jan and I signed off on the pretrial agreement and consultations. And we painfully agreed that if the test were to fail, the respirator would remain off.

It's exceedingly difficult to describe our anxious thoughts at this point in the ICU, so let me just for a moment insert you into the scene. Imagine as a parent—or a trusted friend—you're standing over the bedside of your loved one, not knowing whether in just twenty minutes, you'll be planning a funeral or celebrating a victory. Some of you have lived that moment. In either outcome, your prayer is to hold fast to your faith in God's grace, sovereignty, and his perfect will for your life. Psalm 46:10 holds the only key to sanity when faced with that possibility. "Be still, and know I am God." That morning, we stood very still.

When the respirator dial went to zero, Caroline's blood oxygen level plummeted. Her heart rate, constrained by the sedative, couldn't make up the deficit. But her tiny chest for the first time began to rise and fall and demand a breath of its own, without her life-enabling respirator. Supplemental oxygen gradually carried her into safer territory... and she stabilized.

An ICU environment doesn't lend itself to raucous celebration, but an abundance of joyous bear hugs marked the day. The Ephesians 2:10 girl, after six weeks in ICU, was heading into transitional care— and a host of new challenges. But our *Be still* faith had carried the day, and the mystery of God's sovereignty filled the room.

Caroline's Life Journey: A Snapshot

Our children's trials and triumphs are not only part of their own unique stories but are integral to their parents' stories as well. For that reason, I'll detour for a moment and tell you about the amazing grace God has infused into Caroline's vibrant life—and into her family's life as we have watched her mature.

After the discharge from ICU and a few weeks of transitional hospital care for Caroline (and medical apparatus training for Jan and me), Caroline came home with more life-sustaining contrivances and medical protocols than we could count. The most intimidating was an alarm that would roust us in the middle of the night if her heart rate was too high, her oxygen level too low, or if she suddenly stopped breathing. Initially, these were frightful *Zero Dark Thirty* wake-up calls, but we grew used to them. Although the alarms would rocket Jan and me out of bed and into rehearsed procedures, many times the problem was only a crimped line or loose connection initiated by Caroline's fidgeting. The little rascal was also learning how to yank the oxygen tube from her nose and send her parents into panic mode! Nonetheless, we had her epinephrine and inhalers at the ready.

The feeding routine took an exasperating amount of teamwork and precision. I'd hold a squirming Caroline and keep her as still as was fatherly possible while Jan threaded her feeding tube through her nose and into her stomach. Then, before emptying the syringe of nourishment, we'd listen with a stethoscope to be certain the tube was in Caroline's stomach, not her lungs. If we had miscalculated, we'd have filled her lungs with baby formula and drowned her in milk.

For six months, Caroline was a completely silent baby. Her intubation in ICU had temporarily rendered her vocal chords inoperative, or so we thought. She'd open her mouth and wail with tears streaming down her face, but there'd be no sound. Silence is not all that bad in a six-month-old baby if you can arrange it! But, for Caroline, it indicated bigger issues. Repeated attempts to feed her by mouth resulted in dreadful gags and coughs. She had no swallow reflex.

For the short term, Caroline was fitted with a feeding port in her stomach wall. But there was an urgent need for surgery to release compression on her upper spinal cord and enable her to swallow. That led to another complication. No neurosurgeon had ever performed the needed surgery on a six-month-old.

Again, limited options demanded medical innovation. The surgery was planned and skillfully accomplished by a pediatric neurosurgeon. And in the prosthetic ward, a team of creative medical engineers fashioned a two-piece clam-shell-like device to keep Caroline's neck motionless for the next month. After that, the back half was all she needed, so we made Caroline the kitchen-table centerpiece at every meal. Caroline on the half shell, we called her.

Kniest dysplasia is a rare form of dwarfism. It comes with its own litany of issues, but the most noticeable is short stature. Adults with a Kniest diagnosis seldom grow taller than forty-eight inches. Caroline, fully grown, is forty-two. She's part of a group called Little People (LPs), who are protected by the American Disabilities Act. In her first dozen years, without fail, we would take her to the Little People of America (LPA) Convention to learn how LPs can better cope with their disabilities.

Doctors specializing in different aspects of dwarfism give unselfishly of their time every July Fourth weekend to assist LPA kids, parents, and adults. They're God-sent angels of generosity dispensing vital medical care, encouragement, and counseling to conflicted parents, like Jan and me whose children are facing uncertain futures. Their services are free!

LPA conventions are held in different quadrants of the USA each year to promote maximum participation. Some two thousand Little People come together from all parts of the country—and outside it too. Initially, I struggled with the LPA environment and left some conventions early (and highly discouraged) after Caroline's medical consultations were complete. The raw reality of the future for many LPAers—medically, socially, and opportunistically—threw me into a tailspin. In many ways, I was staring directly into the stark reality of God's sovereignty and what it held for Caroline and her future—and I didn't like the permanence of the harsher pieces of it one bit.

It was Caroline's unbridled exuberance for life, however, that refreshed my ailing spirit and perspective. She continues to live out her Ephesians 2:10 calling as God's unique creation. Caroline faces ongoing physical limitations, but she does so with an unrelenting resolve to overcome them and embrace new possibilities.

Caroline is packaged in a small frame and won't grow another millimeter in her lifetime. She contends every day with bathrooms whose dimensions are frustrating, sinks she can't reach, stairs she can't climb, and kitchen microwaves so high they might as well be on another planet. On Sundays, Caroline always maneuvers for an aisle seat at church. When the pastor says, "Please stand for the benediction," she leans into the aisle, much preferring that vista than the pockets of the guy in front of her.

As I write this, Caroline is twenty-three years old. She's had more than a dozen surgeries to ease a variety of orthopedic maladies. She serves as a Spanish interpreter for a medical ministry in Guatemala and has traveled to Kenya to participate in ministry work with children there. She'll graduate in 2019 from Moody Bible Institute with a degree in ministry leadership. Who knows where she'll go from there! I'm afraid to ask.

Caroline will tell you that her life trajectory is not extraordinary in the least; she's just discovering the good works God prepared for her in advance and following the path he set. "So what's the big deal?" she says. "I wouldn't have life any other way!"

Amazing!

Ecclesiastes 4:12 tells us that "though one may be overpowered... a cord of three strands is not easily broken." Based on that, Caroline is in good shape. Our family is a household of four strands, one more than the Bible grants us. We, her parents, stand strong with Caroline on her God-given foundation. That's the first strand. Her siblings and their spouses also stand with her in unwavering love and support. That's the second. Caroline also has an incredible collection of friends, way too many to list here. That's her third strand. And finally, she's blessed to have a fourth strand of devoted nurses, physicians, and caregivers who are wholly committed to seeing her thrive. One gifted orthopedic surgeon transformed Caroline's physical capacity and mobility through his God-given talent. How do you ever fully thank someone for that!

If you're ever inclined for your own encouragement to read again this mini chapter of God's grace to Caroline—or to share it with someone else—here's something you won't find. Not once have I heard Caroline refer to herself as a victim. It's not in her life narrative or vocabulary. That's God's grace at work as well. She knows she's here for a purpose that's unfolding in her life despite physical and social hardships.

Caroline has spent dozens of nights in children's hospitals. One evening after major corrective hip and leg surgery—the details you don't want to know—I commented to the nurse about her uncanny resolve to sit up in her bed. The attending nurse wasn't the least bit surprised. "Of course, she has resolve," the RN casually noted. "We see that all the time in kids that struggle with affliction. It's the privileged adults who complain that life's unfair."

Jan's journal (from which I took many of the details from this chapter of life), says something similar: "Grace is God's answer to pain and affliction even if he chooses not to change the circumstances."

Caroline has family aspirations like most young women do. We pray those will be fulfilled. She may not be able to bear children, but she'd love to adopt a bevy of them when she marries—maybe Little People from a culture that doesn't value them. Caroline will make an exceptional mom; she's got a great role model in Jan—and she has a faith like Job's.

Africa's Call: Reengaging in Kawangware

In the winter of 1995, Caroline's condition was "normalizing," although things at home could hardly be called normal by most standards. We were still monitoring Caroline's vital signs twenty-four hours a day and getting up for alarms in the middle of the night. But it was also time to consider reengagement with work in Kenya. It had been a year since my first visit. For the immediate future, Jan's role would tilt heavily to Caroline's daily needs and those of her older brother, Bryan, who was now in elementary school. Of necessity, Jan would live our Kawangware experience vicariously through me for a season, but always with her eye on visiting herself.

The fledgling partnership with Pastor David Kitonga was now begging for more of my time and attention. Earlier in the fall of 1995, David had asked me to teach in the inaugural Festival of Learning (FOL) he was organizing for December. The FOL would become an exciting annual learning forum for Kenyan pastors and those from neighboring Rwanda, Uganda, Tanzania, and Sudan. "I want these African church leaders *equipped* with Bible knowledge, practical ministry skills, and church-building passion," said David. It was from David's vision of *equipping* that the Kawangware ministry took its name. Africa Equip Ministry (AEM) stands strong today.

My December visit to Kawangware kindled new aspirations, passions, and life-focus questions. I was developing a passion to learn and teach God's Word. Beyond that, I wanted to engage friends and church members with the vision that was emerging in Kawangware. I was also eager to generate funding for our work in the Kawangware community.

"What do you do for a living?"—the preeminent social gathering question—now took on a new dimension.

"Well, I'm the managing partner of a consulting firm that works in the product-development arena," I'd answer, "but my passion is my work in Nairobi, Kenya. My business fuels my ministry work. My business partners are also involved and we've all agreed to allocate a generous percentage of our earnings to help bring the Kawangware vision to life."

That would open the door to talk about the vision for Kawangware, which I was all too happy to share. "I'm working with a team of men and women committed to economic, social, and spiritual change in a slum community in Nairobi," I would say.

On occasion, that was too lofty a goal for friends and business associates to grasp. But many times, it led to, "Really? Tell me more." And before helping them book a flight with me to Kenya, I'd tell the Kawangware story. I'd tell them how I got involved and how God was working through a team of uncommonly average people like me to bring hope to an otherwise hopeless scene of despair.

Shortly after the December 1995 visit, I brought together in Atlanta a small contingent of volunteers who were strongly committed to helping Kawangware. Together we launched Africa Equip Ministry-USA (AEM-USA) to formally partner with our African contingent. We committed to raise funds, communicate progress, and lead "vision trips" to Kawangware. The latter was intended to get the eyes, hands, hearts, and minds of friends *directly* engaged with the realities of Kawangware.

The legacy of our partnership with AEM-Kenya could easily fill a separate book. But in short, it's a testimony to how God uses ordinary people committed to his purposes for extraordinary impact. It's *so* extraordinary that no AEM-USA team member in his or her right mind would dare suggest that what we have accomplished was absent the hand of God. When you think about it, that's largely the story of men and women in the Bible!

In Kawangware, our first challenge was land. We had to buy the soggy, sewage-saturated, and garbage-strewn field in which I had knelt with the children who first won my heart to Kawangware. That would become the site of Huduma—Swahili for *hope*—the complex we would labor to build over the next ten years. Our vision, to take shape over time, included a church, a preschool, an elementary school, and a high school. We envisioned a kitchen as well, where rice and beans for the school children could be cooked over charcoal. We also saw clean water in Huduma's future. (There was no running water or electricity in Kawangware.) The vision was rounded out with a children's playground, a carpentry facility, a sewing ministry where women would make clothes, a medical and dental clinic, and a pastor training center. We'd also need teachers, administrators, church staff, musical instruments, etc. As important as the vision was a viable financial model that would foster Kawangware's self-sufficiency over time, not permanent dependence on American donors.

The agenda for 1996 included another FOL and our first series of Kawangware vision trips. I made three visits that year. During one, David dedicated the new preschool building to Vanessa's memory. Vanessa Hall accommodated about eighty kindergartners in two classrooms. Jan and I had the memorial plaque at our local church playground recast, translated into Swahili, and hung on the stone wall of Vanessa Hall. It would be two more years before Jan would see it; she still had primary Caroline duty at home.

Vanessa School Dedication

In 1998, Jan was poised to travel to Kawangware with AEM-USA board member John Purser and five other women on a vision trip. Their excursion would turn out to be a tumultuous experience involving a historic and tragic episode in the life of Kenya.

Jan and her team were destined to leave Atlanta on Sunday, August 9. On Friday August 7, the US Embassy in Nairobi was bombed by Al-Qaeda sympathizers, killing 213 people. Incredibly, David Kitonga was in the US Embassy that day seeking a US visa and miraculously escaped grievous injury. He would tell us later that he was covered in blood, only to discover later that most of it was not his own.

Jan, John, and the five women—collectively and passionately—lobbied for the trip to proceed. The mission board at our church who sanctions all mission team travel, however, revoked their approval of the trip. On Saturday August 8, John and I again petitioned the board to reverse their no-go decision. After many hours of prayer and hard debate, they relented, and two days after the bombing, the AEM-USA team headed to Nairobi. In reflection, I admire both the Kawangware travelers *and* the mission board for their faith and courage. It was not in vain… dozens of injured Kenyans were treated at the Kawangware medical clinic.

On the return trip, even more intrigue ensued. The Nairobi airport was shut down for three days in a defensive posture while President Bill Clinton launched Navy cruise missiles at the Al-Qaeda perpetrators in Afghanistan.

Over the next ten years, more than two-hundred friends, family members, doctors, nurses, dentists, and young people made the sixteen-hour flight to Nairobi—many of them more than once. Each set aside their personal and business agendas and invested ten demanding days in ministry work in Kawangware. Some worked side by side with Kenyan painters, some built the playground, and some helped cook the only meal the children in Vanessa Hall would get each day. Some taught Bible lessons to former prostitutes in the sewing ministry, and some organized a soccer camp for Kawangware kids—with genuine soccer balls! The Kawangware variety was a tangled mass of tightly wound plastic bags pulled from the garbage heap.

At the end of each soccer camp, there would be a presentation of the now-famous Huduma Cup. The contest was between the Kawangware kids (and teachers) and the *mzungi*, the visiting Americans. We never won a single match!

Not surprisingly, there were always budget challenges. Construction costs to build Kawangware's elementary and high school, floor by floor and year by year, were skyrocketing. China's appetite for cement was doubling—and doubling again——the cost of construction.

In response, the AEM-USA rabble of volunteers birthed what we called the Big Event. We rented a meeting hall, flew David Kitonga to Atlanta, and challenged local Kawangware supporters to sponsor tables of eight people. We hoped for twenty-five tables and two hundred guests. We'd also conduct a silent auction, enjoy some great worship music, and listen to David's vision for Kawangware. Our much-debated goal? We asked God to grant us $250,000 in one night.

At the end of the evening, we tallied the results. Two hundred and *three* guests had attended the Big Event, and when all the cash and pledges were totaled, we had raised $325,000. Tears, hugs, praise, amazement, and prayers flooded the Metropolitan Club that evening in 2006. And we learned a great life lesson too: when men and women labor faithfully under the banner of God's grace, *nothing* is impossible, and transformational change becomes reality.

Today, there are eight hundred kids enrolled in the Huduma school. Hundreds of students have graduated from Huduma since the school complex was completed in 2007. Education has become the key to breaking poverty's death grip on their lives. Many have thrived in Kenya's best universities, and some have returned to Kawangware to invest in ongoing transformational work.

The Miraculous Huduma School Complex

Tragically, however, if you enter Kawangware today, you will still see men drinking slow death, and on the road to Huduma, you'll see children without shoes to protect their tender feet. Large segments of the slum community still have no water or electricity, and a waft of Kawangware air still assaults your nose. But as you make the turn into the Huduma complex, you will wonder if your eyes are lying to you. "It's a mirage," you'll think, but it's not. It's reality! Rising majestically from the impoverished, shanty-encumbered landscape is a magnificent testimony to God's grace and power. It's the five-story Huduma school in all its glory, nothing short of a modern-day miracle. God's transformational power is at work in Kawangware. As Isaiah said, "He is preaching good news to the poor, binding up the brokenhearted, and proclaiming freedom for the captives" (Isa. 61:1).

In 2012, Jan and I again ventured to Kawangware, this time with Caroline. I taught another Festival of Learning session, Jan conducted a Bible study with the women, and Caroline played guitar with the worship team in the Sunday service. The school children marveled at her fire-red hair and gathered around her by the dozens.

"Caroline," I said, "take note. This is part of the good work God prepared in advance for your mom and me to walk in when he took Vanessa home twenty years ago. This started with a Sunday school class and a conversation over coffee. God can redeem tragedy. These are your eight hundred brothers and sisters in Kawangware."

Nonetheless, the day wasn't all celebration. Caroline visited a young mom in a tiny shanty with a dirt floor. The woman was drowning in sobs of grief, still clutching her stillborn baby. The baby might have survived if given the life-giving care afforded to Caroline many years earlier. It's an encounter seared into Caroline's memory, and it fuels her passion to serve the under-resourced in our world.

Are We Talking About the Same Guy?

As I write this, my forty-fifth class reunion at the US Naval Academy has just passed. Ten years ago, at the thirty-fifth, I sat enjoying a beer with a dozen classmates at the Middletown Tavern in Annapolis. We were catching up on each other's lives, amazed that we could all get better looking while growing older. As is tradition, every USNA and postgraduation exploit was retold again and again, with less and less integrity each time. Somehow, in our own minds, we'd morphed into Marvel heroes.

From my seat at the table, I overheard an exchange between two classmates a few chairs away.

"Yeah, Schuler is here. Did you know he's in seminary, working toward his ordination? He's also an elder at his church in Atlanta."

"No way!" my old friend bellowed. I remembered Bobby. He was a career navy guy. "Are we talking about the same guy, the wrestler from Tenth Company, the troublemaker who went into the Marine Corps?"

"Yup, same guy. He's sitting at the end of the table. Look!"

Bobby turned my way, making eye contact, and flashed me a thumbs-up. "Way to go, dude! I'm ordained too," he blurted out. "I filled out an application online, paid twenty-five bucks, and I got a certificate saying I could marry my wife's nephew. Is that what you're doing?"

"No, Bobby," I replied. "Not exactly!" And that's as far as I got that night as the crescendo of chatter and embellished war stories smothered my attempt at further clarity. Here's what Bobby and my table of warrior classmates never heard.

The FOLs in Kenya stoked my appetite for a better command of God's Word, theological principles, biblical history, and a modern-day approach to mission work. With that as a goal, I enrolled in the Biblical Studies curriculum at Dallas Theological Seminary (DTS) in early 2000. DTS had a satellite campus in Atlanta which was a great option for my tired calendar. Sandwiched between raising a family, running an international business, and making excursions to Kenya, I'd study at night and weekends and write papers on business trips.

With my willingness and enthusiasm to tell the Kawangware story, a growing knowledge of the Bible, well-honed business skills, and a fascination with theology, I enjoyed a busy teaching and mentoring calendar at my church. Ultimately, my leadership profile led to my selection as a church elder. But in parallel with these new tracts of life, I was grappling with a bigger transition, an exit from SDF International, the business I'd started in 1986. I wanted to take on a full-time ministry role at church.

In early 2007, after much contemplation and prayer, I made the career somersault. I left SDF International for the Director of Ministry Development role at the church and transitioned from a lay elder (volunteer) to a staff elder (full-time church employee). The move presented a myriad of new challenges, but none thornier than brokering heavenly inspired ideas from lay elders and members of the congregation with the reality of church staffing and budget constraints. More on that to come.

In early 2008 (which included a leave of absence), I completed my DTS curriculum and wrote a thirty-page ordination thesis. After reviewing it, the Ordination Council gave me a rousing thumbs-up, just like Bobby did at my thirty-fifth reunion... but they never handed me a bill for twenty-five bucks for the certificate!

A formal ordination ceremony followed. Chairman of the Ordination Council and Senior Pastor Dr. Crawford Loritts captured the essence of my journey in his letter welcoming me aboard.

"It gives me great joy to help celebrate with you God's call and commissioning to focused vocational ministry," his letter read in part. "Let's keep encouraging each other... and not settle for anything less than what the Lord has for us. He's done too much for two dudes from Babylon and Newark to do otherwise."

In short order, my ordination credentials would be in demand. My eldest son, Greg, asked me to marry him and his fiancée, Frances, in San Francisco's Golden Gate Park the following September. What an honor! Their marriage in 2009 is another notable milestone in our blended family's reconciliation.

Not long after that, I'd also officiate the funeral of my son Bryan's high school girlfriend. She was killed in a car crash at the tender age of nineteen. Young, blond, and effervescent, she was like a daughter to us. Ironically, her name was also Caroline. At her service, I shared the firsthand testimony of a parent who has given his precious daughter back to her Creator, knowing she's now in his loving care.

In the years to come, the encouragement and joy in the senior pastor's letter would be tested with ministry fire. And why not? "After we have a perfect relationship with God through Christ's atonement and the sanctifying work of the Holy Spirit," says Oswald Chambers, "our faith must be exercised in the realities of everyday life."[16]

In some ways, I wish it was different, but we don't grow and prosper much in our mountaintop experiences; we do so fighting battles in the valleys of life.

Fix Your Eyes: Looking Back

If you're a reader of Psalms, chances are Psalm 46:10 grabbed your attention, because it contrasts markedly with how we live. "Be still." Who does that, except when all other options are exhausted or there's no way out? "Be still and know I am God" is not a default to laziness or apathy. There are simply times in our lives when we've done enough or can do no more, and we must rest in the confidence that God will take it from there. "Be still and know I am God. I will be exalted among the nations. I will be exalted in the earth." Psalm 46:10 concludes with God's glory and his sovereign reign on our planet. There is nothing outside his control including every human endeavor he commissions.

Psalm 46:10 reaches back into biblical history, and there's every reason to believe that the writer knew of its origin in Exodus, the second book of the Hebrew scriptures. In Exodus, Pharaoh's chariots had the nation of Israel pinned with their backs to the Red Sea. That was some two million people. Their slaughter was imminent, and a great cry of anguish and terror arose from the Jewish rabble to Moses. "Was it because there were no graves in Egypt that you brought us to the desert to die?" (Exod. 14:11). All human options for fighting the

---

16 Chambers, *My Utmost for His Highest*, April 4.

Egyptians had been exhausted, and the people God freed from Egypt had no faith in his protection.

Moses saw it otherwise. "Do not be afraid. Stand firm and you will see the deliverance the LORD will bring you today. The LORD will fight for you; you need only to *be still*" (Exod. 14:13–14; italics added). Read the entire exciting story in Exodus, chapter 14, but you know the outcome. The nation of Israel walked to the Sinai Peninsula on dry land… and Egypt's horde of warriors drowned when the walls of the Red Sea crashed down upon them.

Fix Your Eyes is an intense and paradoxical chapter of life jam-packed with Job-like testing, Moses-like faith, and Paul-like purpose. In this chapter of life, I learned to be still, to discern the right things to do, to get them done… and leave the rest to God in confidence, not in desperation.

Be still served my team well in Kawangware. We worked feverishly to prepare for the Big Event, and then there was nothing more we could do. Our ministry vision and backs were pinned to the Red Sea. But there, God provided more people than we hoped for and school construction funding beyond anything we'd imagined. God would be exalted—and still is—in the Huduma school in Kawangware. Our part was just to hustle across the dry land to build it.

Be still also brought Caroline into this world and put breath in her lungs. Yes, it was with prayer and the skilled hands and minds of her physicians, but all in God's sovereignty. Fueled by Ephesians 2:10, Caroline's life reflects an unwavering confidence that as a twenty-three-year-old Little Person, she has a unique life purpose on this planet which continues to unfold.

Be still rests on the precipice of faith. In 1992, all the mustered medical talent in Shands Children's Hospital could not give us one more beat of Vanessa's heart. By human accounts, she was expected to live, yet ordained in God's sovereignty to die. And Caroline, who by medical odds would die at birth, in God's sovereignty was ordained to live.

"As the heavens are higher than the earth, so are my ways higher than yours," says God to the prophet (Isa. 55:9). In the faith journey of life, sometimes that's all we can cling to.

Shepherding Perils

To the elders among you, I appeal as a witness of Christ's
suffering… Be shepherds of God's flock that is under
your care, serving as overseers—not because you must—
but because you are willing, as God wants you to be: not
greedy for money, but eager to serve: not lording it over
those entrusted to you, but being examples to the flock.

—1 Peter 5:1–3

Introduction to Shepherding: The Elder Brawl

I spent five years on the church elder team, serving from 2006 to 2010. I began my service the year before I joined the church staff. I'd characterize the experience as combative and debilitating the first year and confrontational over the next thirty months. But the last eighteen held great promise for healing and renewal under new elder leadership.

In the early years, the elder team meandered in the spiritual weeds. Personal agendas overrode our service to the church body. There was little collaboration and even less civility. We were at war with one another, and the staff hunkered down to avoid friendly fire. At one point, even the senior pastor labeled the elder interactions as "profane."

Since we achieved consensus on nothing, every matter ended in a polarizing vote. From there, the elders engaged in the sport of faction building. They would recruit contingents from the flock to support their view on one issue or another... and then empower their faction of congregants to actively oppose the others.

At an early junction of ministry, I believed the church congregation to be a mix of smelly, mean-spirited sheep. I was dead wrong; the church was divided because the elders were divided. The sheep reflected the disunity of their shepherds. We were embarrassingly ineffective.

Disunity, of course, is nothing new in Christ's sheep pen. The apostle Paul wrote boldly and sternly about this issue to the early church in Corinth. "I appeal to you brothers, in the name of our Lord Jesus Christ... be perfectly united in mind and thought." One of you says, "I follow Paul," another, "I follow Apollos," another, "I follow Cephas." Is Christ divided? Was Paul crucified for you? Were you baptized into the name of Paul?" (1 Cor. 1:10–13).

An elder retreat in September of 2009 came on the heels of a confrontational interval of eldership. We *desperately* needed to chart a new course. "Serving as an elder is the highest calling you will ever experience," said our retreat leader. "It's marked with a sacred trust, submission to God's plan, respect for one another, and it's anchored in scripture. We are to be hope givers, led by the Spirit of God."

Ultimately, our elder skirmish was solved in an explosive climax; two elders were pressured to resign, and another quit, disgusted with the whole shepherding process. The three were replaced after an exhaustive selection process and training regimen powered by lots of prayer. No one dared risk regression to the dysfunctional mean of the last few years.

Then a welcome change in elder leadership finally led our team and church into the fertile land we'd failed to claim over three long years. New initiatives, renewed teamwork, a bolder vision, and a huge dose of humility and prayer brightened the way.

That said, my early elder experience was unvarnished discouragement. It left a bitter taste in my mouth; wore me out physically, mentally, and spiritually; and tore at the fiber of my long-term commitment to church ministry. In reflection, I'm ashamed of my team's failures during these years, and I'm thankful the Chief Shepherd's grace covers spiritual knuckleheads who can't get their leadership acts together.

Inside Ministry: Great Movement and Bigger Challenges

As the calendar marched deeper into 2009, I was learning what I should have already known. For twenty-two years in my consulting business, I was a leader who championed new ideas and change. In my spiritual life, no doubt, that's why I latched on to Romans 12:2: "Do not conform, but be transformed." I had made my living helping organizations create movement toward new futures, but always from the outside in, not the inside out. Change, to me, has always been synonymous with life and survival—personally, organizationally, and spiritually. God gave me a big heart for change. I'm certain that's largely because I've always been in desperate need of it!

I'm also a Malcolm Gladwell fan and gobbled up his book *Outliers*, in which he talks about men and women who live on the fringe of life's traditional bell curve and tend to swim upstream against the current, not with it. Life on the fringe can be frustrating for people like me who are impatient and driven by change. But that's also where excitement and new initiatives are created. They're seldom launched from the comfort and protection of the center.

As director (and newly ordained pastor) of ministry development, I enthusiastically jumped into the church-ministry pool. After seeking a clarified church vision, my team began forging a presence in the local community, where our church was astonishingly underrepresented, given its profile in the international missions arena. Partnering with a dozen local churches and the city council, we assembled a truly incredible array of community services for those in need under the banner of the Roswell Day of Hope. Since its genesis in 2009, the annual Day of Hope has served well over twelve thousand people, enjoyed the commitment of dozens of nonprofit agencies, and harnessed the hearts and backs of thousands of volunteers. On the second anniversary of the Day of Hope, the Flying Wallendas performed frightening high-wire acrobatics over the parking lot at city hall, and from their perch high above the crowd, preached a powerful Gospel message of hope to everyone below.

We also needed a more diverse staff to minister to the large Hispanic population in our community. With help from a few committed elders, I fashioned a detailed strategy to accomplish that vision and presented it to an energetic Hispanic couple I anticipated hiring to lead the initiative.

After reviewing the plan, Miguel and Maria waffled (no good Spanish translation for that). "Who developed this plan?" Maria asked. "We don't see it working. It's built on Anglo church assumptions, not our Hispanic culture and ministry principles."

With some wounded pride, I rescinded the plan, but I understood their hesitation. Who wants to implement someone else's flawed idea? "Okay," I said. "Top line, here's what we're trying to accomplish. Can you retool the plan and launch the ministry?"

"Claro que si," (Of course), they trumpeted. And today, Fellowship en Espanol (FeS), under their leadership, is a flourishing ministry of two hundred men, women, and children with deep roots in the local Hispanic community.

But not everyone was jubilant. At a church "town hall" meeting, a contingent of members confronted me shortly after FeS was commissioned. "We have a real problem with illegal immigrants coming to FeS," they said. "What are you going to do about that?"

With a degree of my signature pugnacity when poked, I said, "Absolutely nothing! If there are illegal immigrants in our community, I hope they flock here to worship. We don't encourage illegal status," I said, "but neither will we check IDs at the door to the church."

This enraged the warring faction of the church and they set about fanning the flames of division on this sparky issue. Finally, I just halted meetings with this fired-up constituency of men and women. I would learn that their penchant for aggressive dissent would not easily fade and I soon faced a barrage of criticism—some highly personal—that mauled my integrity, character, and motivation for this new ministry.

My fellow staffers pressed me for a solution. "What are you going to do about this beehive of criticism and church chaos directed at you?"

Enmeshed in the confusion and anxiety of the conflict, I holed up in prayer and solitude for the weekend seeking an answer. Emerging from my sabbatical, I announced my comprehensive plan-of-action to my ministry colleagues. "I will do absolutely nothing," I told them. "I will not counter the criticism point by point, and I'll also offer grace to those who have thrown me under the bus. I am trusting God to work this out for me."

The staff members—and yes, even the senior pastor—were stunned. They'd expected a slugfest from me. But at this dreadful nadir of ministry, I sensed that God was handing me a "grace ace" and expecting me to use it. "You've always needed grace, and you'll need it again," my conscious whispered to me. "Now, play the grace card God gave you." So, in a rare display of humility and surrender, I did exactly that.

Some months later, after most of the rancor and ministry gale had dissipated, a rival friend called and asked me for a brief get together. To my utter disbelief, Joe showed up in my office with a gift. It was a book—*Spurgeon's Sermon Notes*—which I still treasure to this day. How he knew I was a Charles Spurgeon fan I'll never know. The book has over 250 of the famous British preacher's Sunday messages to include his preparatory notes, questions, commentary, and illustrations. But the biggest surprise was yet to come. Inserted in the back of the book was a card from Joe and his wife, Laura. "Your heart for Jesus, your willingness to lead and serve and your transparency have set the bar high. We are honored to call you a friend."

"Joe," I said, "God has taught me a lot about grace these past few months. I'm learning to be a grace giver, not just a grace receiver. Thanks for affirming that!"

The book and card from Joe and his family are a souvenir of grace and proof that God can set things right-side up anytime he chooses... but it's always on his perfect timing.

Well into my second year on the church staff, the executive pastor decided to accept a senior pastor role in his home state of Texas. Monty was a gifted preacher and aspired to more time in the pulpit. It was an exciting opportunity for him after many years of soldiering as the church's number-two guy. I took on most of Monty's role, adding duties as staff team leader to my responsibilities in ministry development. It was a lot more work and devoured nearly all the time I had available for family and other pursuits Nonetheless, I plowed forward, seeing this as an opportunity to achieve greater effectiveness in our church's ministry endeavors.

"Don't worry," I told Jan when she expressed her concerns. "I'm a high capacity guy. I can make this work. I'll dial things back a bit later." With that heresy, I crossed the line of ministry reality. Astute leaders know that when your ministry RPMs hover in the red zone on your personal dashboard, it's nearly impossible to wind them down.

Ministry Restlessness and Desolation

As my responsibilities expanded, so did a growing sense of personal desolation. *Desolation* is a uniquely spiritual word loaded with history and implication. It describes the kind of heaviness that began to weigh on me and dates to St. Ignatius Loyola (1491–1556). Even today, St. Ignatius remains a recognized authority on spiritual discernment and her cousins, desolation and consolation.

Desolation is a spiritual and physical numbness or *dis*-ease, a restlessness, lack of peace, and sense of distance from God's presence. Desolation can easily escalate to hopelessness and anger with God. It can also be a withering "I'm going it alone" kind of desperation launched from emotional, physical, and spiritual fatigue and a dry, nonproductive prayer life.

In a ministry context, desolation is a particularly deflating emotion. Imagine training for years in your sport of excellence with an eye to a professional career. You're chosen high in the draft by your dream team, earn a starting position, and bang out a few wins—only to discover you dread suiting up for the next competition. You wonder if you're in the wrong game altogether.

Consolation is the opposite experience. It's a peaceful confirmation of God's presence and a deep sense of having a life-giving connection with God. In decision making (and prayer), consolation is an affirming sense of peace that the future will be safe, even if the pathway there is rocky and problematic.

Over the years, I've journaled extensively to capture and process a deep longing for understanding, peace, and God's movement in my soul. *Soul* is another vitally important word. It reflects the essence of all that you or I were created to be—a child of God, made in his image and destined to fulfill a unique purpose in life.

In my third year of ministry, I began a new journal and in short order scribbled sixteen pages of new entries. It was a summary of ministry desolation, which the luster of the Day of Hope and *Fellowship en Espanol* couldn't overcome. When released to fully express its raw sentiment, my heart was clamoring for change and begging for a ministry exit strategy. Here's a journal excerpt:

> Creating movement within the church environment often feels like slogging through hip-deep mud. Small contingents of highly vocal people somehow feel free to forfeit their Christian decorum and attack their pastoral leaders. On occasion, congregational town hall meetings resemble their rowdy political equivalent on CNN!
>
> I am much deeper in capacity-deficit mode than I confessed to Jan. But it's easier to redirect conversation with her than rehash the day's skirmishes. Brick by brick, I fear, I'm building a wall between my ministry work and my marriage. It's becoming very hard to see over it.
>
> High on my Richter scale of frustration is the voluminous energy expended on internal church and staff squabbles. The church, I thought, is supposed to focus on serving the

needs of the congregation and those *outside* the church campus and around the world. I'm wasting dozens of hours of energy untangling the web of *internal* disunity before any *external* movement can be mobilized.

My soul is in distress and my radar is in search mode, perhaps my most perilous self-confession. *Radar* is a code word both Jan and I know. It conveys frustration, lack of fulfillment, impatience, and deep longing. When my radar is in search mode it has dangerous implications because it seeks affirmation, approval, and acceptance—signals for me of a tired and wounded spirit—and they can come from the wrong sources.

My journal musings, when shared privately with my life coach, Gary Franklin, stirred him to quick action. Handing me Ruth Haley-Barton's *Strengthening the Soul of Your Leadership*, he said, "Read this, and then we'll talk." This was followed by a stern warning. "Tom, you must keep your relational hierarchy in order. Nourish your relationship with God first, then make protecting your family boundaries the next priority, followed by time invested in your ministry role. If that pecking order gets upside down, you'll be in big trouble." Gary's advice was deeply personal. Ironically, seven years earlier he'd been seated in the same chair I occupied—and it got the best of him.

In short order, I finished reading *Strengthening the Soul* and raced to read Haley-Barton's second work, *Sacred Rhythms*. Solitude, prayer, self-examination, and deep dives into scripture weren't on my dance card, even in my pastoral role. At the beckoning of *Sacred Rhythm*, I developed my "breath prayer" that would flow spontaneously when ministry pressures pushed me to the edge of cracking. *Jesus, Lord, help me to live within the limits and boundaries you have preordained for me. May your Spirit help me to rest, relax, and release.* It was short and sweet, and it regularly punctuated my day.

Contemplating my future path of life, I penciled ministry-exit options on a blank page of *Strengthening the Soul* and then borrowed a line from it. "Speak to my condition Lord and change me somewhere inside where it matters."[17]

In early 2010, I took those ideas and wrote a letter to the senior pastor outlining my proposal to step out of my ministry role by the end of the year, resign from the elder team, and explore new endeavors outside the church walls. I shared the plan with the church staff and agreed to plug any holes during my transition and help join up a new executive pastor.

In the months to come, the search for a new executive pastor languished, but I held tight to my proposed schedule; I would leave by year-end. For much of the following year, in my newfound freedom, I labored to create a nonprofit entity focused on serving the under-resourced community in the north Atlanta region. The innovative Mall of Compassion (MOC) was an exciting proposition, addressing the plight of those pushed out of the inner city by new growth and into the suburbs. It would house services for immigrants and the poor. But in the final stages, the MOC anchor tenant bolted from the agreement, and the concept died in its infancy.

I knew that in God's sovereignty there was a reason that the plan collapsed, but I was disappointed. Proof of God's master plan is in the pudding, as they say. Later, his reasons would be made clear to me.

Pastor on Call: More Lessons in Humility and Compassion

Although my exit strategy had been hatched and was proceeding, there were still pastoral responsibilities to be fulfilled in the months to come. One of those was serving as a pastor on call (POC), a role some churches employ to establish a first line of defense in meeting needs of the congregation.

POC responsibility is not for the faint of heart, and like its community first-responder equivalent, it requires a readiness to drop

---

17 Barton, *Strengthening the Soul of Your Leadership*, 44.

everything and go when a call comes in. The practice ensures a timely pastoral response to those in urgent need: an accident victim, a dire hospital situation, a single mom threatened with eviction, or perhaps a parent with a critical family issue. The rotating POC role fell to me about one week every two months.

Sometimes too, people outside the congregation ventured into the church office, unannounced, asking for a pastor. They, too, were the POC's responsibility. Most walk-ins have legitimate needs, but some, regretfully, work the church circuit with false and rehearsed stories that leverage churches' goodwill and resources. Compassion is vital to the POC, but wisdom and discernment are also his best friends.

One Sunday, a POC contingency interrupted our family's Sunday brunch; a middle-school boy was stuck in the church elevator.

"Dad! What do you know about elevators?" Caroline blurted out over breakfast.

"Absolutely nothing, Caroline," I said after my last forkful of cheese grits, "but I need to go figure it out." My phone rang a second time; it was the boy's mom. "Yes, ma'am, I'm on my way," I told her. "No, I don't know anything about elevators!"

On other days, POC duties can be a humbling and frightful experience, the stakes sometimes escalating to pivotal family decisions. One day a family was escorted into my office by the receptionist. The chaos in their household had reached boil over. I dropped everything per POC protocol and sat with them most of the day. The mom was working two jobs (and taking a taxi between them) while the unemployed dad was comfortable at home enjoying one of his hobbies. The teenaged son, in the meantime, had dropped out of school, and his sister was struggling with a physical disorder. It was a long and exasperating meeting, particularly with the dad, whom I wanted to take out behind the woodshed for a couple of fatherly responsibility lessons. I finally ushered them out of my office with enough POC wisdom to get them through the week. In passing, I then characterized the family to a ministry colleague as a "dysfunctional circus."

It was a few hours later that my shamefully insensitive comment popped up in my mind to assault me. Even today, the memory of that moment grieves me. Arrogance, apparently, is deeply rooted in my DNA. I begged for God's forgiveness, together with a measure of humility and compassion. A *dysfunctional circus*? I don't recall Jesus ever uttering anything that nasty.

The next day I made a beeline to our staff pastoral counselor to talk about the troubled family. Together we fashioned a remedial plan, leveraging the wealth of his experience. For the next six months, I met regularly with the family. We had many difficult issues to resolve to include a suicide attempt by one of the family members, but God intervened in their circumstances and restored them to a reasonable level of family normalcy.

My last contact with the family was encouraging. I've lost track of them in recent years, but I pray they're still on solid footing today.

Shepherding Perils: Looking Back

Before I left my consulting firm for a church staff role, I leaked my plans to Rejean, a longtime French-Canadian client and friend. Our association had developed into a mentoring relationship while we were both globe-trotting for business. In 2016, I officiated his wedding ceremony.

Rejean knows me well and quickly zeroed in on the challenges I'd face in my new role. "You're not a savior, Tom," he said. "You have a good heart, but you can't fix everything and everyone. That's going to be tough for you in your new job. You don't like chaos and disorder either, and you expect things to change quickly," he added. "The messiness of church and other people's lives will draw you in. Be careful. Don't get in over your head. It will wear you out and won't be good for you and Jan."

Yes, much of the ministry messiness was not good for Jan and me, and the elder fracas remains the most debilitating leadership experience of my career. But despite deeply engrained pugilistic tendencies, I've always had a passion for the underdog and marginalized people. That's what drew me to church ministry—the opportunity for greater "people impact" in my local community and around the world. When engaged with people-centered initiatives like the Day of Hope and the launch of Fellowship en Espanol, I flourished in ministry's sweet spot. When constrained by stuffy church organizational issues and internal policy, I floundered in frustration.

Ministry desolation came unexpectedly and jolted my new career path's equilibrium. The pages of my journal tell that story with painstaking clarity. Rejean's warning proved to be on the mark, not because church ministry isn't a high calling but because I'm not wired for an *inside* ministry role. I'm an *outside* guy with an entrepreneurial, outlier spirit that doesn't conform well to established norms. My call to work in Nairobi's slum community is much more up my alley.

Life experience however, must *always* give way to life change and point to life purpose. But sometimes life change demands a change of *environment* and an acceptance of the fact that, even though your intentions may be noble, you are in the wrong game.

Romans 12:12 tells us to "be joyful in hope, patient in affliction, faithful in prayer." That's always true, but even more so when the change-the-environment messenger pounds on your door.

6

A New Country Experience

Help, Lord,…

—Psalm 12:1

Soul Nourishment

"Help, Lord," is a remarkably powerful prayer in its brevity yet also typical of what we would expect from David. He was despondent over the lack of faithful people and apparently a large contingent of men who honored what is vile. So he called on God.

"When the creature failed, David went immediately to the Creator,"[18] says Charles Spurgeon. David evidently felt *help*-less, or he wouldn't have cried out for help. Yet at the same time, David knew he had to be actively engaged in the solution, for the word *help*, by definition, requires that we take on part of that work ourselves.

I have also learned, like many in the winepress of life, that solutions to life's challenges don't always come through my own grit and determination but rather in partnership with the power and faithfulness of God. "Help, Lord," is the prayer of God's faithful. It serves the strong in desperate circumstances, the weak when confronted

---

18 Reimann, *Morning by Morning*, Day 169.

with their limitations, and the dying in their last gasps of breath before God's eternal embrace.

Is this new spiritual insight? Heavens, no!

In the book of Exodus, Moses learned a lot about God's help. He survived forty years in the desert, found a beautiful wife near an oasis, made his way back to Egypt after a burning-bush encounter, beat Pharaoh at his own game of intimidation (a few nasty plagues *helped* carry the day), led two million Jews across dry land in the Red Sea, saved Aaron and his friends from their golden calf charade, drew water from a rock for his dehydrated pilgrims, and raised up a new leader (Joshua) for the charge into the promised land. Read the full version of Moses's story in the book of Exodus. He was leading a stiff-necked people into a new country. *Help* could have been Moses's middle name.

In Romans chapter 8, Paul digs deeper into the idea of *help*. "For you did not receive a spirit that makes you a slave again to fear, but you received a Spirit of sonship" (v 15a). Cry for help to your "*Abba,* Father" (v 15b) who loves you as one of his children, Paul tells us. What *Abba,* Father—an awkwardly affectionate and very personal name for God—would opt out of giving his children *help,* handing them a stone when they ask for bread? Paul was not the least bit put off by God's help; in fact, he chose to *boast* about it (2 Cor. 12:9).

Why do we plow head-on into life's trials by ourselves? It's the default position of the human spirit. Boasting about our weakness and implying we need help is simply not a common practice in the human experience. But at this juncture of my life, *Abba Father* nudged me into a barren new country with his message: soul nourishment comes only from me, you won't find it anywhere else. Under the ponderous weight of emotional fatigue, marital detachment, and a pitched battle for my spiritual identity, I too called out for help like the Psalm writer David. Help would have many faces and forms in the years to come, but it began in the Transforming Community in May of 2010 and would later include a sabbatical in the forty-ninth state.

Red-Zone Dangers and a New Country Experience

"I am convinced," says Henri Nouwen, "that ministers… and all those who relate to anguishing people need a truly safe place for themselves where they can share deep pain and struggles with people who do not need them."[19]

The intended audience for Nouwen's warning is bigger than you might think. Yes, he's addressing ministers, but his reach extends to all those who find themselves in a work (or ministry) red zone where they feel overwhelmed and under equipped. When you serve people as a primary part of your job description, Nouwen warns, you must protect your own emotional and spiritual health. That may include talking to a trusted friend outside the office who will minister to your own needs and help steer you back to the centerline of life when you've run aground.

Vocational research adds more depth and breadth to the idea of ministry's red zone. Nearly 60 percent of ministry leaders (of which the majority are men) bail out of their roles during their ministry tenures. I became one of them. My emotional battery regularly dipped into low-power mode, and there wasn't much voltage left for family challenges and personal soul care. Ironically, I discovered, a ministry environment can be a *very* arid place emotionally and spiritually; the church family doesn't always take great care of its shepherds. That's especially true of high energy personalities (like me) who can't—or won't—flip the ministry switch to *off*. Ministry leaders often build walls at home to shelter their spouses from the exhausting and unique demands of their work, heightening the risk of emotional distance in their marriage. Not surprisingly, many wives view their spouse's ministry careers as a threat to their marriages and family health. Personally, I found it progressively easier to answer Jan's "How was your day?" with longer runs on the greenway.

Transforming Community founder Ruth Haley-Barton digs deeper into the ministry red zone. Speaking as an experienced minister herself, she warns her audiences to guard the source of their

---

19 Nouwen, *In the Name of Jesus*, 69.

identity, approval, and acceptance—it must come *solely* through their relationship with God. Making her appeal personal, she added this: "If you're a leader or caregiver and you wrongly believe your identity, approval, and acceptance comes from the people you serve, you will begin to feed on the sheep in your pen."[20]

I flinched at the note of provocation in Ruth's warning and wanted to discount it as just another ministry challenge. But her message burrowed into my heart and soul. Who (or whom) was the source of my identity... and did my approval and acceptance come from the sheep in the ministry pen I served?

How and where did I encounter Ruth and the Transforming Community? Shortly after I told the church staff and elders that I would leave my ministry assignment at the end of 2010, I petitioned the church leadership team for money to attend Haley-Barton's Transforming Community (TC). The TC is a two-year life change and spiritual growth curriculum designed primarily (though not exclusively) for ministry workers. My life coach Gary Franklin would join me every calendar quarter for the sessions. The TC was an affirming consolation-based decision that would lead me out of the desolation that had come to cloud my life. More on the TC later.

Ruth's message is timely, literal, and not limited to ministry environments. Just look at today's headlines. If affirmation and approval from the sheep in your pen is your primary source of soul nourishment, whether you are a teacher, doctor, church leader, or a Hollywood director, you're in big trouble. If (or when) those relationships go south, your identity is likely to follow. Parents who live life through Johnny's or Mary's accomplishments face the same scenario; when the kids struggle, the parent's identity tanks.

On the other hand, when your identity is firmly rooted in your relationship with God and not solely dependent on the people you care for, your spiritual health will flourish. Affirmation and approval, of course, are important to human relationships, and God created us to value them. But *true* soul nourishment must come from the Lord.

---

20 Ruth Haley-Barton, Transforming Community Center, "Reflections on Solitude and Community in the Life of the Leader," 2010.

Looking through the rearview mirror of life, I will always celebrate my church role and experience. God orchestrated the whole thing and had many important lessons to teach me. But as the calendar raced toward Christmas of 2010, I found myself frustrated with God for parachuting me into ministry's snare—a desolate landing zone that thwarted my skills and experience. It felt like a bad dream, but it was no dream. It was an upside-down reality that had stripped away the veneer of my confidence and left me in lonely exile.

M. Robert Mulholland Jr. speaks to this new country experience in *Invitation to a Journey*. There's a stage in life, he says, when we think we've got most things figured out; life is on autopilot, and we have a firm grip on our faith and identity as children of God. "We would rather die than hesitate to offer a sacrifice of ourselves and our will,"[21] he says. But then God in his wisdom escorts us into a new country where we realize we've been living a lie. There fear, an off-center faith, and uncertainty attack one's spiritual identity.

I liken my new country reality to Peter's denial of Christ. Peter was a dedicated and energetic disciple, his heart pure and tested (or so he thought) after walking step by step with Jesus for three years. "I will lay down my life for you" (John 13:37), he brashly announces to the Messiah. But then Jesus is arrested, and Peter is confronted with the harsh reality of fear. In the encounter, he proves to be a coward.

"Didn't I see you with him in the olive grove?" the high priest asks Peter (John 18:27). Without hesitation, Peter denies his association with Christ for the third time. And when the rooster crows, Peter is ushered into his own new country.

A new country experience shoves us off a comfortable plateau of life and presents a choice: higher spiritual ground and maturity or a plunge into a valley of despair. Judas chose the latter. Higher spiritual ground can be a frightening call into the unknown, an intimidating ascent we can't envision… and an expedition we might not want to undertake. Mulholland describes it more viscerally. "It's like an abscess which bursts. It's always been with you, but you didn't feel it.

---

21 Mulholland, *Invitation to Journey*, 84.

Now it's out in the open. We know in our heart and mind that the healing process is healthy. It's just painful and very messy."[22]

There is, however, a transformational promise in this new country. It's a newfound spiritual resiliency. David, in Psalms, says the same thing. "He lifted me out of the slimy pit, out of the mud and mire: he set my feet on a rock and gave me a firm place to stand. He put a new song in my mouth, a hymn of praise to our God" (Ps. 40:2–3).

Think about it this way: a new country experience comes with free music lessons!

The Transforming Community, Apollo 13, and a New Country Experience

The sixty-five-plus members of the fifth Transforming Community (May 2010 through March 2012) came from all walks of ministry life. A few were from the business sector as well. We would meet Sunday evening through mid-Tuesday (quarterly, as I've said) at a serene and picturesque Catholic retreat center in Marytown, Illinois, not far from Chicago. The retreat center borders a ten-acre lake and wooded trails where one can lose himself in reflection—which is partially the intent. It's not a Catholic affair; the retreat center just provides the rooms and facility for TC attendees.

In the opening session, Ruth's first two points set the tone for our time together. "Let's talk about the word *retreat*," she said. "What does it mean?" As a former marine officer, I denied any association with the concept. But shrewder colleagues in attendance knew better; even elite fighting forces on occasion put distance between themselves and their foes. They *re*-group, *re*-fresh, *re*-strategize, and *re*-arm before *re*-attacking. Retreat, of course, is not always the face of defeat and can, in fact, lead to strategic advantages. That never came up at the Marine Infantry School in Quantico, Virginia.

---

22 Mulholland, *Invitation to Journey*, 84.

"I want everyone to close your eyes," Ruth said next. "If you're seriously considering exiting your ministry role, or, if you already have and are contemplating what's next, raise your hand."

Mine shot up.

After a short pause, she said, "Now open your eyes."

About two-thirds of the new Transforming Community gathering had their hands in the air. That percentage did not differ much from the vocational statistics I cited earlier, but at that time, I was shocked.

Ruth was not. "Not surprising," she said, surveying the room. "That's why we're here."

What do the Transforming Community, Apollo 13, and a new country experience have in common? Much more than you may think.

Tom Hanks in the classic 1995 flick *Apollo 13* plays astronaut Jim Lovell. In the movie, based on real events, Hanks' character is 205,000 miles from home and knows his crippled spacecraft may not make it back. He radios the command center and barks out, "Houston, *we* have a problem" (emphasis added). The instant those words are out of his mouth, Lovell confesses that the solution to the crew's survival—if there's to be any rescue at all—will come from a *partnership* with the command center. The solution is not solely within his crew's capacity.

As I struggled with the implications of my new country journey, I realized I faced the same dilemma, so I called out too, "Lord, *we* have a problem. Help me out of this crucible of life!" Like the prophet Elijah, who ran for his life after Jezebel threatened to kill him (1 Kings 19), I too was listening for encouragement and God's whisper. In solitude that day, here's what crept into my mind and what I penciled in my journal:

> Have you forgotten my counsel to Isaiah? "I am the Lord your God who takes hold of you by your right hand and says, Fear not, I will help you" (Isa. 41:13). You've shaken loose of my hand... and you won't get out of this new country by your

own strength. There's a long and tough journey ahead, but *we* can travel it hand in hand.

In the movie version, Jim Lovell and his Apollo 13 crew worked feverishly with Houston to engineer a solution for reentry. They got it all worked out and splashed down safely before my popcorn ran out. It would take me much longer, but the dialogue had finally begun. I, too, was on a mission and needed help getting home. Splashdown for me would also involve some reengineering solutions. For me that focused on my spiritual identity and my sources of approval and acceptance. God in his wisdom had shoved me into this new country. He would need to help me out.

Many people struggle with the notion of a *partnership* with God in the life-change process; they are befuddled by the age-old mystery: how does Divine Sovereignty coexist alongside human decision-making responsibility? I've studied the confounding issue for years but have since put it to rest. C. S. Lewis makes it simple. "It's like asking which blade in a pair of scissors is most necessary,"[23] he says. Partnership is God's overarching power *and* his power as he works through us.

Once again, it felt like God had handed me the final exam before I'd had a chance to examine the syllabus. But that's the way he works. He uses life experience and trials as a catalyst for life change. The Transforming Community gave me a fresh start and a new platform to chart a course of personal change and intimate partnership with God. Over the years to come, my view of a partnership with God would take on a new meaning. E. Stanley Jones sums it up well. Jones was an American missionary to India and he brought back fresh ideas about spiritual renewal and discipline. "Trust as if the whole thing depended on God," he says. "And work as if the whole thing depended on you."[24]

Got it!

---

23 Lewis, *Mere Christianity*, 148.
24 Foster, *Devotional Classics*, 302.

The Alaska Reset

Life-change (i.e., true-transformation) principles are not complicated, but it takes a divine partnership to master them. Why? Because we'd much rather fashion and follow our own rules. Fundamentally, transformational change is a three-legged stool. There must be a *motive* for change, often a stark reality check; an *awakening* to what change demands—new habits and behaviors to be learned; and a *process* for change, a means to internalize and sustain it. The fatigue of my soul provided a motive; the Transforming Community, the awakening; and the Alaska Reset gave me the process for life change in a new country. And a way out!

In July of 2013, Jan was headed to Guatemala on a medical Missions trip, joining Caroline, who was already there on a ministry internship. A few weeks earlier, while contemplating what I'd do in their absence, I spontaneously bought a round-trip ticket to Anchorage, Alaska, and announced my decision to Jan.

"You're going *where*?" she asked, puzzled and somewhat concerned. "Where is this heading, and why Alaska?"

"It's a directive from the command center," I told her flippantly, but Jan wanted a better answer. "I need some time away and alone. I'm going with a pile of books and my journal. I leave the same day you do for Guatemala. I've prearranged only one thing. I've hired a bush pilot to fly me to Denali National Park. Denali is the highest mountain in North America. On the trip back, I'll try some salmon fishing, too."

"By yourself?" she asked. "Is it safe? Aren't there bears up there?"

My Alaska decision was somewhat of an awkward moment for Jan and me. I had never ventured off alone in our thirty-plus years together, so why now? She knew the Transforming Community had burrowed deep into my heart, mind, and soul. On my return, I had even pursued a Christian counselor's wisdom at this late stage of life to delve even further into life's challenges.

"The Transforming Community was a launch platform, not a destination," I explained to Jan. "I'm still very much in-process. It's like moving on to higher math. While you're in Guatemala, I'll take the week and sort out all I've learned and how to integrate it into a rule of life—a spiritual rhythm. I want that to be life's guard-rail for my role as a husband, dad, and ministry leader in the years ahead."

There's certainly no formulaic approach to finding a spiritual rhythm. The goal and purpose, however, is crystal clear: to *strengthen* one's faith. Investing in one's spiritual health is a critically important life principle and is ignored at great peril. "So then, just as you received Christ Jesus as Lord, continue to live in him, rooted and built up in him, *strengthened* in the faith as you were taught" (Col. 2:6–7; italics added). Like anything else, life lessons can be unlearned, forgotten, or go stale for a season. Says a close pastor friend who jettisoned his ministry career, "I ceased building up and strengthening my faith, took my eyes off the ball, and got a little prideful. Not surprisingly, trouble followed."

"My experience was similar," I told a group of men at a conference some years later. "In the foxhole of ministry, I loosened my grip on faith essentials, and my spiritual identity became a casualty." I would begin anew in the forty-ninth state; the destination God chose for a remedial assignment.

My Denali expedition was scheduled for Sunday, July 14, the morning after my arrival in Anchorage. Takeoff, I discovered, was only a hundred yards from my hotel, which backed up to Anchorage's Lake Spenard. The lake serves as the runway for a multitude of seaplanes. Racing their engines, they throw up enormous clouds of mist, and about thirty seconds later, they're airborne.

"Anyone else going with you?" the pilot asked. "I can take three, and there's no discount for a solo fight."

"It's just me, sir," I told him, and we were off.

I could dedicate an entire chapter to the breathtaking panoramas I experienced that day as the pilot steered north to Denali. I've flown in small aircraft many dozens of times but never in a single-engine Beechcraft buffeted by Alaska winds curling off the canyon walls and threatening to tear the wings off the tiny airplane. As we gained altitude through the mountain gorges, I tried to separate exhilaration from raw fear.

Approaching Denali

Then my new best friend in the pilot's seat amped up every-thing that I was feeling. "We are at fourteen thousand feet," he said. "The peaks on your right and left rise another five thousand feet above us. The glacier below us is a mile thick. The winds up here are treacherous and can easily shift and pitch us into the mountain. That's why you're flying with me. I've lost pilot friends up here who took too much risk. That's Denali ahead. It's twenty-one thousand feet above sea level. I'll get as close as I can, but the weather up here can change quickly. Then we'll head to the mountain lake, where we'll have lunch and you can fish." Joe Alaska was abrupt, surly, and arrogantly confident, just the kind of pilot you want on a flight to Denali.

"Get your pictures now," he commanded a few minutes later. "I don't like the looks of those clouds ahead, so we're not going any closer." I snapped away as the plane banked southward.

Twenty minutes later, we approached an enchanting mountain lake. We sliced through the glistening water and taxied gently to the shore. It was a postcard setting with the sun arching westward towards the sea.

"Don't get out yet," the pilot barked at me. I was to wait until he strapped a mini-cannon to his hip.

"What caliber is that?" I asked.

"It's a long-barrel .45 magnum," he replied. "Up here, you need enough firepower to stop a bear. I reload my own ammo to be sure."

How encouraging, I thought as we headed upstream. *He's got a .45-caliber artillery piece and I have a fiberglass fishing pole.*

About fifty yards from the plane, we stopped. "This is a good place," he said. "Now listen to me *very* carefully. If you see a bear and she catches your eye, *do not run!* Stand your ground and return her stare. If you run, you're a dead man. *Never* get between mama bear and her cubs. If she runs at you, roll into a ball, protect your head, and yell like hell. *Do not fight back,*" he added in his Alaskan wisdom. "Your only chance is to cover up." With that comforting wilderness counsel, the pilot turned and began walking back to the plane.

"Hey, wait!" I thundered. "Are you leaving me here alone?"

"Don't worry," he said. "I'll hear your shouts from the plane. Hope you catch a few."

Fishing in Bear Country

Anchorage to Seward: An Identity Reboot

The Millennial Hotel in Anchorage is just a few miles from the airport and Anchorage's downtown waterfront. After my Denali venture, I met with the hotel concierge.

"Welcome to Alaska," she said. "What did you come here to do?"

"Well, that's a long story," I said, dodging her question. "Yesterday I flew to Denali, but I need some new ideas."

"You should go to Seward," she said. "You can get there via the Alaska Railroad. It's a relaxing three-hour trip, very scenic, and you can buy a ticket at the railway station, which isn't far from here. While you are in Seward, take the glacier cruise into the Kenai Fjord. You'll see killer whales and amazing glacier sights."

Seward is named after former secretary of state William Seward, who purchased the Alaska Territory for two cents an acre from the Russians in 1867. On the journey, the Alaska Railroad rumbles southward through mountainous terrain with plenty of plucky mountain goats and an occasional bald eagle to keep passengers entertained. At one juncture of the trip, the engineer halted the train and called attention to a mama moose and her "moose-ette" crossing the tracks. As they headed for a dip in the adjacent pond, every passenger jockeyed for position for a once-in-a-lifetime photo.

As I prepared to write this chapter, I scanned the books I carried with me on that summer day, and my Alaska Railroad boarding pass slipped from Miles Stanford's *The Complete Green Letters*. It was one of two books I crammed into my backpack along with my Bible and journal. Interestingly, my railway ticket vouches for a booking in *adventure* class. It would be that... and much more!

The other book was *A Man After God's Own Heart*, R. T. Kendall's epic study of King David's life. The book's subtitle, *God's Relationship with David—and with You*, sparked many questions in my mind. Neither book was on the Transforming Community reading list, but I was anxious to get into both.

My journal records my uneasy peace in being in God's providential grip that day. "The LORD will watch your coming and going, both now and forevermore," said the preprinted verse in the journal margin from Psalm 121:8. Halfway down the page, my own words spill out to a distant God. "I believe you have something important for me on this excursion… but at the core of my soul, I'm despairing, and I desperately need your grace and favor."

St. John of the Cross, a sixteenth-century spiritual icon, calls the feeling a "dark night of the soul."[25] It's a collapse of one's spiritual framework in a season of life and can border on depression. Not surprisingly, people with a shallow faith have no idea what you're talking about.

I grabbed a seat in the spacious, second-deck accommodations on the train and spread out my reading material. I prayed for insights and a booster shot for my tired and depleted soul. As far back as I could remember, nearly everything spiritual had come at a high cost… and again, I was looking into an uncertain future. My reading adventure that day took shape as a three-prong encounter. To my left, I had the perennial truth of old and new life in Romans, chapters six through eight. In front of me was Stanford's *Green Letters*, and on my right, Kendall's discussion of King David's intimate fellowship with God.

As the train rolled southward to Seward, I burrowed into Romans. There is no two-page section in my Bible more dog-eared, underlined, and highlighted than the chapters I turned to that day. Nonetheless, I read the verses again, again, and again, taking the apostle Paul's advice that I should remind myself of what I already know. I reduced each chapter to a word pair that spoke to my spiritual identity: *new* identity (chapter 6), identity *war* (chapter 7), and identity *power* (chapter 8). Unarguably, that's oversimplified, but sometimes less is more.

At a deeper level, Romans, in chapter 6, verses 4 through 8, tells me that in Christ *we live a new life*, our *old self* is dead (in fact, *crucified*), we are *alive* to God in Christ, and in case we missed it, we're told again that we've been brought from *death to life* and been *set free*.

Chapter 7, however, hits us with a painful reality. Everything new, alive, and set free coexists and wars with all that is old, dead, and

---

25 Foster, *Devotional Classics*, 33.

enslaved. C'mon, Paul, tell me it isn't so! But it's true, and sometimes what's old runs roughshod over the new.

Chapter 8 affirms our spiritual identity. "Therefore, there is now no condemnation for those in Christ Jesus" (Rom. 8:1). Further down the page, scripture also tells us that God's spirit holds the power to win life's skirmishes *if* my mind is tuned to the right channel. Romans uproots our tired, guilt-ridden identity like a dead tree in a tornado. It's all we need to know to grow in the fertile soil of new life.

Turning to *Green Letters*, I wrestled with what Stanford calls the *principle of position*. Basically, he says this: my spiritual *position* as a Christ follower never changes, regardless of my failures. That's been taken care of once and for all, the debt of my sin and corruption cancelled by Christ's death on the cross. There's no need for another atonement or more work on my part. Christ himself said it clearly: "It is finished" (John 19:30).

But my human *condition* is variable. I can be cold-hearted and very distant from God... or passionate in my pursuit of him in different seasons of life. "Faith in our spiritual *position*," says Stanford, "brings growth in our human *condition*."[26]

I personalized his proposition that day: If my focus remains on my human *condition* (failures, difficult trials, and bad decisions), it will erode my confidence in my spiritual *position*. And when that occurs, my identity and spiritual vitality will tank.

As the train made headway through the rugged terrain, my focus shifted to *A Man After God's Own Heart*. David is the only person in the Bible for whom God uses this description. (Maybe because he's the best example of *position-condition* living?) As I closed in on Seward and my glacier cruise, David rose to a new standard of positional security. I thought about his contest with Goliath. "I come against you in the name of the LORD, Almighty," says David. "This day the LORD will hand you over to me" (1 Sam. 17:45–46). David's defeat of Goliath was a positional victory; the stone's flight was just the proof.

---

26 Stanford, *The Complete Green Letters*, 81 (italics added).

But there's also the other side of David, the man who has the audacity to write, "For I have kept the ways of the LORD: I have not done evil by turning away from my God" (Ps. 18:23).

"What? You can't be serious, David," was my gut reaction when reading Psalm 18. "What about your adulterous fling with Bathsheba and her dead husband, Uriah?" But as I spent time in deep reflection that day, God handed me clear positional truth. Despite his grievous failures, David never turned *away* from God. Instead, like a first responder to an emergency, he ran *toward* his savior. Grieved in his human condition, he confessed his horrific failures and held tight to his positional security. "My God is my rock in whom I take refuge. He is my shield and the horn of my salvation" (Ps. 18:2).

David claims the same positional identity in Psalm 51. In response, God claims him as a faithful man after his own heart. That theology bruises our common sense, but at another level, it's refreshingly simple. To understand our positional security, we must embrace God's unconditional love, mercy, and grace... and not reason to God from our finite human perspective.

As the train pulled into Seward, a cozy and vibrant fishing town rebuilt after a devastating 1964 earthquake, I reflected on the journey and the rich spiritual insight it had yielded. And I still had the ride back to fine-tune my thoughts and four more days in Anchorage to work on a spiritual rhythm.

At the Seward rail station, I bid adieu to one host and greeted the second. The first had to have been God's Spirit. He'd granted my soul a reboot of my positional-conditional software. My journal shouts out a thanksgiving and closure on my long bout with CIS—conditional identity syndrome. Did the pages in Romans, which I'd read so many times, contain the same ideas that Stanford and Kendall had explained? They did. But apparently, I'd needed the authors' help to get the message from my head to my heart.

The next host, this time an earthly one, held up a sign welcoming me and a half-dozen others to the glacier cruise. After a luscious buffet lunch, the seventy-foot craft headed north into the teeth of the glacier that spilled down the mountain into Resurrection Bay, so named two hundred years ago by a Russian explorer who took life-saving refuge there after a vicious Easter Sunday storm.

As the Kenai cruiser ventured north, the glacier ice wall rose eight hundred feet straight up from the shore. The glacier ice, I learned, was well over a thousand years old, and it displayed a brilliant sapphire blue color, which only added to its majesty and mystique.

There were also pods of killer whales cavorting in the fjord along-side the most fearless (or foolish?) souls on the planet, ocean kayakers enjoying the day in the fjord. I quickly raised the question. And *no*, I was told, Orcas don't snack on kayakers. I love adventure, but I would not spend a nickel on an ocean kayak in Resurrection Bay.

There were other unexpected wonders. As we drew closer to the towering ice mountain, the glacier calved and sent a voluminous shard of ice into the bay. It sounded like a rifle shot, and when the ice crashed into the bay, the resulting wave surged four hundred yards to our boat. As we continued to make headway toward the shoreline, a crewman pointed out sea otter colonies and then snatched a small chunk of ice from the water with his net. "Margaritas with glacier ice will be served on the main deck," he ceremoniously announced.

When mine came up, I asked the bartender, "Are there any thousand-year-old critters in that ice?"

"Nah," he said. "It's the purest water you'll ever drink."

"Down the hatch," was my response.

Anchorage to Seward was a grand spiritual experience enveloped within the wonder of God's magnificent creation. My heart and soul celebrated both, so much so that I vowed to make it a father-son venture the following summer. I made good on the promise, and Bryan and I spent two days deep-sea fishing off Seward's rugged coastline. On the flight home, we checked fifty pounds of flash-frozen salmon, rockfish, and halibut filets. Great eating for the months to come.

Crafting a Spiritual Rhythm

Although I'd practiced journaling for years, I had never integrated other disciplines into a harmonious spiritual rhythm. A rhythm, of course, can have a creative beat, but when the cadence gets random and disjointed, you can't call it a rhythm. A spiritual rhythm is not a slavish protocol; rather, it keeps one's spiritual fire burning. "Keep the draught open, clean out the ashes, and keep putting in fuel,"[27] says the noted missionary, E. Stanley Jones.

The chance to work through a reboot of my spiritual identity before tackling a spiritual rhythm was another grand dose of God's grace. I can't imagine laboring through a spiritual rhythm from a corrupted, upside-down identity. When my position and identity in Christ is secure, I fight the battle of life from high ground. Positional identity fuels one's spiritual energy, vitality, and mind. In fact, our minds are a vital weapon in the identity fight. If we are blinded by conditional reasoning, life takes on a troubled and conflicted existence. But Romans assures us that "the mind controlled by the Spirit… is life and peace" (Rom. 8:6).

Returning late Monday night to the Millennial Hotel, I was energized and spiritually refreshed. I looked forward to another four days with my traveling library and hours of plane watching on Lake Spenard. There, I sketched out my spiritual rhythm. It looked something like this:

Morning Prayer and Devotion. I first determined to take command of my morning calendar. For me, it's important—no, it's vital—to set my spiritual compass on true north early in the day, or I'm apt to be a lost puppy, or worse, take on the demeanor of a junkyard dog. "With remarkable frequency," says the Hitler-defying author Dietrich Bonhoeffer, "the Scriptures remind us that God's people rose early to seek and carry out his commands."[28] I find great comfort and wisdom in well-crafted devotionals. Oswald Chambers (*My Utmost for His Highest*) and Charles Spurgeon *(Morning by Morning)* routinely jump-starts my day. But with assurance that night owls can also embrace spiritual rhythms of their own, Spurgeon also wrote an *Evening by Evening* edition. With a focus on life applications, all these shine a high-beam on scripture, the source of life-sustaining

---

27 Foster, *Classic Devotions*, 303.
28 Bonhoeffer, *Life Together*, 43.

wisdom. There are many worthy devotional guides available today, but I'm drawn only to those that supplement God's Word rather than attempting to replace it.

Informational versus Formational Bible Reading. What does this mean? While in Alaska, I asked myself two questions. *"How could I be so well educated biblically yet still lack a robust spiritual identity?"* And, *"What would be different in the future?"* J. Robert Mulholland Jr.'s *Shaped by the Word* held the answers to my questions.

For years, my Bible reading had centered more on learning facts and *information* rather than any hint of life change and spiritual *formation*. Without much forethought, I had surrendered to an academic norm of mastering a body of information, much like preparing for a college exam. In some areas, I had a headful of knowledge, but it didn't prompt enough life change. Reading God's Word from a formational perspective can be a frightening experience because it zeroes in on our heart, character, and behavior. In the last several years, that shift in focus has been richly rewarded, and it's brought meaningful life change.

Schooling in the School of Psalms. The more I read Psalms, the more I need to read Psalms. The verses help put words to my deepest emotions, my grievances with God, and my exuberant praise that finds its way between the other two. Several years ago, the popular magazine, *Christianity Today* ran a feature article on Psalms (which I still have). "The Psalms… are a mirror; they will reveal you. Yet they are much more. Read them and they will read you. Pray them and they will change you."[29]

Memorizing scripture is difficult for me, but there are many verses in Psalms that are embedded in my heart and mind. I'm encouraged as much by what they say as by the man David, who wrote most of them. Psalms tells me there's still plenty of room in heaven for someone like me who shares some of David's wayward pathways. There's no rule of thumb, of course, for what should go into or be left out of a spiritual rhythm, but the Psalms play an indispensable role in mine.

---

29 Ben Patterson, "Schooled By The Psalms," *Christianity Today*, October 2008, 89.

Journaling the Journey. My Myers-Briggs profile tells me I'm an external processor and a thinker. Journaling helps me *process* life and *think* in reflection and solitude. My journal tells a story, but also reveals the struggle behind the story.

I began journaling after Vanessa's death, and I have faithfully used the process to battle with God, praise him for his grace and favor in my life, and blow off spiritual steam. From my journal flows much of the narrative chronology of *Metamorphyx*. Even today I make it a habit to periodically review what I have penned over recent months and meditate on the good, the bad, and the ugly of my story as it continues to unfold.

A journal also demands honesty from its author; facts and events over time easily give way to biases and spin when not hard-wired to the written account. I rarely open my journal to anyone in its truncated and naked transparency. But on occasion, when I trust in the confidence of the listener, I'll unveil it. On my Alaska reset, my journal helped me reevaluate, retool, and redirect my life's trajectory. In fact, the mandate for writing *Metamorphyx* came from my journal notes. I don't journal every day (not even close), but when I do, it's a rich experience.

Soaking in Solitude. In one sense, solitude is the gateway to all spiritual disciplines. However, the busyness of life frequently pushes her off the calendar. I gave her a louder voice in my emerging spiritual rhythm and in the charge to gauge the effectiveness of other disciplines. Solitude takes practice but easily melds with other elements of a spiritual rhythm. I use an age-old acrostic, ACTIP, to kick off a session of solitude. I address God in humble *A*doration, am repentant in *C*onfession, bountiful in *T*hanksgiving, purposeful in *I*ntersession for others, and bold in my *P*etition for my own needs. ACTIP can be a meaningful launching point for morning prayer, introspection, and a deeper relationship with God.

Getting away for a day or two of solitude (or just a long afternoon) can be a real challenge with our demanding schedules, but the discipline serves me well. Jesus frequently went off by himself to pray and draw close to his Father. That's reason enough for me to do the same. There's a rock outcrop with my name on it at Woodall Shoals, that mysteriously treacherous class 5 rapid on the Chattooga River in North Georgia. Like an old friend, it invites me to sit with my thermos of coffee and reflect, relax, and meditate. I've written dozens of pages in my journal on that rock, watching kayakers readying to make the plunge around (or through) the keeper hydraulic.

Making Time. I still do some life coaching and spiritual mentoring. It's a rich opportunity to build unselfishly into someone's life. I meet regularly with younger men who in some facet of their life are wrapped around the axle. I listen carefully to the issue at hand, usually a problem to be solved, a goal to be achieved, or a new behavior to be mastered. When it's my turn to talk, regardless of the issue on the table or their age, I always ask the same first question: "Tell me about your spiritual rhythm." Most of the time, my question is met with a blank stare; most men have no idea what I'm talking about, which is often the reason they're in a life crisis. When I explain the basics, I'm frequently greeted with the same canned answer: "Oh, I don't have time for that."

No one *has* time to develop and live within a spiritual rhythm; one must *make* time for it and implant it into his or her routine. Many years ago, I came across an old black-and-white photo of Oswald Chambers in his World War I army fatigues. I taped the picture and its caption to my current priorities "in-basket" so that it would never be out of my view. Apparently, someone greeted Chambers with the same canned answer I have encountered. "Of course, you have the time," says Chambers in his quintessential wisdom. "Strangle some other interest in your life and *make* time to realize the center of your power is in the Lord Jesus Christ."

A Nathan Accountability. "The Lord sent Nathan to David" (2 Sam. 12:1). That's *not* the kind of interruption I want on my calendar. In the biblical account, Nathan confronted David about the mess he'd gotten himself into with Bathsheba. He was David's truth serum, but his words came too late; Bathsheba was pregnant, her husband murdered, and the baby of David's illicit liaison with her was destined to die in God's justice. Shortly thereafter, David wrote, "Have mercy on me, O God... blot out my transgressions" (Ps. 51:1). When David spied Bathsheba, he should have been out with his troops in the field, not in the palace sipping margaritas and watching her take a bath. The error in David's priorities started small, but absent accountability, it escalated to disaster.

Accountability is vital to a spiritual rhythm, because small, everyday stumbles can trap us and grow into destructive life scenarios. Gary has been my source for accountability since our days together in Chicago. God didn't *send* him to me. Rather, he gave me the wisdom to *invite* Gary into my battle of life. Imposed accountability often goes badly. But since Gary is invited, he's free to challenge me when I seem to be heading in a wrong direction and he can ask tough questions when I'm evasive. He's my "pre-emergent" for fighting weeds, and I keep him posted on what's growing in the backyard. I cannot encourage you too strongly to get a Nathan in your life!

A Wife's Grace

I could make this whole chapter of life about a tired and depleted soul, Apollo 13, the Transforming Community, my sabbatical to Alaska, and the power of a spiritual rhythm. If I did, I'd do Jan a great injustice.

Earlier, I called attention to the railway boarding card that slipped from the pages of *Green Letters*. It marks a day, a time, and an event. What I didn't mention were the cards and letters from Jan I could shake from nearly every book in my library. They're mementos of encouragement from rough-and-tumble chapters of life we endured together, including my new country experience. From her perspective, some of those cards and letters must have been painfully difficult to write. However, without exception Jan has stood by me with unconditional love, unbridled encouragement, and gracious support, honoring me as her husband, the father of our children, and a seeker of God's grace.

Jan wrote me a note shortly before my Alaska trip that said, "All of my earthly blessings are richer with you as my husband." I can't imagine working through the challenges life has presented, some of them precipitated by my own hand, with a marriage partner who withheld grace, scorned me for bonehead decisions, or allowed me to stew in my own juices.

Jan, during thirty-five years of marriage, has been the embodiment of Jesus's love and grace. No one ever could ever guess that our oldest son and daughter are from my first marriage, because her love is equally shared with all our kids. Jan is a wife of noble character, "clothed with strength and dignity" (Prov. 31:26); she is gentle and a patient reservoir of grace, overflowing with biblical wisdom. Perhaps more than anything, she's my unfailing advocate—and not just on the good days.

"Husbands, love your wives, just as Christ loved his church and gave himself up for her" (Eph. 5:25). I'll never fully live up to that standard or sacrifice, but for me, it stands as the true north bearing for my role as a husband.

A New Country Experience: Looking Back

Ministry's red zone dominated this stage of life. It was a painful and unwelcome reality. But it helped me redefine the concept of God's *help* and understand what it means to have a *partnership* with him. I also learned that *self*-help in many life crises is a *self*-defeating oxymoron.

No one, I dare say, likes being shoved off a plateau of life into the wilderness of a new country. But that's where life experience gives way to life change. The Alaska reset, and my identity reboot remain pivotal events in my spiritual life. Even today, my summary understanding of Romans, chapters 6 through 8; the positional-conditional truths made clear in Stanford's *Green Letters*; and the practice of a spiritual rhythm revitalize my soul and keep my spiritual fire burning.

That said, my new country experience precipitated another confrontation with my *Abba*, Father. "Why," I complained, "did you wait until this stage of life to teach me such important lessons? I could have been much more productive in life if I'd learned this ten to twenty years earlier."

I've not received a direct answer to that question, but my morning devotional companion, Oswald Chambers, answered it for me. A saint's life (i.e., the life of a Christ follower) "is in the hands of God like a bow and arrow in the hands of an archer. God is aiming at something the saint cannot see, but our Lord continues to stretch and strain. The saint may say, 'I can't take it anymore,' yet God pays no attention. When His purpose is in sight, he lets the arrow fly."[30]

Everything in life is appointed in God's sovereignty and perfect timing. God let my arrow fly on his perfect timing, not mine. There is only one "master plan." The apostle Peter had the same experience. He ventured into a new country the day the rooster crowed in his life and not a day earlier. From there, Peter would discover life change and his unique life purpose. It's the same for most of us. Life experience is the springboard to life change, and life change lights the pathway to enduring life purpose in another chapter of life.

---

30 Chambers, *My Utmost for His Highest*, May 8.

7

Life Purpose Contemplation

The righteous will flourish like a palm tree, they will grow
like a cedar of Lebanon planted in the house of the LORD,
they will flourish in the courts of our God. They will
bear fruit in old age, they will stay fresh and green.

—Psalm 92:12–14

Deep Water Experience

"How did it go at the range?" Jan asked.

"Not too well," I grumbled as I dropped my golf clubs by the front door. "The guy next to me got the bucket with the straight balls. All mine hooked left."

"You're home early," Jan observed, glancing at the clock.

"Yeah, it's weird," I said. "I have this nagging pain. It's like a catch behind my left shoulder blade. I can't think of anything I did differently today," I added, attempting to dismiss the issue, "but it makes it difficult to get a deep breath. Maybe it's the heat?" Summer's ninety-degree temperature and 90 percent humidity held a tight grip on Atlanta that August afternoon in 2015.

"It's a normal summer day," said Jan. "I doubt it's the weather."

Over the next two hours, my "catch" intensified. Jan watched guardedly as my pain level escalated and my breathing became more labored. In short order, I lost the outlandish argument that I could drive myself to the emergency room. Good thing. When Jan delivered me there, I couldn't open the car door.

ER attendants quickly loaded me onto a gurney. Every breath was met with a searing spasm that radiated viciously from my back into my chest. My mind was arguing with my body. "I desperately need a breath. Why won't you give me one?"

As a former triathlete with a resting heart rate still in the sixties, I have a keen sense of my vital signs. When my pulse zipped past 110 bpm that evening, I knew I was in deep water. Ironically, just a few days earlier, that had literally been true. I'd been eighty feet underwater on the stunning coral reefs of Belize. I wondered if there was a connection between my dive trip and this sudden, intense pain.

Before the morphine shot, my eyes focused on Jan's. I could read her concern, but she never panics. I love that about her.

If you can't breathe, you don't have much to say, but my eyes took in all the life-monitoring contraptions in the ER. Having watched Caroline's monitors in years past, I found that these machines were surprisingly familiar. Some training you never forget.

As the morphine began its curative work, the acute pain diminished, and my breathing eased. The ER doctor popped in fleetingly and handed me the CAT scan results. "Read this," he said, "I'll be back in a minute and we'll talk. I'm admitting another critical case."

"What? Am I *critical?*" I asked myself.

"What's a pulmonary embolism?" I whispered to Jan, passing her the diagnosis. She hunched her shoulders and launched Google on her phone; neither of us knew. How can anyone not love Google and WebMD? In thirty seconds we learned a pulmonary embolism (PE) is a blood clot in your lung. They are life threatening—and often lethal. A PE blocks the normal pathway of blood from your heart to life-sustaining oxygen in your lungs and wreaks havoc with every muscle group in your back and chest. Between spasms, I learned from Google that a PE had nearly killed tennis star Serena Williams a few years back—and that PEs take many home!

Did I contemplate the deep issues of life purpose that first night in the ER? Not even close. When stricken with a PE, you quickly narrow your focus to getting your next breath and worries about survival are not far behind. That's plenty to occupy one's thoughts. Contemplation would come later, but sooner than I envisioned.

In the wee hours of my second night at North Fulton Hospital, friends and family had gone home for some needed rest of their own. Apparently, they had assurance I'd be okay until the morning. I don't recall anyone sharing that snippet of good news with me.

As my morphine dose wore thin again, every attempt at a sip of breath became an agonizing contest—and I was losing. Minutes became hours on that lonely night, and the work of breathing extracted its physical and mental toll. I started to contemplate life—and death. I reached for my Bible, cracked it open, and began to read Psalms between muscle spasms that convinced me I wouldn't make it to the morning.

I found myself musing over who would officiate my funeral, what Jan and my kids would say about me—and whether I'd draw a large crowd. Pretty vain thoughts, I confess in reflection, but don't we all want our lives to count for something in the eyes of family, friends, and our God before the buzzer goes off?

The answer to whether I'd live or die that night came from a compassionate night-shift nurse. (If I knew her name I'd shout it out!) Watching the irritating clock hand click its way to 2:30 a.m., I squeezed the red button for the nurse. When she appeared, I appealed for another dose of morphine.

"Honey, I am *sooo* sorry," she sympathetically responded. "That's not in the doctor's orders for another two hours. But I'll check on that for you. Don't you worry."

"I'm not worried, ma'am," I managed to eke out, "but I'm exhausted, in a lot of pain, and I'm working *very* hard to breathe. If I fall asleep, I don't think I will wake up!"

Ms. Midnight Nurse took a step closer to the bed and gently patted me on the shoulder. Tears well up as I recall her response. "Honey," she whispered in her sweet Georgia cadence, "that's why you're on oxygen! You get some rest. You'll wake up in the morning. I see you're reading your Bible. Psalms?"

I nodded, too worn out to utter a word.

Her caring eyes locked onto the desperation in mine. "Mr. Tom, don't you know you can't *work* to breathe? Let the oxygen work for you. God has more days for you."

Life Purpose Pivot Points

Reviewing this chapter in an early draft of the manuscript, my ever-insightful editor asked me a probing question. "Did your PE experience *heighten* your urgency to fulfill your life purpose? If so, tell your readers why."

"*Heighten* my urgency? No, not in a nervous-Nellie context," I told her over a Starbucks latte. "If you *begin* thinking about life purpose in a hospital bed when you're shackled to life-monitoring apparatus, well, you've largely missed the game. But did it *strengthen* my resolve to grab hold of the sweet spot of life purpose that God has for me in the years ahead? You bet!"

Think about it. No one knows their specific life purpose pathway at birth (although God does). But as human creatures, we seek to discover it, often battling to grasp and fulfill it over our lifetimes. For most of us, clarity of life purpose hinges on a *pivot point* in life, a change in direction brought about by a desperate situation or circumstance. Those trials often birth a spiritual awakening—and with that new awareness, we're better able to zero in on God's call and his signature imprint on our lives.

Let's face it: nearly everyone comes to a pivot point—a change in life's direction—at some time in their life. Prior to my deep water experience, I could easily identify three that significantly disrupted my pathway in life and forced me to think more deeply about my life purpose. These included my divorce and subsequent encounter with Father Ulrich, the dreadful lonely evening in Scunthorpe, England, after Vanessa's death, and my more recent new country experience in Alaska. With my PE episode, I added a fourth. Each produced its own unique brand of life purpose tension, challenge, and demands.

Even Jesus struggled with the excruciating demands of life purpose. In the garden of Gethsemane, he asked, "My Father, if it is pos-

LIFE PURPOSE CONTEMPLATION

sible, may this cup be taken from me. But not my will but yours be done" (Matt. 26:39). Jesus's struggle with his Father's will in his life should encourage each of us. There's no human scale that can begin to measure Christ's agony, but if he can confess his humbling scuffle with God's will, we can surely do the same.

Jesus, of course, is the perennial model for life purpose. He was looked upon by many as a kook on the fringe of life and was rejected by the people he came to serve. But his life purpose was *always* inspired by his Father's will. Ultimately, Jesus suffered a humiliating and agonizing death, but he never for a moment lost sight of his life purpose. Most of us, however, as did Christ's disciples, need a circumstantial pivot point to embrace it.

"We are going up to Jerusalem and everything that is written by the prophets about the Son of Man will be fulfilled" (Luke 8:31). Luke's Gospel account tells us the disciples had no idea what Jesus was talking about. Their pivot point would come on a bloody Friday afternoon in Jerusalem, and thereafter, they would lock in to their life purpose as witnesses of Christ.

The Tenets of Life Purpose

The words of Psalm 92 that headline this chapter hold astonishing promise for the man or woman seeking to embrace and live out his or her life purpose. The *righteous* (those who love the Lord) are likened to a *palm tree* and *cedars of Lebanon,* both of which symbolize strength, longevity, and resilience. These folks will *flourish* under God's watchful care in *his courts* and will *bear fruit* as a reward for their service well into *old age.* We could also say it this way: if you're laboring in God's garden, you're in good hands, and his favor rests upon you!

How is this promise lived out? Largely by embracing three tenets of life purpose. Each is best posed as a question.

Tenet #1: Am I surrendered to God's purposes and producing life change? God sends rich blessings into our lives, but he's also the author of trials and refining fire, which burns off the dross of life experience and moves us toward the "likeness of his Son" (Rom. 8:29) and his perfect will for our lives. We may squirm in our trials, but if we surrender to his purposes, we will increasingly reflect God's image to a broken world.

It's not unlike the process ancient jewelers used in refining silver. The jeweler adjusted the fire to achieve the perfect temperature—and when he saw the likeness of his face perfectly reflected in the metal, he knew the refining process was complete.[31]

Is your journey in life increasingly reflecting God's image through the refining fire of life experience and life change?

Tenet #2: Am I exhibiting a working faith? A plumber's work is characterized by his effectiveness in using his training and trade to serve others. A working faith is similar. It's the outward expression of what constitutes a man or woman's faith.

After healing a crippled man on the Jewish Sabbath, Jesus was roundly criticized for his working faith by the religious leaders of his time. He dismissed their criticism as rule-following nonsense and told them, "My father is always at his work to this very day, and I too am working" (John 5:17). Jesus was not distancing himself from the Sabbath commandment. Rather, he was giving divine credence to what the disciple James would later write: "Show me your faith without deeds, and I will show you my faith by what I do" (Jas. 2:18). "Faith without deeds is dead" (Jas. 2:26).

In a recent sermon, a pastor described an elderly woman who simply won't release her grip on tenet #2 though stricken with severe disabilities. Every Friday her caregiver delivers her to the church, where she folds Sunday bulletins. In that tedious but majestic work, she honors God, gives him glory for her capabilities, and exhibits her working faith. She's not working for divine approval—she's already got that—but in her work, God's favor rests upon her.

Advancing God's kingdom through personal connections with our neighbors locally and globally is a vital part of a working faith. It's the role of an "ambassador," that high and noble pursuit Paul outlines in his letter to the church in Corinth. "We are therefore Christ's

---

31 Reimann, *Morning by Morning*, Day 232.

ambassadors, as though God were making his appeal through us" (2 Cor. 5:20).

Frankly, I'm stunned that God delegates any of his reconciling work to people like me. I'm better qualified for grilling chicken or some other kind of menial workmanship! But no, ambassadorship is the call!

St. Francis of Assisi is credited with saying, "Always preach the Gospel of Christ—and when necessary use words." The same could be said of ambassadorship. There's unfinished work delegated for us to tackle on this messy planet. "Start by doing what's necessary, then do what's possible—and you'll soon find yourself doing the impossible," said St. Francis. His wisdom has endured for nine hundred years.

The last time I checked, God is still hiring, and every applicant is accepted, no matter what the résumé. The only requirement is an open heart. Have you signed on?

Tenet #3: Am I being strengthened in my faith and standing firm in it? Tenet #3 ensures that everything else in life will find its rightful place. Moreover, you have no chance of successfully living out tenets #1 and #2 if tenet #3 is built on sand. Why? Because what is *strengthened* stands strong and testifies to the source of its strength. But don't take my word for it. Dig deeply yourself into the writings of the apostles Paul and Peter and see for yourself how the foundational underpinnings of their faith—and their certainty of life purpose—fueled their dedication to the Lord. Here's a few biblical snippets to get you going.

In Peter's case, he concludes his second letter to the first-century faithful with an imperative: "But grow in the grace and knowledge of our Lord and Savior Jesus Christ" (2 Pet. 3:18). Why? Because it's a practical and powerful corollary of life learning. Who can understand the wonders of the human body without growing in the knowledge of biology, cell theory, anatomy, and brain function? Knowledge helps us to embrace truth, maximize our effectiveness, and seek solutions to problems. It's no different with our faith and pursuit of life purpose.

The apostle Paul, on the other hand, encourages us to cultivate our knowledge of the Lord. In that pursuit, he says, we become "rooted and built up in him and strengthened in the faith" (Col. 2:6). To what endpoint? Trees with deep roots stand strong and don't topple in a gale. We are no different when the roots of our faith run deep. Ultimately, Paul tells us, that teaching, wisdom, and correction lead to "maturity in Christ" (Col. 1:28). And in that maturity, we're equipped to *stand* and fight the battle of life.

The verb *stand* can't be ignored in Paul's discourse in Ephesians chapter 6; he uses the word four times within three short verses to be sure we get the point. *Stand* conveys the ability to endure successfully, to tolerate without flinching, to remain firm, and to exhibit courage in the face of adversity. "Put on the full armor of God so that you can take your stand against the devil's schemes. For our struggle is against the powers of this dark world and the spiritual forces of evil" (Eph. 6:11–12).

Finally, when equipped to *stand* in our faith, we're able to give glory to God and testimony to our resolve. Says the apostle Peter, "Always be prepared to give an answer to everyone who asks you to give the reason for the hope that you have" (1 Pet. 3:15).

Are you faithful to Peter's imperative and Paul's teaching? Are you being strengthened in your faith? Are you standing firm in the battle of life? Are you able to give an answer for the hope you have in your trials?

Threads of a Life Purpose Tapestry

As it turned out, what I thought might be an early departure to heaven on that July evening in the hospital was thwarted by a divine directive.

"That's true," said my pulmonologist. "Apparently God has more for you on planet Earth, but he took you right to the edge!"

Apparently so, but Jesus, a caring nurse, and a healthy dose of oxygen held me in their safe grip. There was unfinished work for me to tackle. The book you're reading is partial evidence of that.

Have you ever contemplated the mesmerizing truth that as you live out your pivot points of life—and engage with the tenets of life purpose—that God is weaving a one-of-a-kind life purpose tapestry with your name on it? In fact, the Master Weaver was at work before you were born. "For you created my inmost being; you knit me together in my mother's womb" (Ps. 139:13). Ultimately, God's desire is to create a stunning piece of human artwork with the threads of your life.

A beautifully crafted tapestry, let's call it an oriental rug, serves as a simple metaphor for digging deeper into the nuances of life purpose. Rarely do I visit a mall department store, but when I do, I like to wander to the oriental rug display. I'm fascinated by the artistry. The blended strands and colors that complement the patterns and shapes in a carpet speak to the creative genius of its creator. Carpet making is now aided by technology, but a $29,000 price tag on the *New King of the Jungle* design by Manhattan Rugs tells me there's still plenty of artistry in the process. But don't fret about the price tag; Manhattan Rugs will ship it to you for free!

An oriental rug has two truths. The first lives in its finished top side and reflects the intentional and intricate design of its maker. The naked back side reveals the second truth. It looks to be a random and chaotic collection of threads which contradicts the majesty of the first truth. The underbelly wants to tell us that the designer was hopelessly confused and had no tangible plan to rescue his work. Our purchase decision, however, isn't driven by what we might see on the back side. We buy the finished pattern on the top, a design that serves as proof that the craftsman had a vision of the outcome—a masterpiece in his mind's eye.

The "top side" of life purpose isn't any different. There's a Master Craftsman guiding the process. He's a sovereign God who has a vision of the finished product. He sees threads in our life tapestries that are peculiar colors and some that have odd textures. But he never panics. He weaves them into the finished products, *every* thread contributing its own story line to the top-side panorama. Some strands on the undersides are knotted and hastily tied off; they may represent failure or fault. Nonetheless, their contributions are fully reconciled to the larger work at hand.

Think about the threads in your own unfinished tapestry—those of your childhood, your high school and college experiences, your relationship with your parents, or your young married years. Other strands may represent your relationship with your spouse, health challenges, shameful failures, athletic prowess, the joy of children, grief over the death of a child, fear of rejection, or the perils of overachievement. These life experience threads define you as the person you are now—but also help create the finished product you are becoming as you embrace your life purpose.

Are you living life with the confidence that your tapestry is worthy and destined to be hung in the hallowed halls of heaven? You may ask, "Can that be true? What about the ugly underpinning of my life, the defiant threads of my younger years, the betrayals that have hurt my friends or family, and prejudices hidden in my identity? My tapestry is hopelessly flawed. It's anything but a masterpiece." You might feel more like a tangled ball of yarn abandoned to no purpose—or to hell, as I was once told.

Ephesians 2:10 says otherwise. God at any time and under any circumstance can lead you into a finished work. "For you are his masterpiece, created in Christ Jesus, to do good works which he prepared for you in advance, so that you may walk in them."

To a bewildered carpet salesman (who might roll his eyes), I might say this: "Did you know that *I* am a tapestry in process? I share God's identity, he's given me some work to do, and it's my heart's desire to enjoy and glorify him in my life purpose."

There's free choice in tapestry making, freedom to *flourish* or *flounder*, but God can help us turn our lives into magnificent works of art. For that to happen, we must commit our lives to the Master Craftsman and opt onto the loom of life purpose. What he began in each of us at birth, regardless of the outrageous detours we may have chosen, he can redirect to a great finish. Did I make that up? Absolutely not. It's right out of the book of Philippians. "Forgetting what is behind and straining to what is ahead, I press on toward the goal to win the prize which God has called me heavenward in Christ Jesus" (Phil. 3:13–14).

Every life tapestry of God is beautifully and meticulously created. Some are brief but are priceless handiworks nonetheless. Vanessa's tapestry was completed in six short years. Others extend fifty, eighty, or ninety years. But I've learned this. The Divine Craftsman never abandons our looms. He ties off the horrific threads of our wanderings, rebellion, and recklessness. He did that for Israel's King David, the prodigal son of Luke's Gospel—and for me as well. His focus is the top-side panorama, which is *always* distinguished by the grace signature of the Master Craftsman. How else could David be called "a man after God's own heart" (1 Sam. 13:14, Acts 13:22)?

No doubt, there will be some striking surprises in heaven's art gallery. There will be tapestries on display that we never dreamed would make the cut. We will also search for tapestries of friends and family members that we thought would be there, only to discover that these loved ones did not surrender to the hands of the Master Craftsman, rejected the invitation of their Savior, never offered praise or glory to a sovereign God—and couldn't find time to fold a single church bulletin. They opted off the life purpose loom.

The Woodall Shoals Encounter

Woodall Shoals on Georgia's Chattooga River

171

To place my 2015 Woodall Shoals encounter in proper context, I must rewind the calendar to Memorial Day weekend of that year, three months before my PE adventure. At that time, I was burrowing into Henry Cloud's *Necessary Endings*. His book prompted some personal recalibration and ultimately a Cloud-inspired revelation that I relayed to Jan. "Did you know you can't grab hold of a new beginning in life if you're unwilling to trigger a necessary ending?"

"Sure," she said. "That makes sense. But what's your point?"

"The work I'm doing now is fruitful and keeps me busy, but I think I'm doing it for the wrong reason," I said. I was referring to a bevy of project work I'd taken on after leaving my church assignment. At that time, I was working with two church planting organizations to expand their footprint, teaching leadership principles to aspiring young pastors, helping Fellowship of Christian Athletes (FCA) develop new growth strategies, and sharpening the focus of Metamorphyx, the business entity.

"I have a sense God is calling me to a new assignment in this stage of life. I don't know what it is, but I'm going to cut ties with all my project work before we leave for our August dive trip to Belize. Then, after we get home, I'll head up to my favorite rock shelf on the Chattooga Rive and have a 'new beginnings' chat with the Lord."

What I didn't factor in, of course, was the schedule-busting hospital soiree a few days after the dive trip. That monkey wrench torqued my new beginnings timeline out of kilter. My riverside heart-to-heart chat with the Lord would have to wait until mid-October. During my recovery, I'd spend the next few months in contemplation, reviewing old journals, reflecting on my Alaska trip, perusing Transforming Community notes from years past, and waiting for an idea to leap onto my calendar as the next thing I should do. But nothing did, and my impatience began to kick in. "C'mon, Lord," I thought. "I wiped my slate clean. How about putting something on it?"

As October approached and the doctor cleared me for a few days away, I connected again with friend and spiritual soul mate Kent Shaw. We've been great friends since my days on the church staff. One of the project cords I had severed after Memorial Day was a church-planting initiative we were jointly working on. Kent, nonetheless, fully supported my decision. Now, five months later, he asked, "So what's on your plate?"

"Nothing," I told him, "but I'm heading up to my favorite spot at Woodall Shoals to sort that out. Hopefully, God will fill in the blank."

"Do you remember the assignment I gave you a year ago to memorize Psalm 92?" asked Kent. "Brush up on that Psalm. It will serve you well on your retreat. Let me know what you come up with." On rare occasions, I do precisely what I'm told, and I complied with Kent's counsel. My reward would come in short order.

The road to Woodall Shoals is remote and mostly unpaved. It begins near some apple orchards about five miles from Clayton, Georgia off Highway 76. If you're a kayaker or river-tour guide, you know the exact location of the bend in the road that takes you deeper into the Chattooga National Forest. If you're a curious tourist, you'll never find it. After the bend, it's another three miles to the kayak drop-off point—with a final quarter-mile hike down to the Chattooga River.

Woodall Shoals has claimed dozens of lives since the film *Deliverance* made the river popular in the mid-seventies—or a place that most would never dare to venture. Early on the morning of October 15, 2015, I set my camp chair on the same rock outcrop I've claimed for a dozen years. I kicked off my agenda by shouting out my favorite verses of Psalm 92 to the river, trees, and treacherous rapids. "The righteous will flourish like a palm tree. They will grow like a cedar of Lebanon planted in the house of the Lord. They will flourish in the courts of our God. They will bear fruit in old age. They will stay fresh and green" (vv 12–14). I'm sure the Good Lord was tuned in that frosty morning—but no one else was. I didn't see another soul the entire day.

Settling into my chair, I pulled from my backpack notes from a 2011 Transforming Community homework assignment. In the margin, I had penciled a series of questions. Now, four Octobers later, I sat ready with pen in hand to ponder them again. "Lord, what is the best use of my gifts, skills, and abilities? What is it you have for me next—and when? Is it a book, a new business, or another ministry opportunity?"

Much had changed in life since I first wrote those questions, but I opened the future once again to a new script. "Lord, I'm moving past this PE episode," I said. "I believe I've got at least ten more years of ministry spunk left in me. Where should I direct it?"

Much of the day I spent rereading my journal, reflecting on excerpts from favorite books, and meditating on verses I've marked in my Bible over the years. But midafternoon, it became mysteriously clear that it was time to pick up my pen and listen. I can explain it no better than that. And in rapid succession, five phrases found their way into my journal: *Trust in the character and promises of God; Invest in people and kingdom work; Flourish in a ministry calling; Pray with confidence; and, exhibit Patience in all things.* In about twenty seconds, God handed me the framework of my ten-year vision—and then he went silent for the rest of the day.

On that brisk October afternoon, TIFPP became my Five Pillars of Ministry. If I can't match an idea or assignment to those pillars, I reasoned, I would need to consider it outside my life purpose focus in any new stage of life. My only regret in writing down exactly what I heard is that *Patience* made the inspired short list. I was hoping to get a bye on that!

Venturing out of the National Forest later that day, I called Kent the minute I had cell phone coverage. He was more excited than I was about my Five Pillars. "Tom," he ribbed me, "were the words handed to you on stone tablets by a guy with a beard, or did you just write them in your journal?"

Early in 2016, after marinating in the juices of TIFPP through the entire winter, I scheduled coffee with longtime colleague, Dick Ducote. Dick, as you may recall, was my business partner for twenty-two years, and we go back another seven before that when we worked together at Procter & Gamble. Dick has always been a great advocate and encourager.

When we sat down at Starbucks, he asked me the same question he's asked me a dozen times over recent memory. "Are you ever going to write that book?"

"I am," I told him, and I explained my Woodall Shoals encounter, the meaning of TIFPP, and how the idea for *Metamorphyx*, the book, had grown out of my riverside chat with God. I also shared with Dick another insight. From the rearview mirror of life, I could now see clearly why God had called on me to break ties with other projects that pivotal Memorial Day weekend, endure the torture of a PE, and venture up to Woodall Shoals. It was to make it clear that *Metamorphyx* should get on my calendar.

"I have a new vision and pathway," I told Dick. "It's another pivot point in life. I'm taking some risk in this life purpose venture because I don't know anything about writing a book. But on the other hand, I don't want my life experience and story to rot on the vine. We'll see what God does with the idea."

I still visit Woodall Shoals periodically for personal retreats, contemplation, and as of late, for encouragement and perseverance in the writing process. I'll go again when my writing assignment is complete. I'm thinking I'll have just two agenda points. First, I'll ask God what's next. And secondly, I'll lobby again to drop *Patience* from TIFPP.

Life Purpose Contemplation: Looking Back

Fulfillment of life purpose remains the compelling topic of any age. Many have passed judgment on the subject. Even Solomon, the wisdom standard bearer of the Bible who wrote Proverbs and Ecclesiastes, toyed with the idea that life is meaningless and has no overriding purpose. But a penetrating study of Ecclesiastes tells us just the opposite. True life purpose, Solomon discovers, *always* has a spiritual component. Life is only meaningless when we pry the fingers of the Master Craftsman off our tapestries of life.

That said, living life according to God's purposes (versus our own) can be a bewildering and exasperating journey. Take Jesus, for example. From every perspective other than his Father's will, he was a miserable failure. Hurriedly nailed to a cross on a Friday afternoon so that the Passover Festival could proceed unencumbered, he was destined to be forgotten as just another casualty of Roman occupation. But Sunday was on the horizon.

Life experience in a broken world will always lead to pivot points, life change, and life purpose examination. Ultimately, contemplation hinges on a single premise: will I allow God's sovereign call to shape my life purpose on his terms?

In this chapter of life, God introduced a new thread of life purpose. TIFPP gave me the framework for the vision, and *Metamorphyx* emerged as my assignment. What comes next? I have no idea. But when the time arrives, I'm willing to search for it; I have faith God knows precisely what's he's doing in my tapestry of life.

Where does that confidence come from? I'm a student of Psalm 139; it's God's encouragement to us from the pen of King David, a man who spent much of his life fighting for clarity and success in his life purpose. David writes Psalm 139 for a choir director, so it could be an ancient song. Here are some of the lyrics. "I praise you because I am fearfully and wonderfully made, I know that full well. My frame was not hidden from you. When I was woven together in the depths of the earth, your eyes saw my unformed body. All the days ordained for me were written in your book before one of them came to be" (Ps. 139:14–16).

I can't overemphasize the importance of life purpose *contemplation*—that is, understanding life backward, reconciling pivot points of life, holding tight to the tenets of life purpose, petitioning God to let you know what's next, and living life forward. How does life purpose contemplation square with God's sovereignty when all your days (according to Psalm 139), are preordained? It's a divine mystery but also a dynamic truth. God will orchestrate pivot points in your life—and when you come to a new fork in the road, contemplate wisely and ask for his help in choosing the right pathway.

PART II

Living Life Forward

Life Purpose Visioneering

Now give me this hill country that the LORD
promised me that day.

—Joshua 14:12

A Warrior's Life Purpose

Young Caleb of Old Testament fame was one of twelve men chosen by Moses to spy on Canaan, the Israelite's promised land. At that time, Caleb was a man of forty, highly trusted, ambitious, and an Israelite leader but essentially untested. In their report to Moses, ten of Caleb's colleagues recoiled in fear after their foray into Canaan and sowed panic into the wandering Nation of Israel. Some, it seemed, would have preferred to die in slavery in Egypt rather than face the perils of conquering the promised land. Others even considered choosing a leader to take them back to Pharaoh's Egypt! Read Numbers chapters 13 and 14. It will give you all the cowardly details in the dismally discouraging report the spies gave to Moses.

Caleb and Joshua, however, broke ranks with their friends' timid nonsense and lack of faith. They countered with a gutsy response. "It is a land flowing with milk and honey. It is exceedingly good. We will swallow them up. The LORD will give it to us" (Num. 14:8). For

Caleb, life purpose was taking shape. He would help lead the fledgling Nation of Israel into the promised land.

Run from anyone and everyone—and suggestions from the Evil One—that you should dumb down life purpose aspirations and settle for something that is lukewarm. "The lust for comfort murders the passion of the soul—and then walks grinning in the funeral,"[321] says Kahlil Gibran in his captivating classic, *The Prophet*.

In our final reckoning with God, may he not say, "Welcome to the Kingdom, my friend. I had so much more in life for you—but you never grabbed hold of it."

"Now give me this hill country that the LORD promised me that day," comes from the mouth of Caleb, a man who had fulfilled his life purpose vision. The wrinkled and battle-seasoned warrior was calling in his chips, the land promised to him forty-five years earlier by Moses. Caleb's hill country is modern day Hebron. It's still a hotly disputed territory in Israel's West Bank. In Caleb's time, the "hill country" was occupied by Anakites, a race of people who produced the likes of Goliath. Caleb's passion in life purpose, however, was undiminished. "So here I am today, eighty-five years old! I am still as strong today as the day Moses sent me out: I'm just as vigorous to go out to battle now as I was then" (Jos. 14:10–11).

Forging a Life Purpose Vision

Vision is a familiar word and the subject of much debate in businesses, churches, and nonprofits. It should be; it's vitally important to organizational health. Even the Bible recognizes vision as important. "When there is no revelation [commonly translated as *vision*], people cast off restraint" (Prov. 29:18). That simply means people (and organizations) tend to wander aimlessly without a compelling purpose (a vision), something that points to a "future state" or destination they seek to achieve. Vision is directional, and channels effort and initiative into calculated *movement* toward a goal.

---

32 Gibran, *The Prophet*, 33.

"Visioneering," on the other hand, encompasses the overall *process* of creating and nurturing a vision. Life purpose visioneering has similar intent, but there are some distinct differences between it and its business cousin. Life purpose for you and I isn't scripted during long sessions in a boardroom; we don't spend countless hours revamping a vision statement. Instead, it comes from *listening* to God's call on our lives and *submitting* (a very irksome word) to a life purpose vision that *progressively* unfolds in our lives according to his plans.

God is *always* at work shaping us into his finished product. (That's Tenet #1 from the last chapter.) He wants us to become fully transformed men and women who increasingly reflect his image on our life purpose journeys. That's not to say we're lifeless clumps of clay on the Divine Potter's wheel with no active role in the visioneering process, but God knows much better than we do how to create movement toward a compelling life purpose vision.

That's great news because my vision of life purpose now becomes dependent on the sovereign power of God and his ability to guide me into stages of life (and assignments) that accomplish his purposes over my lifetime. Think of that as the "process of life." We can remain calm because God's "purpose *is* the process itself."[33]

Here's more great news. If we follow God's dynamic script and accept that it may change direction on a dime (i.e., a pivot point in life), we're destined to flourish in life purpose and bring God glory. Visioneering pleads a bold truth; God didn't create us to waste our time on planet Earth.

Proverbs 16:9 also keeps us on a clear visioneering pathway. "In his heart a man plans his course, but the Lord determines his steps." So, if you're looking to develop a rigid life purpose vision with a fixed drumbeat, I suggest you ditch the idea. You're part of the process, but not fully in control of where you're headed. Responding to God's call has always meant embracing new challenges and life change, but never apart from intimate conversation and partnership with the

---

33 Chambers, *My Utmost for His Highest*, July 28.

Caller. If you're listening and acting on what you truly believe God is revealing to you, you'll do just fine in life purpose visioneering.

Cameron Strang, founder and publisher of the wildly popular magazine, *Relevant*, says it this way: "The key [to calling and life purpose] is making sure we're following God in all seasons… and not looking for shortcuts of fulfillment in places that will never satisfy."[34]

I hope it's clear that we're talking more about the *process* of life than a fixed destination. With that understanding, we're now prepared to discuss our Caller, along with the core elements of life purpose, stages of life, assignments, and sweet spots. Finally, we'll get into how all those ideas converge in the fulfillment of life purpose. In other words, we're going to dig deeper into life purpose *visioneering*.

Awakening to a Caller

"Nothing short of God's call will truly fulfill your life-purpose aspirations." That's a bold declaration to pitch to anyone undefended, but that's what I told Matt one summer day over lunch.

Matt and I were meeting at the request of his future fiancée. She and Matt were contemplating engagement. But after weathering messy divorces a few years earlier, they were both rattled by their differences in spiritual grounding.

"I don't know anything about life purpose or God's call," said Matt. "Why should I? I have a good job and life is going well. Besides, how will I ever know if I've fulfilled my life purpose until my dying day? Then it's too late to change anything!"

I notched up our debate a click or two. "Matt, your heart and mind tell you that you're missing something, or you wouldn't be here today. You're wandering through life like Alice in Wonderland, thinking any road will lead to fulfillment and a happy marriage. You know that's not true. You lack a Caller whose passion is to steer you into meaningful life purpose. You seem unsure of God but very sure of yourself. How's that working for you?"

---

34 Cameron Strang, "Restless to Find Your Calling," *Relevant*, July–August 2016, 8.

Matt was silent; he pondered my question but couldn't answer it. Neither could Tom Brady, the fabulously famous and brilliant quarterback for the New England Patriots. Brady has more Super Bowl rings than ring fingers, more money than he can spend, and more notoriety than most on planet Earth. By all accounts, he's a gentleman off the field. But in an interview with *60 Minutes* earlier in his career, Brady confessed, "There has to be more than this!"[35] Who knows? Maybe by now Brady has filled in the blank to that important question in life. Can football qualify as a fulfilling life purpose endeavor? Sure, if it's played in a way that honors God.

Os Guinness's purpose-provoking book *The Call* was a Christmas gift from Jan in 1998. The subtitle zeroes in on the critical issue, *Finding and Fulfilling the Central Purpose of Your Life.* In his book, Guinness brilliantly expands on the notion of a calling. It's a scholarly account and well worth the read. I share a lot of common ground with Guinness, including a refrigerator well-stocked with his family's brand of Irish beer. My thoughts on life purpose are distinctly my own, but unashamedly enriched by the wisdom and insights of Mr. Guinness.

Each of us has a responsibility to honor God with our lives. Some of us accept that responsibility, but many don't. Those opting out prefer to launch their life purpose journey on their own terms, as did Matt, and invite God into the game as long as he doesn't inconvenience them too much. True life purpose is quite the opposite. We are seekers—and the life purpose journey is launched by a Caller. Says Guinness, "We think we are looking for something; we realize we are found by Someone… the 'hound of heaven' has tracked us down."[36]

For many of us, God's call results in a radical reshuffling of priorities. This is especially true for those of us who are successful and independent. We much prefer choosing our own paths, using our powers of reason, and asking God to get with the program.

---

35 HabeebScott, "Tom Brady—There has to be more than this."
36 Guinness, *The Call*, 14.

Life purpose, however, pokes at our souls in this broken world. Why? Because as we mature and graduate into adulthood, the human heart sifts through life experience and raises profound questions that beg to be answered: "Why am I here? Why is life so chaotic? Who or what is this Hound of Heaven? Can I trust him? What is the meaning of [my] life? Can I chart a course to achieve my life purpose on my own terms?" Those questions tug at the very essence of who we are created to be. Church leaders, theologians, and writers of all sorts have offered varying answers over the centuries. The same can be said of secular philosophers. We'll get to them later, but let's start with Jesus.

Jesus kept it simple in the Sermon on the Mount. "Do not store up for yourselves treasures on earth... For where your treasure is, there your heart will be also... But seek first his kingdom and righteousness and all these things will be given to you as well" (Matt. 6:19, 21, 33).

Augustine, the eminent fourth-century theologian, puts it this way in a prayer: "You have made us for yourself, and our hearts are restless until they find their rest in you."[37] Pastor and popular writer John Piper elevates life purpose to "living for the glory of Christ crucified."[38] He describes it as a point in which our "single, soul-satisfying passion... is to live for the supremacy of God in all things."[39] Bob Buford, author of *Half Time*, describes life purpose as a focus on the most important thing "in the box of life—for him, Jesus Christ."[40]

Let's be clear. The headwaters of life purpose flow from the Caller. Says Os Guinness, "There is no calling unless there is a Caller."[41] Acknowledging a Caller, I've learned, changes everything. Be forewarned; when Jesus wedges himself into a corner of your life, you're in a heap of trouble. He'll penetrate every nook and cranny of

---

37 Guinness, The Call, .
38 Piper, *Don't Waste Your Life*, 44.
39 Ibid., 43.
40 Buford, *Half Time*, 51.
41 Guinness, *The Call*, 20.

your existence until you increasingly take on his character. But don't take my word for it; ask the apostle Peter.

Peter's calling was, admittedly, unique. He was a present-day disciple of Christ, and because of that, scripture gives us an up-close and personal account of his life. Ken Boa, noted writer and teacher, points to Peter as an outstanding example of "character built from the inside out."[42] What's the source of that inside-out change? Peter's relationship with Jesus, who awakened his calling.

Think about it. Peter in his younger years exercised little restraint. He could be "comically impulsive," as Boa likes to put it.[43] Twice he jumped out of a perfectly good boat into the Sea of Galilee; he resisted Jesus's foot washing, fell asleep during Christ's agony in Gethsemane, hacked off the ear of one of Jesus's accusers, fled in fear when Jesus was arrested, denied knowing Christ when confronted by an observer, and skipped the Crucifixion. Not a stellar résumé when it comes to character.

But like many great leaders, Peter survived himself. In his ministry calling under Jesus's teaching, Peter developed his leadership skills, sharpened his theology, and spearheaded the growth of the first-century church.

Beyond that, Peter was commissioned, under the inspiration of the Holy Spirit, to write two letters to new believers in Asia Minor. These are forever captured in the canon of scripture that bears his name. Peter's first letter reads like a PhD thesis on character development. I encourage you to read it. You will find it to be the best short course on that subject you will ever lay eyes on. Ironically, the uneducated fisherman and acclaimed hothead twice exhorts his readers "to be self-controlled" (1 Pet. 1:13, 5:8). *Really, Peter?* Yes. That's the new man speaking—the Peter who survived himself under Jesus's teaching.

In his second epistle, Peter offers keen insight into the Hebrew scriptures, skillfully educating his readers on Old Testament prophecy, warning them of the perils of false teachers, and pointing to the

---

42 Kenneth Boa, "Character," *Reflections,* July 2016, Part 1.
43 Ibid., Part 2.

future Day of the Lord. All this from an uneducated trout fisherman? How could Peter have possibly pulled it off?

There are only two possibilities. One is that the Bible is lying to us and Peter is a complete fabrication. The second, my friends, is that Mr. Comically Impulsive serves as testimony of how one man's life purpose was divinely engineered from the inside out. Since I've lived a lot of Peter's foibles and failures, I'm going with option number two: his relationship with Christ, the transformational power of his calling, and a kingdom-first mind-set dedicated to God's glory. But you decide.

Leveraging the Four Core Elements of Life Purpose

In its simplest form, life purpose, by my count, has four core elements at play: **(1)** *God's call* on our life; the **(2)** *passion(s)* in life he's implanted in us; the supernatural **(3)** *giftings* and talents we've been granted; and his **(4)** *provision* for us, the financial sustenance we need for the basics of life. We can leverage these in powerful ways— or painfully neglect them. We'll explore that in the next section, but first we need to understand the *role* of the four core elements in the life purpose journey.

I encourage you to let the description of each element soak into your heart and mind so that you're able to visualize and understand how God has wired you. This will help you see your Creator's signature on your soul and how he may ultimately deploy you on the life purpose journey.

#1 God's Call. A call is a clear instruction or directive from the Caller that announces a *specific* stage of life. In a life purpose context, God's call is unmistakable and musters intentionality as you set off to live out your life purpose. It may come as *leave this job, pursue this one, go into ministry, get out of ministry, stay home with the baby, acquire these skills, serve this group of people, sell your house, play baseball, or start a new business*—you get the picture. Calling emanates from our relationship with God and our trust in the integrity and character of the Caller. Otherwise, why would we listen?

Heeding a call demands a well-tuned ear to help you discern God's whisper over the ambient noise of life. The lure of technology and social media in our day makes listening exceedingly difficult. The Old Testament patriarchs, Moses, Israel's prophets, and David—all sought God's instruction as common practice. In the New Testament, even Jesus was subject to his Father's call and instructions, a point he made very clear to his disciples.

God's call may come "inconveniently," and it may not line up with your well-intentioned visioneering efforts or any path you were taking on your life purpose journey. It can snatch your breath away like a dunk into frigid water; it can demand the courage of your first sky-diving venture. It may also come absent any assurance of success, survival, or method. What? A call without safe passage, guarantees, or method? Yes, God's ways are not ours, and his assignments can't always be understood by our finite minds. How else could a simple coffee with a Sunday school teacher introduce a fifteen-year stage of life in the slums of Nairobi?

An answer to a calling, more than anything, is a faith decision. It's often discerned (though not always) within the discipline of one's spiritual rhythm. I am writing this book because God made it clear in my daily prayer focus that I was stuck in a stage of life that didn't align with his purposes for me. Calling always functions as a present-day reality, but often births a future life purpose breakthrough.

How does God's call come to us? In August of 2017, Caroline spoke via a video link to two thousand souls at Uganda's 2017 Women's Empowerment Conference. As she stood forty-two inches tall on her Ephesians 2:10 life verse, Caroline's words profoundly impacted the temperament of the conference. "I flourish in life purpose because God is my shepherd and I am one of his sheep. Jesus is very clear," she continued. "'My sheep listen to my voice; I know them, and they follow me'" (John 10:27). Ask the Shepherd, to *call* you to his purposes—and then listen intently for his response."[44]

An awkward silence fell over the conference after Caroline delivered her captivating message. Caroline, as you know, barely sur-

---

44 NewtonCarl, "Caroline."

vived her dwarfism challenges in her early years. In rural Uganda, even today, she would stand no chance—and every woman at the conference was aware of that dark truth. As a marginalized infant with a cloudy future, Caroline would have been abandoned by her parents to certain death in the jungle. Yet in God's grace that day she stood tall before them as a witness to God's compelling power in life purpose.

Oh, I should confess before going further that it was that mischief-minded Caroline who, on her twenty-first birthday, hatched a skydiving adventure for our family. Her instructor-partner judiciously rejigged her parachute so that her smaller-than-average body wouldn't pop out of it when the chute opened. Then, in tandem, they launched from the plane when the pilot announced we had reached fourteen thousand feet. With unparalleled courage, I followed right behind her.

#2 Passion. The hunger and thirst of your soul define your passion. For some, it's a penchant to right a social injustice. For others it's a proclivity for music, teaching, reporting on the weather, athletics, counseling, technology development, or evangelism, each to be used in some way to honor God. My precious daughter-in-law Sharon has a passion for music. She's a worship leader at our church, lives to sing and play the keyboard, and teaches piano to both kids and adults. When Sharon is leading worship or teaching music, she glows in her passion and gives thanks and glory to God for the musical fire in her soul.

God provides an overwhelming abundance and diversity of passions. Medical professionals, fire and police officials, leaders of community nonprofit organizations, entrepreneurs, social workers, athletes, schoolteachers, and family caregivers flourish in their passions. Only a few of these men and women are in their line of work to get rich; for most, their joy in life comes from fulfilling their God-given passions.

Tabitha Kimani, a dear friend living in Nairobi, knows this firsthand. "My passion," says Tabitha, "is to help rescue marginalized women from prostitution and give them a word of hope. With God's help, I lead them into a new future."

#3 Gifting. God grants each of us skills, abilities, and capacities—ordinary to extraordinary—that exhaust the spectrum of possibility. They include uncanny abilities to comfort others in their sorrow, develop business strategies, solve complex problems, build houses, work with numbers, preach on Sundays, play scratch golf, or lead men into battle.

Giftings and passions are sometimes intermingled, but they can also be miles apart. Like Sharon, I have a passion for music, but, unlike her, I have no gifting to produce it. (I was a horrible clarinet player in high school.) I'm intrigued by men and women who are great musicians, mathematicians, artists, athletes, and writers. I particularly admire communicators who effortlessly speak or preach without a single prompt from notes. How do they do that?

Caroline has a gift for foreign languages and memorization; she speaks Spanish like a Latino. I don't. From my mouth, *gracias* sounds like *grassy-as*, and I can't roll my *R's*. I also have a ministry friend who can spend all day visiting the sick and injured in hospitals; he has the gift of compassion. I've gone with him on occasion, but I'm often at an awkward loss for words.

My gifts are different. If someone needs help untangling a messy personal issue, crafting a strategic plan, or developing a job change strategy, I'm their guy.

#4 Provision. Provision is a twofold proposition. First, it's the financial or in-kind means to sustain our physical existence, allowing us to at least live meagerly with enough food and clothing and sufficient shelter for ourselves and our families. Provision can be earned or donated by like-minded followers. God knows we need the basics of life and often uses provision as an acid test of faith and life purpose calling.

Secondly, provision is required to carry out one's calling. I'm well acquainted with this beleaguering truth. I've fought the gnawing anxiety of defeat that accompanies a grand idea when provision is scarce. The Huduma school in Kawangware was once a pencil sketch on an architect's easel with a staggering price tag. Earlier, I told you about the $325,000 miracle that God engineered to meet that need. But I've never forgotten how provision is intimately linked to a call from God—and how it can bring about a stalemate in the quest toward a life-purpose vision. Today, the Huduma School is transforming lives, shattering the cycle of poverty for God's dirt-poor, and sending graduates to some of Kenya's best secondary schools.

I'm also reminded of Fennel, a warmhearted Haitian immigrant who lives not far from me. She possessed both a passion for serving the poor and the gift of evangelism. Fennel desperately longed to serve in the Kawangware ministry, and it was my job as the ministry leader to help guide her aspirations. "Fennel, the test of whether God is truly calling you to Nairobi *may* be in his financial provision for you," I said to her one day as our trip to Nairobi neared. "Other team members are pitching in for your trip expenses, but you're responsible for the down payment on the airfare. I'm scheduled to buy the tickets tonight, and you have no money in your account."

"Can you wait until Sunday?" she begged. "Can you just give me two more days?" Provision, of course, *always* has a faith component.

Randy Pope is the lead teaching pastor at Atlanta's Perimeter Church. He tells a similar story. Randy's call while at graduate school in Mississippi was to plant a church in the northern suburbs of Atlanta. His call, passion, and gifting were clear, but provision eluded him. He finally arrived at the painful conclusion one Sunday morning that his ministry quest in Atlanta had run aground.

At a church service on that final gloomy Sunday, Randy bumped into an old college acquaintance. Randy and his buddy caught up on family life and their mutual aspirations, but Randy felt God nudging him *not* to share the financial needs of his wobbling ministry in Atlanta. When the offering came around, Randy's friend wrote a check—but instead of placing it in the basket, he tucked it into Randy's shirt pocket. That $600 gift carried Randy's ministry into the next month and it became the financial seed of momentum that propelled Perimeter Church into the future. On September 24, 2017, Randy led the celebration of Perimeter's fortieth anniversary.

Oh, about Fennel. Her husband at that time was a taxi driver. He was keeping the family fed, clothed, and sheltered, but just barely. On Sunday of that pivotal weekend, a passenger handed him a "tip" after the cab fare. "Use this for your family," the rider told him. Fennel called me the instant her husband got home. "I have the money for my plane ticket," she yelped through her tears. "I'm going to Africa."

I could hardly choke out a reply through my own sniffles. While in Israel, I stood on the shore of the Sea of Galilee where Jesus told the crowds not to worry about the small stuff of life. "O you of little faith" (Mat. 6:30) he reminded them. On that Sunday, Fennel had taught me the same lesson.

Navigating the Stages of Life

It's common in our culture and conversation to speak of stages of life. For example, we may refer to our teenage years as a "difficult" stage of life. We may think of our college years as an "exciting and fun-filled" stage of life; raising our children might be thought of as a "challenging" one.

But what constitutes a stage of life and what are its boundaries? How does one navigate between stages of life, and how do *assignments* fit within a stage of life and the broader life purpose journey? How do we get to a point, like Caleb did, where we can look back with feelings of fulfillment but still long for more of God's adventure? We'll tackle those questions later, but first we must get our terminology straight.

Stage of life is a phrase I've used consistently throughout *Metamorphyx*. Typically, it's a multiyear span of time (though with some exceptions). It's usually framed by a significant life event or "pivot point" that marks its beginning and ending. On either end that could be a marriage, birth of a child, death of a loved one, a family relocation, or a major shift in one's career focus.

I see four distinct stages of life within a life purpose journey. Three, **vocational excellence**, **tent making**, and **retirement** grant their owners great freedom of expression. "Whatever you do, work at it with all your heart, as working for the Lord, not men. It is the Lord Christ you are serving" (Col. 3:23–24). That's great motivation in any stage of life. Most of us have bosses; some of us also have a Boss.

The fourth, **perseverance**, by its nature, offers much less freedom. It's a character, humility and discipline building stage of life. But even there, we can take encouragement from the apostle Peter who reminds us, "Humble yourself under God's mighty hand, that he may lift you up in due time. Cast all your anxiety on him" (1 Pet. 5:6–7).

An *assignment* is a specific role or dimension *within* a stage of life that fleshes out the landscape of that stage. Typically (though not set in stone), a life purpose traveler takes on more than one assignment within a stage of life. An assignment has the same hue as the stage of life itself while adding the daily focus and practical dimension of the required tasks. For example, if a man or woman is called to vocational excellence in the marketplace, they may very well have assignments in accounting, marketing, and sales which brings focus to their roles.

Not everyone passes through all four stages on his or her life purpose journey. There is no fixed pattern, sequence, or time frame for entering (or exiting) a stage of life. Caleb, for example, lived his whole life as a military leader on the front lines of Israel's conquest of the promised land. He then clamored for more engagement in the only stage of life he ever knew. But we can be assured that Caleb had many different assignments throughout the military campaign.

It is God's sovereign work in our stages of life… and the assignments within them that ultimately define our life purpose mosaic. No, we're not passive observers in the journey of life, but God's sovereign hand at any time can trump our visioneering work and catapult us into a stage of life that we never anticipated. It's in faith that we listen to and discern God's will, discovering and fulfilling our life purpose on the journey. But it's also in faith that we can be certain that God has his fingers on all the buttons on the master panel.

I encourage you to develop a working knowledge and understanding of the stage-of-life descriptions that follow with an eye to identifying the one or two that most accurately describe where you are at this moment. Note that you may occupy more than one stage.

As you assess your call to a stage of life (and an assignment within it), remember that God's voice is distinctly personal—but nearly impossible to hear amidst the distractions of daily life. For that reason, when you finish reading the descriptors below, hit the pause button for a few hours (or days) and listen for God's voice in silence and solitude. When you sense God's movement in your spirit, reengage your visioneering software and then wrestle with these three questions:

1. *How did you arrive at your current stage of life?* Were you called to it, or did you randomly parachute into your present situation? Are you working in an assignment that is unfulfilling and contributes little to your personal growth or any tenet of life purpose? If that describes you, it may be time to reassess your pathway in life and ask God for new insights into the future.

2. *Should you stay where you are?* If your call is clear and you can attest that your passions, gifting, and provision align with your stage of life and assignment, then celebrate your good fortune and give thanks! But remain vigilant, because the storms of life change and life purpose often come unannounced in God's sovereignty.

3. *What does the future hold?* Visioneering is a future-oriented endeavor. If you're on an even keel now, then sail boldly into the future with confidence and God's grace—but never haphazardly. An astute life purpose traveler keeps his or her radar in search mode and actively scans the horizon for the next stage of life, a new assignment, and greater utilization of their passions and gifting.

Outlined below are descriptions of the four stages of life. The boundaries of each description are *not* uncompromisingly rigid. Stages of life, by definition, have nuances and gray zones, and you may need to flex a boundary to come up with a good fit. There's also no hierarchy of importance in their order, but I'll begin with the most easily recognized and universally experienced stage of life.

Perseverance. If trials and suffering haven't yet pounded on your door, you're indeed fortunate, but it's unlikely you will avoid their visit over the long haul of life. The need for perseverance reflects our human existence in a broken world. It's a theme that is echoed from Genesis through Revelation in the Bible. "Why have you brought this trouble on your servant?" Moses asks God when burdened with the complaints of his rabble in the desert (Num. 11:11). We ask the same question today, but like Moses, we are often called to persevere through life's trials in faith without knowing all the answers.

Perseverance is both a call *and* an assignment from God. It's often uninvited, unwelcome, undesirable, unsought, and can be nearly unbearable. Perseverance rides on the cusp of personal or family tragedy, illness, calamitous betrayal, a dead-end job, unemployment, infertility, shattered expectations, drug rehabilitation, divorce, catastrophic failure, natural disaster, prodigal children, or, as the God-stricken Job experienced, the loss of family wealth, health, and friendships. "Though he slay me, yet will I trust him" (Job 13:15), says Job, profoundly aware that he, like us, is only privy to knowledge on the human side of life's equation.

This stage of life may take us into a bone-dry spiritual valley that demands a new expression of faith. It may also require our blood and sweat. Jesus tells us clearly that in him alone we have peace. "In this world, you [we] will have trouble" (John 16:33), he said. Perseverance is no one's sweet spot in life, because it doesn't align with anyone's passions and gifting. Rather, it's the boot camp of life purpose. Perseverance etches character, teaches vital habits of life, and *prepares* us to flourish in another stage of life... if we live through it! It's in God's sovereignty and our trials that our hidden passions, gifting, and grit are often revealed or reinforced.

Take our family friend Lisa, for example. Lisa endured the rigors of advanced colon cancer, "I had nothing left to surrender but my will to God's purpose in my life—or what remained of it." Lisa's chemotherapy and radiation treatments proved to be a monumental trial. In bizarre medical collusion, her chemo and radiation killed her cancerous adversary, but they nearly took Lisa's life with it. Lisa miraculously survived her testing, and perseverance is now in her rearview mirror. As she looks ahead to a new stage of life, Lisa's passion to serve orphans in Uganda has never been stronger.

Cathy Tolk is another woman intimately acquainted with this stage of life. Cathy is the wife of my USNA wrestling teammate, Andy Tolk, and mother of four boys. "That alone speaks to my lot in life," she jubilantly declares. But in 1995, she was rocked with a multiple sclerosis (MS) diagnosis and the disabling disease has progressively attacked her body... but not her spirit! "Life is 10 percent circumstances and 90 percent attitude," Cathy will tell you, thirty seconds after you meet her. "Do you think God makes mistakes?" she recently asked me. "Of course, he doesn't!" she added before I could get a word in edgewise. "My body is sick, but my zest for life is as vibrant as yours. God has given me a badge of honor. It's called MS. He chose me to wear it in this life... and that's what I will do until the day he takes me home."

Jan and I were also residents of this stage of life after Vanessa's death upended our family's serenity—and then we entered it again when Caroline's challenges overwhelmed us. Today's newspaper tells me there are thousands of others who are now enrolled in this stage of life. Hurricane Irma just pounded their lives into oblivion and changed everything. In perseverance, however, there's always a pathway in faith to a new stage of life—from the remnants of what was to the promise of what can be. But it's never easy.

Vocational Excellence. It's easy to be marginally effective at work—but God's call elevates work to vocational *excellence* in a stage of life. One can flourish in vocational excellence as an entrepreneur, a bookkeeper, a Walmart employee, a flight attendant, a city engineer, a police officer, a music teacher, or a car salesman—as long as God has a grip on you at work.

That doesn't mean you must wear a "Jesus Saves" T-shirt to the office, but vocational excellence demands we exhibit a working faith while on the job, produce a high-quality outcome, maintain steadfast integrity, and surrender offensive behaviors—because all those things honor God! In our work settings, we reflect the values to others that are most important to us. Every day our work settings plays a pivotal role in our life purpose journeys.

That shouldn't surprise anyone. Many of us spend nearly one-third of our lives in some vocational endeavor. At work, our character and faith are on display in all their glory—and their unfinished ugliness. God obviously knows that and uses our work environments to chisel our character, add skills to our life purpose inventories, and make us aware of irritating behaviors we persist in displaying to others. A person's work environment is an important agent of life change.

There are at least five distinct arenas for vocational excellence. I'll briefly list them to illustrate the broad array of life purpose choices and people impact we can have. Says the apostle Peter, "Use whatever gift you have received from the Lord to serve others, faithfully administering God's grace in various forms" (1 Pet. 4:10).

Marketplace Workers. By a wide margin, more men and women are represented in the broad scope of business roles than in any other niche of vocational excellence.

I serve on the advisory board of A Step Ahead Physical Therapy (ASAPT), a small business that recently celebrated its tenth anniversary. Brad, the founder, loves the Lord but he's also a tenacious businessman. ASAPT's mission is to honor God and serve the men, women, and students who come through its doors. It's a business that reflects the values of care and compassion through each employee.

Caregiving. God's call to be a caregiver can be a difficult assignment full of personal sacrifice and challenge. It can easily take on shades of perseverance as well when a caregiver surrenders his or her passions, gifting, and even provision to care for an elderly parent, a disabled sibling, or a young child suffering from a chronic medical condition.

Caregivers include but are not limited to hospice workers, elder-care specialists, and stay-at-home moms and dads who choose to delay (or forfeit) career aspirations to more purposefully imprint the lives of their children.

Those called to caregiving are extraordinary people. Carol, for example, flourished in life purpose for twenty years as a missionary and hospital nurse. But for the next fifteen years, God called her to hospice work—guiding men and women on their deathbeds into the arms of eternity. "I can't think of anywhere I'd rather be than comforting a dying soul," she once told me.

Ministry and Nonprofit Workers. This grouping, of course, includes pastors, ministry staff, missionaries, and volunteers who lead people in worship and help them grow in their faith. It also includes dedicated workers around the world who flourish in humanitarian work. These God-sent people serve marginalized populations and those suffering the ravages of natural disasters, disease, and the wrath of corrupt governments.

Community and National Service. God's call to a select group of men and women in the community service sector seems to hinge on a single gene in their DNA profile. Whereas almost everyone else runs *from* the grip of nature's fury, malevolent perpetrators, and raging infernos, those called to roles as EMTs, police officers, and firefighters run *to* life's most frightful emergencies. Included in the broader spectrum of community service providers are our nation's teachers who invest in the next generation of students and research scientists that will make our world a better place.

On the national service spectrum are our nation's political leaders and the men and women of our armed forces who unselfishly guard our way of life from foreign adversaries. They're men like Lt. Gen. John Sattler, USMC (retired), another wrestling teammate at the Naval Academy and commander of the Fallujah Campaign in Iraq. John is now an adjunct professor of leadership at Annapolis and enthusiastically imbues men and women with the highest ideals of military service.

Professional Service Providers. In this niche of service, a short (and admittedly incomplete list) counts social workers, doctors, nurses, and counselors who heal minds and bodies and enrich the lives of their clients.

Armann, for example, is a friend and certified professional counselor who is called to help men "talk it out, not tough it out." Armann's focus is to free men from their dysfunctional past—and clients with lingering PTSD brought on by their combat experience in Iraq and Afghanistan. Armann, like many other professional service providers, goes home at night with the confidence that through one-on-one relationships with his clients, he's helping men retool their life-purpose journeys.

Tent Making. Beyond vocational excellence, tent making is a stage of life where committed men and women celebrate a unique call from God that links their passions and gifting to the achievement of something noble in the world. They may be passionately committed to eradicating a grievous social evil or advocating for a marginalized people group—but there's no financial provision or committed donor base associated with their call and passion! What's the answer?

Become a tent maker like the apostle Paul. After encountering the blinding light of Christ on his murderous foray to Damascus, it was Paul's passion to take the Gospel message of Christ to gentiles (non-Jews) in Asia Minor and plant churches. But to finance his efforts and avoid dependence on fickle supporters who often turned on him, Paul moonlighted and sold tents. Tent sales paid his bills, so he could pursue his ministry calling.

If you aspire to tent making, you will join the company of other like-minded souls like George Foreman in his earlier life. Surprisingly, the world champion boxer also lived as a Baptist preacher in a stage of his life. "Preaching was my calling," said Foreman. "Boxing was only moonlighting."[45]

I, too, found great fulfillment in this stage of life. My call was to school building in Kenya; my consulting business was the tent making operation. Tent making became my stage-of-life sweet spot for many years. Other members of the Africa Equip Ministry (USA) team also saw their calling in a new context and likewise, became tent makers. Collectively, we were creating a bloom of empowerment and new opportunity eight thousand miles away from home—and funding it through our local tent making shops.

Retirement. Former president of the *Florida Times-Union* newspaper Robert Feagin achieved a high-profile legacy in northeast Florida's growth and development. He was a business innovator extraordinaire, a world-class bass fisherman, and founder of the Greater Jacksonville Open—the professional golf event which was the prelude to the Tournament Players Championship (TPC Sawgrass). The TPC Sawgrass is now played every spring in northern Florida. Bob golfed with the likes of Gary Player and Jack Nicklaus and was a man of mammoth vision and accomplishment. Feagin was Jan's stepdad; we called him Papasan.

In early 1982, only five years into his retirement, Bob crafted a handwritten letter to his wife, Jan's mom. With typical Papasan panache, he opens the letter, "To You from Me." Papasan then offers

---

45 Guinness, *The Call*, 52.

a penetrating x-ray into the heart and mind of a brilliant man trying to discover life purpose outside the framework of his business career.

"I know for some time it has been increasingly difficult to live with me. I am not a happy person and I am not sure of the reasons. But it has nothing to do with my love for you, this I'm sure of. Then what is it? I do the things I want whenever I wish. Maybe selfishness itself taints the joy of living. I am desperately sick of being sick, though not physically.

My zest for things—the anticipation of new places—the exhilaration of planning—the old feeling about a new project or problem to overcome—the excitement of challenge. I don't know where those emotions have gone.

As you know, I am not very religious, but I have seriously started asking for His help. If this is the way the years after seventy will continue, I honestly want little more of it."

Papasan came to faith shortly before his death fifteen years later, so we know he's at peace and in good company. We also trust he's knocking out five-hundred-yard drives on heaven's fairways. But on this side of eternity, he struggled with life purpose despondency in retirement. What's the solution in this stage of life? It's found in how one defines and characterizes retirement.

Some believe the most productive decade of a man's or woman's life is his or her sixties. Those with a firm grip on life purpose charge into retirement. They see it as an unparalleled opportunity for deeper spiritual rooting, investment in one's family, contributions to local community initiatives, leadership in one's church, commitment to nonprofit work, and engagement in mentoring relationships with the next generation of men and women. Retirement is all about finishing well, carrying the good work God began in us "on to completion" (Phil. 1:6) and ultimately investing life experience and life change in others.

More commonly, however, this stage of life is a quagmire of spiritual and life purpose vagueness such as Papasan endured. That's the consequence of a meandering life purpose that never fully matured in earlier years. It is then further conflicted by the artificial finish line of retirement. Not surprisingly, many people believe that relaxation will make them happy. They want to work less and spend more time at the beach. But repeated studies reveal just the opposite.

Mihaly Csikszentmihalyi, the world-renowned behavioral scientist (no, I can't pronounce his name either), concluded that our "best moments usually occur when a person's body or mind is stretched to its limits in a *voluntary* effort to accomplish something difficult and worthwhile."[46]

No wonder seniors struggle in retirement! They've been schooled in the life purpose myth that pursuit of leisure time is the answer to happiness… and they don't possess a vision that transfers into retirement. Many seniors don't know what to do with their remaining days on planet Earth—and life becomes unrewarding and boorishly grueling.

To be truly fulfilling, retirement must be *outwardly*, not inwardly focused. It presents unmatched opportunity to invest decades of life experience into others. Can you imagine the epic impact in our families (and the world at large) if countless millions of men and women redefined retirement not as a finish line, but as a fruitful stage of life in which they ask God for a potent new assignment? From that perspective, retirement can be exceptionally rewarding, openhanded, and a highly productive stage of life before we're called home.

Diane, a neighborhood friend for many years, has a rich perspective on retirement that could help many seniors. I recently caught up with her on the golf range. Here is Diane's story.

"Can you believe it? I'm learning to play golf in retirement. I've got a lot more time on my hands, but my retirement isn't all about golf," she told me.

Diane works part-time for a company that finds employment for people with developmental and mental health disabilities. "That's my passion," she said. "My background is in health care, and in that stage of life, I formed partnerships with many local hospitals. Now, I'm putting that experience to work. Over the last few years, we've placed nearly 150 adults with disabilities in those hospital workforces—and they're good jobs! They stock medical carts, assemble procedure packs,

---

46 Newport, *Deep Work*, 84 (italics added).

deliver lab results, and do other meaningful work. I've thought about fully retiring several times, but the company owner knows me too well. "Diane," she says, "you *know* retirement isn't a biblical concept." So I'm working again in retirement—but for much more than money."

One Man's Stage-of-Life Pathway

Earlier in this chapter, I challenged you to identify your current stage of life within the grid of choices I presented. I also encouraged you to wrestle with three life purpose visioneering questions following your stage of life assessment: How did you get to that stage? Should you stay there? And what does the future hold?

To help bring a practical perspective to those questions, I'll hold the rearview mirror of life to the life purpose pathway I've traveled over the last thirty-five years. I've mentioned previously that *Metamorphyx* is largely a stage-of-life narrative that fleshes out my life purpose mosaic. I must say again, however, that despite great personal commitment and intentionality to life purpose visioneering, the fruit of life purpose is *always* the work of God—never wholly attributed to our own efforts, God delights in his sovereign work and partnership with the men and women he loves… and with those who delight in him.

My stage-of-life pathway begins with an *awakening* that a Caller exists and that he is indeed, a partner in the process. For the first thirty years of my life's journey, I had no Caller, nor was I listening for one. But after the tragedies of my divorce, the loss of my daughter, and the challenges of Caroline's birth, God awakened me and shoved me into **perseverance**. In his timing, **perseverance** blossomed into **vocational excellence** and **tent making**, where for fifteen years I flourished in dual stages of life with a commitment to my consulting business *and* work in Kenya. God's call, however, is dynamic. When it changed and pointed me to Dallas Seminary and a future pastoral role several years later, I grasped another dimension of **vocational excellence** in church ministry. But I was destined to enter **perseverance** once again when I discovered my passions and gifting didn't align with my pastoral role.

Metamorphyx the business was born in that conflicted stage of life, and it nudged me back into *vocational excellence*, this time in the nonprofit arena. But something was still missing, and through prayer and discernment, I discovered it during my Woodall Shoals encounter a few years later. God's call drew me into *retirement*, though not with the lure of an arbitrary finish line but instead with a new assignment… write *Metamorphyx*.

When *Metamorphyx* is complete, I'll listen again for God's call—and perhaps bid for some time to play a little golf.

Looking Forward: Life Purpose Visioneering

Forging a life purpose vision isn't easy work, but it brings clarity, focus, and meaning to the journey of life. More than anything else, perhaps, visioneering reminds us that the most important thing in life is our relationship with our Caller. His desire is not necessarily to maneuver us into a stage-of-life sweet spot where our passions, gifting, and provision are maximized, but rather to bring us into a maturity of our faith and a sweet spot with our Savior. We walk only in the light of the vision given to us individually, not in competition or comparison with that given to anyone else.

"Now give me this hill country that the LORD promised me" (Josh. 14:12), said Caleb to his commander, Joshua, after a pause in the conquest of Canaan. The hill country west of the Jordan River was Caleb's reward for a life "wholeheartedly" (Josh. 14:9) dedicated to God's purpose in his lifetime.

Our reward is similar. Rather than a patch of ground in the now disputed West Bank of Israel, it's the joy and peace of living a life dedicated to God's purposes, wholeheartedly though never perfectly. It's the blessing of being able to flourish in life purpose, bear fruit, and finish well—even in crushing life circumstances. Imagine the indescribable delight that will accompany our last moments if we too can utter the words Jesus spoke to his Father, "I have brought you glory on earth by finishing the work you gave me to do" (John 17:4).

For many of us, visioneering is the most difficult endeavor we will ever undertake. Why? Because it may require us to chart a new course in life—from life experience to life change and then onto the pathway of life purpose. Says Oswald Chambers, "The greatest crisis we will ever face in life is the surrender of our will. Yet God never forces a person's will into surrender, and he never begs. He patiently waits until that person willingly yields to him."[47]

Have you accepted the charge to identify your current stage of life? Have you charted your stage-of-life pathway? Have you seen God's hand in your rearview mirror? Have you probed your future through prayer and discernment?

Your Caller can confirm that you're *exactly* in the stage of life and assignment he has for you today. He can also guide you into a *new* stage of life and fuel it through a grand vision only he could engineer.

Jesus again makes things very simple. "I have come that [you] may have life and have it in abundance" (John 10:10). In that right-side-up revival of life purpose, I pray that millions of men and women will embrace a renewed commitment to life purpose, particularly in retirement, where their passions, gifting, and life purpose will benefit those they (we) leave behind.

---

47 Chambers, *My Utmost for His Highest*, September 13.

The Notion of Convergence

Only blocks dressed at the quarry were used, and
no hammer or chisel or any other tool was heard
at the temple site while it was being built.

—1 Kings 6:7

A Stone-Cold Reality

Jan, Caroline, and I went to Israel in the spring of 2017. The tour was arranged through Dallas Theological Seminary (DTS). At times, it had more of the intensity of a traveling classroom than the feel of a vacation, but it was amazing nonetheless. Dr. Mark Bailey, the president of DTS, was the lead teacher. At every site, our entourage of fifty-plus "students" of all ages found a bench or patch of holy ground where Dr. Bailey and his able teaching assistant, Dr. Stephen Bramer, unfurled the accounts of biblical events that transpired in that very spot two to three millennia ago.

The tour was masterfully choreographed. We traveled with Old Testament prophets from the heights of Mount Carmel (where Elijah scorched the pagan prophets of Baal in 1 Kings, chapter 18) to the still bubbling Spring of Harod. That's where Gideon culled his fighting force from thirty-two thousand to three hundred tough dudes to engage the pesky Midianites in Judges chapter 7. God would grant

Gideon no perceived advantage in manpower. The victory would come through faith.

Then, after marveling at the treacherous Judean wilderness where Jesus fasted for forty days, we entered Jerusalem from the southwest. There, we found our way to the Mount of Olives (where there are still fifteen-hundred-year-old olive trees), plopped down piously in the garden of Gethsemane, and gazed across the Kidron Valley to the remnants of Solomon's Temple. On the temple's original foundation today sits the Muslim Al Aqsa Mosque. The mosque was built in 691 AD and is reflective of the turbulent cultural and religious turnovers that have prevailed in Jerusalem's history. Muslims call the mosque the Noble Sanctuary; Jews call it the Dome of the Rock. Nearby, stands the remains of Roman Praetorium, where Jesus was condemned to death by Pontius Pilate.

Early the next morning, we ventured to Jerusalem's Western Wall, endured the rigors of security checks by Israeli soldiers, and gazed at the foundation of Solomon's temple. I reminisced, "No hammer or chisel or any other tool was heard at the temple site while it was being built" (1 Kings 6:7).

My mind drifted to utter disbelief and opposed the stone-cold reality in front of me. "How was it humanly possible—three-thousand years ago—to *precisely* place a fully dressed block of limestone [about the size of a small pick-up truck!] at the base of this wall?" But that's exactly what Solomon and his army of workers had done. Still wrestling with the feasibility of the confounding reality that my hand traced that day, I launched a question to our Israeli tour guide. "Are you telling us this stone came from the quarry *exactly* as we see it today?"

"I am," said Dan, "and archeology confirms the truth of the Bible. You can't even squeeze a credit card between the blocks of stone you're looking at [which I promptly attempted]. These blocks of stones came to this site *perfectly* dressed, just as you see them today."

Dan, our Jewish-Christian tour guide, then seized the tour offense. "But now I have a question for you, Tom. Why is that an important truth for us today?"

In an instant, a dozen pairs of eyes shifted from Dan and locked onto me and my DTS legacy. All were anticipating a worthy theological response.

My reply was bathed in all the wisdom and candor I could muster that day. "I have no idea, Dan," I confessed. But in that instant, I endeavored to find out.

Converging on Convergence

What I came to learn is that the answer is tied in with the idea of convergence, whose meaning I had not yet begun to explore in its fullest sense.

"I love the notion of convergence," says Suzanne Phillips, a member of my *Metamorphyx* advisory team. "The word is loaded with life purpose application and fulfillment. The idea that life experience can be perfectly chiseled by God's hand into life change… and helps us close in on the sweet spot of life purpose, is an exciting premise of life."

Long before I understood the depths of its meaning, the word *convergence* became lodged in my life purpose vocabulary. It came from the pages of Dr. J. Robert Clinton's *The Making of a Leader*, the book my life coach handed me when we first met twenty years ago. At that time, I could tell you little about convergence, but the idea that a peak of life purpose existed on the distant horizons of life experience and life change captured my imagination and stirred a passion to know more.

As we have discussed throughout the pages of *Metamorphyx*, God's call leads us into various stages of life throughout our journeys. Some of those align with our passions and giftings; others don't. But our God is not a God of chaos. There's divine intentionality and order in our journeys of life if we're listening to his call and building up skills and knowledge on the pathways of life.

Convergence is the phase of life we encounter when we look to God and shout out ecstatically, "I was made for this! This is the sweet spot of all I've experienced in life. Everything I have learned *converges* in this stage of life and this assignment. *These* are the good works you have called me to do. I can do this for the rest of my life because it makes the best use of my gifting and passions to help others and impact God's kingdom. It's not been an easy road, but *this* is the destination you had for me and reflects your glory and faithfulness to me."

Heap all the praise on God that you can muster. He will love your monologue as you celebrate the embrace of convergence.

But be wise in your exuberance. Convergence rarely comes at an early age and not everyone passes through its gates. Some declare it too early and then crash and burn in discouragement or disappointment because they never acquired enough life experience to distinguish the summit of convergence from the pathways leading to it. Søren Kierkegaard, who established the foundation for *Metamorphyx* many pages earlier, might have put it this way: "You don't have enough understanding of life backward to prove you can gainfully live life forward." The journey to convergence often takes decades; it's not an easy jog around the block. It's more like a marathon.

So how does one know if they've entered convergence on their life purpose journey—or the innocent foolishness of declaring it in error? There are three telltale markers on the life purpose journey that will tell you that you're on the right pathway. The first signpost is that you have become like a *living stone*. The second is the extent that *wisdom* permeates your life, while the third is the unmistakable shifting of God's hand from working *in* your life to working *through* your life to impact others. Grab a coffee… and we'll explore each of those points.

Convergence and Living Stones

Let's venture back to the Western Wall and Dan's bewildering question to me about the important truth reflected in the chiseled stone at the Temple Mount foundation.

The apostle Peter, in keeping with his hardheaded character, positions the answer to marker number one in a unique context that incorporates the idea of human stones. "As you come to him [Christ], the living Stone—rejected by humans but chosen by God—you also like *living stones* are being built into a spiritual house" (1 Pet. 2:4–5; italics added).

In fact, there are *two* vital truths at work in Dan's question and Peter's answer. The first is profound and simple. The Lord has provided plenty of materials for his spiritual house (then and now) but these need to be prepared for construction.

In the building of the temple, the cedars of Lebanon had not yet been cut down and hewn into the planks that would beautify his temple, and rough stones for the temple still needed to be quarried, squared, and chiseled into shape. In our context, this represents Christ's work in the heart and soul of every individual believer as we are being prepared, polished, and made ready for our place in God's *heavenly* temple. And after we've taken on whatever God-appointed design he has for us on planet Earth and his work in us is complete, we are transported across the threshold of death into his presence as a finished product. Our identity and security in Christ are as perfect as a fully dressed stones, polished to millimeter specifications. We are being made ready in earth's quarry.

The second truth lies within the first and speaks to the purpose of quarrying, chiseling, hewing, and polishing. Although invited and predestined into God's future presence, we nonetheless have important work here that is individually and uniquely scripted for us. "Living stones" are engaged in God's work! We practice visioneering, are called to stages of life, deploy our gifting and passions, endure trials and afflictions, and seek life purpose convergence, where the whole body of our life experience can be used to impact and benefit others in our spheres of influence.

Jesus, speaking to us as friends (not only as servants), reminds us, "You did not choose me, but I chose you and appointed you to go and bear fruit—fruit that will last" (John 15:16). Yes, we are chosen to be quarried, chiseled, and polished, but also to live lives that matter on our small planet in the universe. *Here* we are to serve others, love one another, engage in issues that matter to God, and bring him honor and glory—all rolled up in the work we've been called to do while he's making us ready for his heavenly temple in eternal Jerusalem.

Convergence and the Call to Wisdom

Convergence also carries wisdom's signature. Wisdom is demonstrated excellence in the art of living—the application of life skills, knowledge, and lessons of perseverance we've acquired in our stages of life. No one has ever defined wisdom more accurately and succinctly than J. I. Packer in his extraordinary life-shaping work, *Knowing God.* "Wisdom," he says, "is the power to see, and the inclination to choose the best and highest goal, together with the surest means of attaining it."[48] You may want to permanently stow that definition in your life purpose archives. It's an indispensable maxim on the life purpose journey.

Interestingly, Packer's definition of wisdom invokes both divine and human implications. In the divine realm, it introduces *omniscience* as an attribute of God—his all-knowing, all-seeing nature. God himself employed wisdom in the marvels of creation. "By wisdom the LORD laid the earth's foundations, by understanding he set the heavens in place; by his knowledge the deeps were divided, and the clouds let drop the dew" (Prov. 3:19–20).

The writer of Proverbs also speaks to the value of wisdom to mankind. "Listen, my sons, to a father's instruction; pay attention and gain understanding. Get wisdom, get understanding. Do not forsake wisdom, and she will protect you: love her and she will watch over you. Wisdom is supreme: therefore, get wisdom. Though it costs all you have, get wisdom" (Prov. 4:1, 5–7).

In wisdom lies assurance that *everything* God appoints in our lives is part of a *perfect* plan to help us reach *perfect* life-shaping goals along with the *perfect* means to attaining them. Often, those perfect means involve a white-hot personal trial or suffering because those are the classrooms in which we learn best.

Sure, on occasion it would be nice to know the life-change target God is aiming at, but like Job, who became the focus of Satan's evil intent in his wager with God, we don't always get the inside scoop. Acknowledging that infuriating conundrum, British journal-

---

48 Packer, *Knowing God,* 90.

ist Malcom Muggeridge adds his own dose of wisdom. "Every happening, great and small, is a parable whereby God speaks to us… and the art of life is to get the message,"[49] he says.

Ultimately Packer and Muggeridge say much the same thing about wisdom. Spiritual discernment and practical life application should be the signature pursuit of men and women dedicated to excellence in the art of living. No human being, of course, has the omniscient power of God to see the future or the inclination to perfectly choose the worthiest goals in life. Nor can we guarantee the surest means of attaining the goals we choose. But for those who are maturing in their faith, intent on listening to God, learning from life experience, embracing life change, and seeking excellence in the art of living, the acquisition of wisdom will be the game changer which leads to the summit of life purpose.

Wisdom in the Bible is such a fascinating and passion-inspiring topic that the books of Job, Proverbs, Psalms, Ecclesiastes, and Song of Songs are all dedicated to it. They're commonly called "wisdom literature." These books of the Bible frequently address the tension between God's idea of an ordered and balanced society and the reality of corrupted human values and life's injustices. Those committed to a deep understanding of what it means to live wisely know the answer to Job's penetrating questions, "But where can wisdom be found? Where does understanding dwell?" (Job 28:12)

"Certainly not from within ourselves!" they would affirm. "For the LORD gives wisdom and from *his* mouth comes knowledge and understanding" (Prov. 2:6; italics added). Says Ken Boa, "True wisdom can only be attained by cultivating the fear of the Lord… the fountain of all wisdom."[50]

"Fear of the Lord" (Prov. 9:10) is a phrase that often burns holes in our sensible natures. Few embrace it; most recoil from it. But it nonetheless prods us to a higher level of understanding as we wrestle with its true meaning. This *fear* is not the raw terror one feels when cornered by a rabid dog. No, to *fear* God is to nurture an attitude of

---

49 Kenneth Boa, "Wisdom," *Reflections*, February 2018, Part 1.
50 Kenneth Boa, "The Fountain of Wisdom," *Reflections*, March 2018, Part 2.

awe, supreme reverence, and humility before a Father to whom we are all ultimately accountable. It is a show of respect to the Creator, who speaks to his people, expects them to obey his precepts, disciplines like a loving parent, is jealous for their worship—and grants them wisdom.

If God is adding wisdom to your spiritual portfolio, he may be pointing you to convergence, where your continuing teachability and life processing skills will become a rich source of discernment and counsel to others. How will you know that you are there? You probably won't, but others will see that wisdom and understanding dwell in your heart and mind, and God will increasingly use you to produce lasting fruit in the lives of others.

Convergence and Growth *In* and *Through* Us

Twenty years ago, Jan and I wrangled with leaving our old home and Vanessa's legacy in it, but we finally decided in a positively motivated decision that it was time to relocate to a new neighborhood as our family grew. Shortly after we moved, Jan and her then Bible-study-leader-friend Debbie, walked the neighborhood together, put informational flyers in mailboxes, and prayed to expand the reach of the Neighborhood Bible Study[51] concept to our new neighbors. But Debbie wanted Jan to flex her spiritual wings. "You didn't move here just to have more closet space," said Debbie. "God has been working in you over these last five years. Now it's time for him to begin working through you."

Jabez is a man in the Old Testament book of First Chronicles who cried out to the God of Israel, "Oh, that you would bless me and enlarge my territory!" (1 Chron. 4:10). We don't know much else about Jabez or how his prayer was answered, but we are told that God granted his request. If Jabez's prayer led him to the same impact

---

51 Neighborhood Bible Study is a ministry of CRU created by Debbie, Jan and a team of volunteers. Access to the materials and curriculums are free at: www.NBS2Go.com.

Jan has had in our neighborhood, he would no doubt have been a busy guy.

Jan's Bible study in 1999 began with a fledgling gathering of a half dozen interested neighbors. Today it reaches fifty-plus women and their families and includes an annual Christmas and Easter outreach to under-resourced families in our city. Sometimes when I hear the "enlarge my territory" kinds of prayers (or speak them myself), they are always accompanied with a caveat. "Be careful what you ask for. You may get it." It's like the proverbial dog chasing the car. What does he do with it when he catches it?

To that question, I'd say, "Ask Jan!"

Convergence calls into play the *in* and *through* dimensions of life purpose. This means God tends to work in the lives of men and women before he works through them. If Jabez was around today, we might coach him with that wisdom. "Hey, Jabez, God may grant your territorial aspirations, but not before he's done some chiseling in your life and introduced you to a few 'process checks' to test your resolve and maturity." After he has worked in your life, you can expect that he will work through your life in ways you never imagined possible.

What are process checks? The Agent of convergence, God's Spirit, holds those cards. He walks alongside us through our whole life-purpose journey. But on the trek into convergence, he's more intimately engaged and increasingly seizes opportunities to reach into our life purpose narratives and inserts tests to confirm (or refute) that we are steering the right course. God, of course, knows if we are ready for more territory... we often don't.

Process checks test our resilience and candidacy for convergence. They often arrive on the heels of adversity or personal trials and enter our lives as character appraisals, relational upheavals, integrity examinations, humility assessments, conflict-resolution evaluations, and discernment reviews. Process checks are God-ordained maturity markers on the journey to convergence. They're pass-fail hurdles strategically embedded in our life purpose syllabus. They must be mastered because they reveal the internal state of affairs of the convergence traveler.

It's on that road that many high-profile businessmen, politicians, or pastors in an overly confident stage of life take a catastrophic detour to moral failure, compromised integrity, or destructive behaviors that marginalize their effectiveness to the people they serve. If your eyes are tuned to the daily headlines, you will have little difficulty finding the pass-fail scorecards of those who too eagerly or carelessly pursued convergence.

Process checks have a lot in common with kudzu. Yup, pronounced just like it sounds. Kudzu is a famously noxious vine that somehow transplanted itself from Southeast Asia into the southeastern states of America. Every Southerner (including transplanted Yankees like me) knows about kudzu. If it creeps onto your shrubs or trees, you must take aggressive action. If you don't rip it out by the roots and burn it, kudzu vines will gain a stranglehold on its host and kill it by shading it from sunlight. The outcome is no different for men and women shaded from God's light. When spiritual kudzu grows unchecked in the life of a convergence traveler, it will topple a strong and proud personality on the backroads of his or her life.

I don't want to overplay the perils of retirement, but if there's any spiritual kudzu growing among your life purpose shrubs as you approach retirement, get some turpentine and a match and burn it out of your life. If you don't, it will strangle any notion of convergence in your final years—and your spheres of influence and life purpose initiatives will collapse.

The apostle Paul tells us that "love, joy, peace, patience, kindness, goodness, faithfulness, gentleness, and self-control" (Gal. 5:25) are the fruit of the Spirit. These attributes are the harvest of convergence. But the greatest joy of convergence is *not* the knowledge that we are living in the sweet spot of God's will, as fulfilling as that may be, but rather the jubilation that God is working through us to bring others into relationship with him… and to jog alongside us in their own life purpose journey.

The chart below presents a top-line overview of the two dimensions of convergence. God, of course, in his omniscience sees the *in* and *through* of convergence as one continuum. We may not. Instead, we labor in life experience for life change so that we can more fruitfully live out our calling and life purpose.

The *In* and *Through* of Convergence

Foundational Life Experience and Surrender (Rom. 8:28–29)	Transformational Life Change (Rom. 12:1–2)
Life Learning: Discovery of Gifts and Passions (Eph. 2:10, John 10:27)	Life Application: Effective Utilization of God-Given Gifts and Passions (1 Pet. 4:10)
Inner-Life Growth and Development (Character Appraisals, Integrity Examinations, Relational Challenges, Humility Assessments) (2 Pet. 3:18)	Outward-Life Maturing and Kingdom-Impact Coaching, Mentoring, and Discipleship Relationships (Rom. 15:17, John 17:4)
Growth in the Knowledge of Your Faith (Eph. 3:17, Col. 2:6–7)	Fruit of the Spirit and Maturity in Christ (Gal. 5:22–23, Col. 1:28–29)
Trials, Affliction, and Failure (John 16:33)	Faith, Hope, and Perseverance (Rom. 5:3–4, Eph. 6:10–18)
Understanding Life Backward	*Living Life Forward*

Looking Forward: the Notion of Convergence

"The big challenge about life, faith and work is making sure we're always pursuing God's purpose for us. What is the dream he's put in your heart for your life?"[52] asks *Relevant* magazine founder Cameron Strang.

No, you won't hear heavenly bells tolling and welcoming you to convergence—but you will know when you get there. "Delight yourself in the Lord and he will give you the desires of your heart" (Ps. 37:4). Ponder this verse in your life purpose journey because God in his grace can take it in two directions. When you delight in him, God will either *give* you desires, which he may ask you to fulfill—or he will *fulfill* desires he's already given you. Either way, you're in the clover of his grace.

Convergence is the summit of life purpose and the full fruit of its labor. If you're a hiker and have scaled Alaska's Denali, convergence is the wisdom and experience of your frigid ascent, nearly calamitous missteps, and the memory of every grueling switchback—all invested in others on their own mountain-climbing ventures.

If you're an Iron Man triathlete, convergence is the wisdom and experience of your training strategies, regimens, and psychological preparations, which prevail over dehydration, debilitating muscle cramps, and delusional headaches—all invested in others in similar pursuits.

If you're a recovering cancer patient, convergence is the wisdom and experience that overcomes lost hope, the trauma of chemotherapy, and the rigors of radiation. It's the oncologist's declaration, "You're clear!" It's your perseverance culminating in triumph—all invested in others on similar life pathways.

So, while it's easy to casually dismiss the vitality of God's calling, life purpose visioneering, stage-of-life discernment, and the notion of convergence, we do so at great risk. For convergence is beyond the reach of casual life travelers. They may live productive and meaningful lives, but the higher calling of convergence will elude them.

---

52 Cameron Strang, "Restless to Find Your Calling," *Relevant*, July–August 2016, 8.

But for those who embrace the full potential of convergence and pursue its call, the reward is great. Convergence is the apex of a life fully committed to God's purposes. It's the Master's affirmation that we have reached the high watermark of life purpose we long for. "Well done, good and faithful servant! You have been faithful with a few things: I will put you in charge of many things. Come and share your master's happiness!" (Matt. 25:23).

3

The Premise of Eternity

He has made everything beautiful in its time. He has
also set eternity in man's heart, yet they cannot fathom
what God has done from beginning to end.

—Ecclesiastes 3:11

A One-Word Sermon

In November of 1932 in Sydney, Australia, a hapless World War I veteran named Arthur Stace was homeless and a self-confessed alcoholic. Stace couldn't hold a job and supported himself with petty crime. Having failed at everything he attempted, he stumbled one Sunday into St. Barnabas Baptist Church. In God's providence, preaching that evening was Rev. John Ridley. His sermon topic? Eternity. "'You're on your way somewhere brother! And God made you long for the place you're headed for.' Ridley proclaimed the truth of every person's march toward eternity; he preached the only true Gospel that prepares men and women for that inevitability."[53] In his eloquent sermon, he pounded home the destination of every human being, repeating the word *eternity* again and again.

---

53 MacDonald, *Vertical Church*, 34.

The word *eternity* captured Stace's heart and mind and set him on a new course of life. The God of the universe had invaded Stace's soul. Struck by the message of salvation and Christ's provision for his own eternity, Stace discovered his life purpose. He would help people find the God who had found him. Every day for more than thirty-five years, he rose early in the morning to go out into the streets of Sydney with his yellow chalk and write the word *Eternity*.

Thousands of times, he wrote the word, each time in the same enticing script. People in Sydney would see the word everywhere—on the sidewalks, outside coffee shops, or on the backside of street signs. Reminders of *Eternity* mysteriously appeared all over town. Somehow, instead of being angered by Stace's spiritual graffiti, people embraced it as a signature of their hometown.

In 1956, the townspeople discovered the identity of the message bearer. Arthur Stace had been unmasked, but no one put a stop to his morning routine. Instead, they supported, even celebrated his message of the life to come. Somehow, it resonated within the soul of the city. If you travel to Sydney today, there's a bell inside one of the government building towers where you can still see Stace's original scribble.

He died in 1967; he was eighty-three years old. His gravestone reads, Arthur Malcolm Stace—Mr. Eternity, repeating a word he had written "more than five hundred thousand times on Sydney's pavements."[54]

Interestingly, Stace's legacy endures. Sydney's fireworks are frequently the first to be telecast around the globe each New Year's Eve. As the new millennium crept into our lives in 2000, a spectacular display of fireworks greeted the world—along with the word *Eternity*—which was emblazoned in Stace's handwriting across the face of the Sydney Harbor Bridge. Later that same year, Mr. Eternity's message again appeared at the opening ceremonies of the XXVII Olympiad in Australia. It lives today as the testimony of a man who heard the voice of his Creator and committed his life to preaching a one-word sermon.

---

54 Murphy, Damien. *"Eternity: How Arthur Stace's handwritten chalk message became a symbol of Sydney." Sydney Morning Herald,* 28 July 2017. https://www.smh.com.au/national/nsw/arthur-stace-one-word-wonder-20170727-gxk7ow.html.

Eternity: The Breath of Life and Solomon's Complaint

"Eternity: it's a powerful word that penetrates deep into the soul of every human being," says Chicago pastor James MacDonald. "And every time we make a choice that detours our search for fulfillment, eternity shouts within us, 'You're getting colder.'"[55]

Do the words of Ridley and the Chicago preacher ring true in your soul? Did Arthur Stace have a spiritual chip or inner compass within him that pointed to eternity? Do we? What moved in Stace's heart and soul and put him on a new course of life? What moves in ours? What, if anything, distinguishes you and me from every other living thing on the planet?

Three thousand years before Stace scrawled the word *Eternity* on the sidewalks in Sydney, Solomon, King David's son and the successor to ancient Israel's throne, grappled with those questions. Scripture tells us Solomon was granted extraordinary wisdom and wealth. You would think this would make him happy and fulfilled. It did not!

Solomon's affluence was so overwhelming and his possessions so opulent that world leaders visiting his palace were stunned. Young people of the sixties may have birthed the sex, drugs, and rock and roll revolution, but they had nothing on Solomon's indulgences. Leveraging his power and wealth, he tried to find satisfaction and fulfillment in every earthly pleasure. He had seven hundred wives (and another three hundred snooze partners), he was the biblical originator of the eat-drink-and-be-merry tune and had more celebrations than he could sleep off. He was denied nothing from life's epicurean menu. Yet his self-modeled, self-scripted formula for living failed to satisfy his cravings.

Solomon, like many wealthy, smart, and powerful people today, was devastated by the realization that on his own, he was unable to find happiness or any enduring meaning in his life. Like Solomon, many today know something is missing, but they can't find it.

---

55 MacDonald, *Vertical Church*, 35.

As the richest and smartest guy alive, this frustrated the stew out of Solomon, and he vented his anger at God. "So I hated life because what is done under the sun was grievous to me, for all is vanity [meaningless] and a striving after the wind" (Eccles. 2:17).

My interpretation of Solomon's frustration: "I'm mad as a stepped-on snake because I have everything I want and nothing I need."

Solomon is the writer of Ecclesiastes. He lived around 950 BC. We can reasonably assume that Solomon read the Psalms authored by his father, David, and that he also knew the ancient Hebrew Scriptures backward and forward—to include the Torah, the first five books of the Old Testament. In his own words, he tells us, "I devoted myself to study and to explore by wisdom all that is done under heaven" (Eccles. 1:13). Why is that important? Because Solomon's knowledge is the basis of his complaint. He knew that "God set eternity in man's heart." He tells us that in verse 3:11. Yet he couldn't take hold of it by grabbing another plate from his buffet of riches. Solomon's complaint is the collision of these two truths; God planted something in his soul (and ours), but it calls to something outside of us to satisfy the longing.

If Solomon hated life, we can also assume he distanced himself some of his father's Psalms. Why? Because their focus is to encourage an intimate heart-to-heart connection with the all-powerful God of Moses and the patriarchs—exactly the thing that Solomon resisted. In fact, if Solomon started reading the 150 Psalms in the order we see them today, he wouldn't need to go beyond Psalm 17 to discover the answer to his problem. "O LORD, by your hand... save me from men of this world whose reward is in this life" (Ps. 17:14). In the mirror of his day, Solomon was staring at that man.

Although frustrated by his own corrupt theology, we can also assume Solomon drew two important truths from his study of Genesis. First, he knew that from the dust of the earth (signifying that we came from nothing), "God created man and woman in his own image" (Gen. 1:26–28), whereas birds, fish, and creepy-crawly things were *not* created in the image of God. Secondly, Solomon also knew of the attribute which differentiates mankind from animals.

"God breathed into his nostrils the breath of life… and the man became a living being" (Gen. 2:7). That's *ruah*, the Hebrew word that in the Genesis context identifies you and me as spiritual beings possessing the very nature of God. The breath of our Creator rests in our souls before we are born… and it begs to be awakened. Yes, birds and chipmunks are breathing entities of God's creation, but they don't possess ruah.

Ruah is the seed of eternity set in the souls of every man and woman on planet Earth. It births the "inconsolable longing" for something beyond ourselves that dominates the writings of C. S. Lewis and led him to declare in his signature wisdom, "If I find in myself a desire which no experience in this world can satisfy, the most probable explanation is that I was made for another world."[56] It's as if God stamps his "made in heaven" trademark in our being… and then commissions the search to find its Maker.

Only God holds the key that unlocks the mystery of his transcendent and otherworldly nature. (More on transcendence in chapter 4.) Only his key opens the great storehouse of his grace, where we will find his invitation to salvation, fulfillment of life purpose, and meaning in life. Not one of those jewels is within our reach without him, though countless men and women, including Solomon himself, have attempted to prove God wrong and develop their own life purpose curriculums.

Viktor Frankl, in the horrors of the German death camps in World War II, also discovered this truth, though he substituted a humanist's "future hope" for ruah and God's eternal promise. To survive, Frankl clung to a greater purpose than the misery of his barbed-wire enclosure. He learned that the last human freedom to be grasped was one's ability to persevere in their circumstances. In *Man's Search for Meaning*, Frankl tells the tragic story of a man who forfeits that final freedom. The "hope" of that fellow prisoner rested solely in a human rescue—the rumor circulating within the camp that Allied Forces would liberate the camp on a specific day. When that day arrived with no rescue, the man stopped eating, became hopelessly

---

56 Lewis, *Mere Christianity*, 136–37.

despondent, and died shortly thereafter.[57] Where there is no eternal hope, life forfeits its meaning.

In another setting, I witnessed a similar story unfold. I call him the "man in grief recovery." As the facilitator of a small group of parents who had lost young children, I had the responsibility of gently peeling back the layers of pent-up pain, anger, spiritual disillusionment and lost hope that each parent was experiencing. I could then help them see a speck of God's love and grace in their futures. In the round robin of tearful storytelling and tragedy accounts, I would sometimes guess in my mind the timing of their loss and the duration of their grief journey. Through these sessions, I had learned to recognize some of the mile markers of the grief process. It was now time to invite the fidgety man to speak.

In fact, he didn't speak at all; he raged for twenty minutes. His anger knotted his face and contorted his whole being until he was barely recognizable. As he seethed, his eyes attacked each person in the room until his stare defeated theirs. He blamed the opposing driver, the police, the EMTs, the hospital staff—and even the design of the intersection—for his son's car accident and death. He discounted the compassion in the room and the group's purpose in being there. And in his finale, he launched into a tirade against God that the Evil One himself might have applauded. Exhausted in his fury, he finally shut things down.

In the awkward silence that followed, I ventured a silent guess that the man had lost his son three to six months prior. I was wrong. It had been twelve years! Where there is no eternal hope, life forfeits its meaning, and where there is no meaning to life, bitterness often fills the void.

One's focus on eternity changes things. It did for Arthur Stace, it did for me—and it will for you. Eternity helps us live above and beyond our circumstances. God promises "a new heaven and a new earth… the Holy City, the new Jerusalem" (Rev. 21:1–2), a place and time where there will be no more death, mourning, or pain. God said to the apostle John, "I am making everything new" (Rev. 21:5).

---

57 Frankl, *Man's Search For Meaning*, 96.

I take him for his word. That's the future hope we live in today. Joy and fulfillment are often well beyond our grasp in this world, which is why we must reach into the next.

I'm convinced that nearly everyone deep in their souls knows eternity exists. But there are those who squelch the voice of eternity and suppress its truth. These are people like Ron Reagan Jr., an unabashed atheist who serves as a spokesperson for the Freedom from Religion Foundation. Mr. Reagan boasts brashly on TV that he is "not afraid to burn in hell," the eternal place he disavows. Go for it, Ron—and bring a fire extinguisher!

Why does an atheist's or agnostic's mind-set play out in their life's scripts? It's not an easy question to answer, but Oswald Chambers nonetheless takes a stab at it. "The conflict is waged over turning our *natural* life into a *spiritual* life."[58] One's natural life has no Creator guiding the journey; a spiritual one does. That critical decision point in life is no small potatoes in our dominantly godless world. But when we leap over that decision point in life, many men and women will reach the pinnacle of what life offers in this world and then echo a Solomon-like reflection, *"So I hated life…"* You know the rest of the verse.

No doubt our plunge into the realm of eternity holds tough questions. It may be one thing to acknowledge eternity's existence, even hesitantly. But how does one take hold of it?

Good question. Let's get into that.

Eternity: A Glimpse of God's Revelation

If the cosmos imploded today, the *only* decision in your life that would matter a hoot is whether you have responded to God's invitation to join him in eternity—or join up with Ron Reagan Jr. and the gang from the Freedom from Religion Foundation. Eternity is a binary proposition; your switch is either ON to God's call or OFF to oblivion. There are no other programming choices. Yes, it's true that

---

58 Chambers, *My Utmost for His Highest*, September 8.

life in general is not binary; it is full of wonderful nuances, but the question of eternity can't be nuanced. Even "I'm not sure!" isn't safe middle ground, because by binary definition, if your switch isn't ON, it's OFF!

God reveals himself to us in many ways. Through his Word in the Bible, he provides insights into his creation, his character and power, what he loves and hates, his moral code, and yes, some highly disturbing snapshots of his justice. But more than anything, he gives us a mind-boggling picture of his grace, mercy, and love for mankind.

A *glimpse* of God's revelation is all I can attempt in this slice of *Metamorphyx*. But the slice I'll serve up could not be more central to every person's eternal destination, because there is a fork in the road—and the will of every man and woman is confronted there.

Jesus stands at that fork in the road and says, "I am the way, the truth and the life. No one comes to the Father except through me" (John 14:6). He greets everyone that gathers there by name and points to the pathway where his unconditional love, peace with God, and eternity is celebrated. This is an essential truth in the remarkable story of God and his relationship with mankind. God created the heavens and the earth and sanctioned mankind to rule over his creation. Then, a few millennia later, he sent Christ into earth's mire to rescue us from ourselves. It's God's passionate desire that *all* should rest in his eternal presence and none should perish, not one (John 3:17–21). But on the journey of life, there are those who will reject Christ and in so doing, cast-off the grace of God as well. They are destined to take another road into eternity.

Ravi Zacharias, the world-renowned Christian theologian and apologist, is credited with reminding people that they should not argue friends into God's kingdom, because someone smarter will come along and argue them out. I've also learned that persuasive theological arguments change little in a person's heart. Resistance to God's revelation—his revealing of himself—seldom pivots on more facts, information, or a compelling rational argument. The issue is much deeper and hinges on the human heart, not the mind. Absent the penetrating Spirit of God, convincing arguments accomplish little. Embracing eternity (and God's kingdom) comes with movement *in* one's spirit (an awakening of ruah)—*from* the Spirit of God who put it there! The divine invitation is always followed by a human decision to receive it. Together, these two events flip the eternity switch to ON in a man or woman's life.

Jesus, of course, knew the futility of arguing with the Pharisaical leaders and gentile doubters of his time. That's why his wisdom is regularly salted with lots of *ifs*. "If anyone desires to come after me, let him deny himself" (Matt. 16:28) and, "If you love me, keep my commands" (John 14:15) are just a few.

God speaks to us about eternity in two different ways. The first is through every day "natural revelation"… using things that are seen, experienced, and evident to every man, woman, and child on planet Earth. Psalm 19 speaks to God's natural revelation in his creation. You *hear* it every morning in the pastels of the sunrise… and *see* it in the evening in the overwhelming expanse of the night sky. "The heavens declare the glory of God; the skies proclaim the work of his hands. Day after day they pour forth speech; night after night they display knowledge. There is no speech or language where their voice is not heard. Their voice goes out into all the earth" (Ps. 19:1–2). This is God speaking through his megaphone of eternity, reaching out to every human being on earth.

But inside each of us, there's a Mr. Hyde, our own personal version of the wicked manifestation of the sociable Dr. Jekyll. Mr. Hyde stalks the back alleys of our minds and private lives. His evil tendencies in each of us give rise to humankind's penchant for suppressing truth.

In that sense, Romans 1:18–20 shouldn't be read by the faint of heart; it speaks to another dimension of God's revelation. "The wrath of God is being revealed from heaven against all the godlessness and wickedness of men who suppress the truth, since what may be known about God is plain to them. For since the creation of the world, God's invisible qualities—his eternal power and divine nature—have been clearly seen and understood from what has been made, so that mankind is without excuse" (Rom. 1:18–20). That's a hard and jagged truth. Yes, God's revelation cuts both ways. He offers buckets of grace to each of us… but doesn't invite anyone into eternal fellowship that denies his glory and presence.

"Special revelation," on the other hand, is God's salvation pathway, an unveiling of the truth and living existence of Jesus Christ, the Son of God—the Messiah, the Anointed One, the One heralded by the Old Testament prophets and introduced in the apostle John's Gospel as the "light that shines in the darkness" (John 1:3) and the "Word of God [who] became flesh and made his dwelling among us" (John 1:14). Jesus is God's ambassador who came from eternity past, lived in the swamp of mankind, and awaits us in a perfect eternal future.

Christ is the great rescuer and reconciler of a sinful people to a perfect God. His mission was to clear the books of mankind's sins—past, present, and future—and settle all accounts with their God. By means of Christ's sacrifice, the apostle John declares, "Yet to all who receive him, to those who believed in his name, he gave the right to become children of God" (John 1:12). Every child of God is destined for eternal peace with the King of kings. There, I'll meet Jesus, my daughter Vanessa, Arthur Stace, King David, and the comically impulsive apostle Peter.

Before Christ rejoined his Father in heaven, he introduced his circle of friends to the Holy Spirit of God. The Spirit's job, even today, is to sustain us with his supernatural power in this crazy, upside-down world. Our justification before God is a one-time, done-deal occurrence through Christ, but the battle of life greets us at the crack of dawn every day, and we need supernatural power to get through it.

Scripture confirms God is "mighty to save" his human creation" (Isa. 63:1, 59:1; Zeph. 3:17; Heb. 7:25), but always within his self-imposed limitation to never override human free choice. While we need God's providential hand to jostle the eternity switch, he won't oppose any human effort to keep it OFF. God does not compel obedience; he invites it. Even Christ's life was not taken from him; it was yielded to the Father on behalf of mankind as a one-time redemptive payment.

But of course, not everyone sees it that way. Take my friend Cam. She's a Buddhist and has been cutting my hair and trimming my eyebrows every six weeks for the last seven years. "Tell me about your Jesus and how you pray to your God," she once asked me. So over coffee one afternoon, I did.

"Jesus is my savior," I told her. "Christ gave his life for me and every imperfect person like me on this planet so that I'd be worthy to stand in the presence of the Holy God of eternity. I've always pictured God saying to me, 'By what right do you dare stand before me?' But then Jesus chimes in and says, 'It's okay, Father. I've got him covered.' And with that, the all-powerful God of the Universe ushers me into his presence. That's the God I pray to, Cam. What about you?"

"That's too easy, Mr. Tom. I can't believe it. There's got to be more to it than that."

"For a good part of my life, I thought so too," I told Cam. "But God's grace in my life has convinced me otherwise. I assure you, Cam, it's not any more complicated than that."

"It still sounds too easy, Mr. Tom. It's too simple for me to accept."

I love that a glimpse of God's revelation can be so simple. Yet, disappointed of course, that Cam isn't ready to accept God's grace.

Special revelation also unveils another uncomplicated truth. Jesus says, "You did not choose me, but I chose you" (John 15:16). That's God's irresistible grace, and it points us to the fork in the road that guarantees eternal peace with him. It's what Solomon came to realize. Everything else is meaningless—like chasing the wind.

Eternity: God's Glory and Life Purpose Fulfillment

"I am the LORD; that is my name! I will not give my glory to another or my praise to idols" (Isa. 48:2). We serve a jealous God who does not want his children messing around with ideas and ideals that don't bring him glory. Throughout the Bible, God often likens his relationship with his people to that of a marriage covenant; adultery is to be shunned, and if committed, it must be confessed and put behind us.

Glory is not a word spoken much outside church circles. For that reason, it's a good idea to define it. We can start with what it's not. For example, we don't use the word around the office. We may *honor* our bosses with hard work and with our integrity, but we don't *glorify* them in the workplace.

A working definition of God's glory might look like this. God's glory is our acknowledgment of his manifest presence in our lives and his supreme sovereignty over all creation; it's the highest order of our worship, adoration, praise, respect, dedication, obedience, grandeur, and thanksgiving—ascribed *solely* to the mystery of the one living God of the universe. "Show me your glory" (Exod. 33:20), said Moses, but God knew a human being could not take it in, so he shielded Moses in the cleft of a rock. "Our God is a consuming fire" (Heb. 12:29) and "lives in unapproachable light" (1 Tim. 6:16). His glory is that commanding.

Jesus shares in that glory because of what scripture tells us about who he is and where he dwells. "The Son is the radiance of God's glory and the exact representation of his being, sustaining all things by his powerful word. After he had provided purification for sins, he sat down at the right hand of the Majesty in heaven" (Heb. 1:3). So, whether we glorify God the Father, God the Son, or God the Holy Spirit individually, we glorify their unity in God's Trinity.

So how is life purpose fulfillment linked to the idea of God's glory? If we, like Arthur Stace, are faithful to the one-word sermon, are drawn to the truth of eternity, embrace the revelation of God in its full bloom, and venture to honor God with our lives, we will bring God glory. Glorifying God with our lives is part of our "holiness journey." That's called *sanctification.* It's the ongoing process of life experience chiseling our characters and forging our likenesses to Christ (though imperfectly, of course). Sanctification ultimately delivers us into heaven's eternal grasp. And if we bring God glory in our life purpose journeys through all the switchbacks, stages of life, failures, tragedies, and triumphs, we will fulfill our unique life purpose missions and offer them to God's glory.

The apostle Paul says it this way: "If we live, we live to the Lord: and if we die, we die to the Lord" (Rom. 14:8). What does Paul mean? I think this. If we love the Lord, love others, exhibit a working faith, bless others with random acts of compassion and kindness, and share the Good News (the Gospel of Christ) with those who don't know him, we will glorify God by living out the life purposes he's designed for each of us. Nothing more (or less) is asked of us.

And if we die in those endeavors, so be it. Yes, we live to the Lord in life. And in death, we're invited into the presence of God's consuming fire and unapproachable light. If we become vessels of God's purpose, he will make his appeal to the world through us (2 Cor. 5:18–20).

The blessings of heaven await those who write *Eternity* on their hometown street signs, bridges, and walkways; and invite friends, family, and neighbors to etch it onto their hearts.

Looking Forward: The Premise of Eternity

How God draws people to himself and provides for their salvation—the theological doctrine of soteriology—is *not* the primary focus of *Metamorphyx*. But you can easily embrace soteriology through the threads of life experience, life change, and life purpose that run through every chapter of this book.

Embedded in these pages are answers to vital and personal theological questions. Theology, some complain, poses questions no one is asking. But questions that center on eternity are questions every man and woman should be asking. Those questions must produce answers that not only satisfy our theological curiosity but also make it south from our heads to our hearts. There, theology shapes our daily lives, feeds the work of life change, and fuels the process of sanctification and life purpose.

It's possible that nothing I've said in *Metamorphyx* will motivate you today to seek a deeper relationship with the God of eternity. That's okay, for I have no power to invade your soul. But God's Spirit does, and I hope this section of the book will at least make you think and ask the question, "Is there something out there I'm missing?" If you do, open the debate with God and ask him to show you why you need him more desperately than anything else in your life. You certainly won't be the first (or last) person to do that. In fact, you may join the company of rock star Bono of U2 fame.

In 1987, Bono and his U2 colleagues recorded their second consecutive number-one hit single, *I Still Haven't Found What I'm Looking For*. The song's lyrics are poetic and captivating like one of King David's Psalms... and they unmistakably reflect the eternal Gospel of Christ.

> "I believe in the Kingdom come
> Then all the colours will bleed into one
> Bleed into one
> But yes, I'm still running
> You broke the bonds
> And you loosed the chains.
> Carried the cross of my shame
> Oh my shame, you know I believe it"[59]

What was Bono looking for? Only he knows for sure, but it appears he was in debate mode with God. Has Bono found today what he was looking for many years ago? It seems he has. In a culture that routinely discounts the Gospel of Jesus and the premise of eternity, Bono is a voice of truth, a beacon of hope, a model of Christ's love and compassion, and a witness to eternal truth.

C. S. Lewis also found the comfort of eternal truth after exiting from his battle with atheism. "There have been times when I think we do not desire heaven but more often I find myself wondering whether, in our heart of hearts, we have ever desired anything else."[60]

Sometimes, the message of salvation gets overly complicated, but it doesn't need to be. It's likely you've seen a snippet of the simple Gospel on a street corner or at a sporting event. "For God so loved

---

59 Genius Lyrics entry on "U2—I Still Haven't Found What I'm Looking For," Genius Media Group accessed on May 9, 2018, https://genius.com/U2-i-still-havent-found-what-im-looking-for-lyrics.

60 Lewis, *Problem of Pain*, 145.

the world that he sent his one and only Son, that whoever believes in him shall not perish but have eternal life" (John 3:16). In the endgame, it remains simple. "For God did not send his Son into the world to condemn the world, but to save the world through him" (John 3:17).

4

Coming Home to Truth

The younger one said to his father, "Father, give me my
share of the estate." So he divided his property between
them. Not long after that, the younger son got together all
he had, set off for a distant country and there squandered his
wealth in wild living… When he came to his senses…

—Luke 15:12–13, 17

The Embrace of a Father

Rembrandt's Return of the Prodigal

I hope you can pull up a full-screen color image of Rembrandt's *Return of the Prodigal Son* on your phone or laptop and let its imagery soak into your heart and soul. Study the characters, their body language, their individual expressions, and other details of the scene as if you were witnessing it firsthand. Even better, if you have lots of time, book a flight to St. Petersburg, Russia, and find your way to the famous State Hermitage Museum. There you will find the original painting, purchased in 1766 by Russia's Catherine the Great. The Hermitage Museum is on my bucket list. If you go, send me a postcard.

The guess is that Rembrandt painted *The Prodigal* just a few years before his death in 1669. Some claim it as the greatest painting ever put on canvas. For longer than I can recall, a miniature *Prodigal* reproduction has sat on my desk as a reminder of from whence I came. No, I never ran off to a foreign land and squandered my wealth in wild living. My judgment has failed me on occasion much closer to home.

If you look closely at Rembrandt's painting, you'll notice five distinct characters. In the foreground, one's eye is drawn to a disheveled young man whose father tenderly embraces him. His older brother is dressed in the same scarlet robes as his father and stands, hands clasped, in judgment of his brother with just enough light on his face to highlight his scornful countenance. I can almost hear Mr. Scornful say under his breath, "You are such a loser, bro! You're grimy, you smell like the pigs you've been feeding, you've come home in rags, and your sandals are full of pig filth." The brothers' mom seems to be taking in everything from the rear, and no one really knows who the fellow in the black beret is.

A gifted painter knows how to direct the eye of the observer, and the light in Rembrandt's work puts the focus on the younger son's disgrace, humility, and repentance before his father. One muddy sandal lies beside his foot as he kneels in bowed surrender and shame, his face buried in the bosom of his father, who lovingly conveys his compassion and acceptance to his wayward son.

Notice, too, the hands of the father. One is large, manly, and commanding while the other is smaller, womanlier, and seemingly more tender. Together, there's no mistaking their message: "Welcome home, my son. You were lost and now you're found. You were dead, and you've come back to life. I love and accept you unconditionally. How can you ever *not* be my son? Our family is going to celebrate your homecoming to this truth."

This parable in Luke's Gospel comes from the mouth of Jesus. It's a heart-rending lesson centered on God's unconditional love for his children. If you're not intimately familiar with the story, I encourage you to find a comfortable chair or a corner in a nearby coffee shop and dwell on it. When you do, you'll discover another truth. The younger lad had no time to tidy up or spit out an apology for the chapter of life he spent in a foreign land. Why?

Because while the young man was still a long way from the farm, his father ran to greet him with a bear hug. Biblical historians love to focus on the cultural recklessness of the patriarch in running to meet his wayward son. According to them, it should have been the other way around. Maybe so, but my heart zeroes in on the warmth of the father's embrace. It's the first wonderful truth of the prodigal's homecoming—and it can be ours as well. Our Father can't wait to wrap his arms around us, no matter where we've traveled or how long we've been gone.

Rock Bottom and a Young Man's Pivot Point

The father's embrace in the parable hinges on a key point in the story. The young man had experienced an epiphany. "He came to his senses" (Luke 15:17) and confessed before God that he had taken a disastrously wrong turn in life. His new compass heading had steered him homeward, but he made the journey without knowing what to expect. In making the decision to return home, he hoped that his father might at least hire him for menial farm work. But he also knew he had squandered that relationship. After all, in violation of every cultural norm of his time, he had demanded his inheritance while his father was still living.

But his dad, symbolizing our Heavenly Father, would have none of his son's bogus reasoning. Instead, he threw a coming-home-to-truth party. Like the father in the parable, God loves us unconditionally and *never* turns away from a relationship with his children. When that unrelenting ruah within us reaches for the hand of God, it becomes a pivot point in life, and we're instantly headed in a new direction. Yes, we may wander and shake ourselves free from God's grip for a season of life, but the Hound of heaven will always be there for us when we decide to come home.

But let's take a half step back and look at what triggered Younger Bro's venture home. It's another captivating truth. Luke's account tells us plainly that while the prodigal had money and means, he did just fine in his distant country. It was *after* he had spent every shekel in his wallet that a severe famine ravished the land. Why is that significant? Because men and women with a lot of money survive famines and other disasters; they buy themselves out of trouble. So God brought the prodigal son to the end of his tangible means, where nothing in his human inventory could sustain or save him. Bro hit rock bottom. His human compass and battery pack had failed him. Only at that point did he come to his senses and turn homeward.

Such is our human nature, and this is the reason God must sometimes take us to the hollow depths of it before we surrender our will to him. But our God is patient. He's content to wait as long as necessary for us to come home to truth, the joy of our surrender, and the warmth of our grubby faces pressed against his chest.

A Reckless and Extravagant God… and an Inconvenient Truth

In the embrace of his father, the prodigal son had to reconcile still another stunning truth. He had fled to a father who was more reckless and extravagant with his love than he had been in his rebellion. The wayward prodigal had met the Father of unconditional love. Much like the son in the story, we may come to the end of ourselves but also to a new beginning in our relationship with the God who longs for our soul. There, human nature gives way to spiritual truth.

The conflict between a person's human and spiritual identity is not new. It's been at the forefront of human existence since the days of the Bible's patriarchs. It was Solomon's conflict too, as we've learned and the Greek philosopher Aristotle as well, who lived three hundred years before Christ. Aristotle fought the same battle as a rationalist thinker. We'll delve into that identity conflict shortly, but first, a peek at a more modern-day thinker.

Abraham Maslow was a purveyor of life wisdom. He was determined to weigh in academically and settle the human-spiritual identity conflict that had swirled for centuries. In the early 1940s, Maslow tirelessly studied humankind's motivation and societal norms. He concluded that all people have the same basic needs, which he illustrated in his famous hierarchical pyramid.

At the pyramid's base, said Maslow, are physical necessities like food, clothing, and shelter. Who would argue that these are not essential for human existence? At the next level, Maslow determined that humankind needed to be loved and to belong to something or someone. Family and a like-minded community, of course, still play a critical role today in a healthy society. We each need relationships with one another and a place to be known. The highest strata of the pyramid Maslow reserved for self-actualization.

Self-actualization is a philosophy of life centered on the ideal of an unconquerable power of the human mind and spirit. Even in the conservative bastion of the Naval Academy in the late sixties, Maslow's views were in vogue. For no reason I can recall, I enrolled in a philosophy course, where Maslow's hierarchy of needs was presented as the missing jewels of life. The idea, I guess, was that future naval officers should know what makes their fellow sailors and marines tick. But I can't recall a single field exercise where debate on Maslow's pyramid upped our operational readiness. But within his own famous hypothesis, Maslow himself was destined to experience a pivot point in life, a reversal of his thinking, like the one experienced by the younger brother of Luke's Gospel.

A few short decades after Maslow first presented his ideas, the resilience of his pyramid assumptions had already begun to crumble. In fact, Maslow's ongoing research ultimately confirmed the prevalence of complaints much like Solomon's; self-actualization was leaving men and women empty and unfulfilled. Put another way, ignoring the tug of the ruah in their souls made for an empty life. In 1971, during my junior year at USNA, Maslow wrote *The Farther Reaches of Human Nature*. In that pioneering study, the noted thinker backtracks and criticizes his own conclusions, acknowledging that people are *not* finding satisfaction in their own accomplishments and experiences but are looking for meaning in life beyond themselves.

Maslow was heading in a new direction. But his philosophic pivot point garnered much less fanfare than his earlier work. Why? Because *Farther Reaches* was inconvenient truth. It was buffeted by the winds of a cultural storm that was raging on the heels of the Vietnam debacle, a society enamored with self-actualizing smoke from a popular weed, and a proclamation by Bob Dylan that "the times they are a-changin'."

Maslow's inconvenient truth collided with emerging societal norms. "Our need for transcendence is much more pervasive than our need for self-actualization,"[61] says Maslow affirming that there is something beyond our own human reach we yearn for. Why should that surprise anyone? Even the ancient Egyptians and Mayans of Latin America understood the notion of transcendence. No, I've not been to the Great Pyramids of Egypt, but I have climbed the Mayan Temples in Cozumel and Belize, and I've witnessed firsthand what their cultures embraced. The temples (and I'm told the pyramids) all point *up* to something!

Transcendence is not a common word in our jargon today, even within our churches, but we should add it to our faith lexicon. But, before we press on and discover more about its meaning and implications in society and our personal lives, let me challenge you with two life perspective questions.

---

61 MacDonald, *Vertical Church*, 42.

First, as you read the daily newspaper, watch the evening news, observe the trends in our schools, plug in to social media, observe the teen suicide rate, dig in to the political scene, and reckon with the opioid crisis, are you confidently upbeat about what you see, hear, and read?

And secondly, would you say society is flourishing and moving in a united, noble, and God-honoring direction, or are we flying into a mountain?

You decide.

A Short Course in Rationalism, Self-Actualization, and Transcendence

Why should you even care about the philosophic bent of rationalism, self-actualization, and the notion of transcendence? For one reason only. Understanding the implications of rationalism and self-actualization might markedly alter your worldview and perhaps create a "come to your senses" moment for you or someone you care for deeply.

Beyond that, perhaps the topics will inspire some lively debate around the family dinner table and give you a chance to weigh in with truth against the incessant drumbeat of today's culture. You may also discover, as you heighten your awareness of rationalism and self-actualization, that their subtle (and sometimes in-your-face) messaging invades nearly every facet of daily life. The kudzu of this way of thinking is wrapped around educational norms, social media platforms, advertising themes, television programming, pop music melodies, and political discourse at Starbucks.

Let's wade into the deeper water.

Rationalism is a doctrine of belief that rests on the pillars of human reason and intellect, scientific logic, and self-evident propositions. It's Aristotelian thought! For example, we know and observe that bricks fall down, not up. We call that gravity. Yet, as magnificently self-evident as God makes himself in the universe and on our pea-sized planet, a dyed-in-the-wool rationalist can't accept a

God-ordained creation reality because the premise has gaps of reason that can't be pragmatically bridged. Rationalism leaves little space for mystery. What can't be known today (or ever) is labeled *luck* or *happenstance* and left to another generation of smarter people and artificial intelligence to be reasoned out.

I once thought rationalism was the default position of uninformed skeptics. I've since learned it is commonly just the opposite. There is more resistance to faith in the higher circles of learning because there, mystery is the enemy. So, if you sit down with family and watch a recent National Geographic special about the origin of the universe (which Jan and I recently did), you'll see all the mystery of creation distilled to the lowest common denominator of silliness. You'll hear that "seven *lucky* factors"—I kid you not—somehow made our planet hospitable in the Goldilocks zone between Venus and Mars. And in that fortuitous place where the earth's porridge is not too hot but not too cold for human existence, a single-cell amoeba in the slime of a swamp became our ancient ancestor.

On a spiritual level, I'll never prove to my rationalist friends that God exists or that they have a desperate need for him (only God's Spirit can do that). The best I can do is hold up a mirror to my own life and confess, like John Newton, "I once was blind and lost, but now I'm found and can see." Therein, I believe, is enough pragmatic evidence to sway any wavering rationalist to faith.

Self-actualization is rationalism's kissing cousin. It is a philosophy of life (and motivation) based on the belief that fulfillment can best be reached through human ingenuity, initiative, creativity, brain power, independence, and hard work. Each is an outstanding human attribute, but in a self-actualizing framework, there's no divine Giver of those gifts. I find it interesting (and somewhat convicting) that even at the first level of Maslow's pyramid, food, clothing, and shelter in excess or extravagance tend to move human nature's needle toward pride and self-actualization. How quickly we discount the source.

At their core, self-actualizers deny or ignore the ruah of eternity buried in their souls. Consequently, they are particularly vulnerable to shipwrecks on the painful shoals of life experience. When they're upside down in the churning surf, as we all are in some stages of life, many don't know which direction to swim—or toward whom.

God, of course, knows this perfectly well. As he did with the prodigal son, he rescues many self-actualizers from themselves by sovereignly dipping them into painful circumstances beyond anything they can endure without his help. Some in those circumstances come home and bury their faces in their Father's chest. Others will take darker paths to agnosticism or atheism. Or they may, like the man in grief counseling, tilt to bitterness.

Taken at face value, some principles of self-actualization make a lot of sense. To some degree, we're all self-actualizers, and the American ethic of independence, entrepreneurship, and personal freedom adds no small contribution to that bent. Yes, there are demands in life and life purpose which we should *actualize*—that is, bring to certainty, fruition, and full bloom. But the rub comes when we believe the pinnacle of life purpose is achieved by self-actualizing our goals and aspirations and shoving God's Spirit into the margins of life. Self-knowledge is important and provides valuable insights into how God has wired us, but self-actualization breeds an inflated view of human capacity—and a lack of awe at what God's transcendent power can do.

One self-actualizing blogger I read went so far as to pin his desperate human condition on God himself. "He goes out and creates faulty humans and then blames us for his own mistakes. He's a pretty poor excuse for a supreme being." If I was jogging with this fellow and saw lightning on the horizon, I'd let him run a few steps ahead.

Transcendence is the fraternal twin of eternity. She lives apart from rationalists and self-actualizers, but she is often a misunderstood player. For example, if you go to Sedona, Arizona, as Jan and I did one weekend, you're likely to find people seeking a *transcendent* experience in the multicolored sandstone architecture of the mountains. They're seeking a higher power in a desert "vortex," some mystical and magical location that allegedly exudes transcendent vibes.

"Are you with the group going to the vortex?" asked the friendly woman in the hotel gift shop.

Chuckling, I said, "No, ma'am, I find all the higher power I need in Jesus."

The woman's eyes quickly darted around the shop, and then she whispered, "You know, I do too. But so many people come here looking for something they're not going to find in the desert. I just hope God speaks to them out there. Why do people seek meaning in created things rather than their Creator?"

Good question. I would have loved to have chatted more with her, but other customers needed help with vortex maps and meditation trinkets. Here's what A. W. Tozer says about a "higher power" in *Knowledge of the Holy*. "We must not think of God as highest in an ascending order of beings starting with the single cell, then the fish, the bird, the animal, then man and angels and cherubs and God... This would be to grant God eminence or even preeminence, but that is not enough. We must grant God *transcendence* in the fullest meaning of that word. He's wholly other. He breaks all the categories of being and knowing."[62]

I find a lot comfort in Tozer's wisdom, because when my battery of life runs low or my circumstances overwhelm me, I want to know Someone Else has the power to get me through life. Speaking to our human limitations, Oswald Chambers, in his signature bluntness, adds this: "I cannot save and sanctify myself: I cannot make atonement for sin; I cannot redeem the world; I cannot right what is wrong, purify what is impure, or make holy what is unholy. That is all the sovereign work of God."[63] Amen!

A short course in anything should have a few teachings and learning objectives. Otherwise, it's much ado about nothing. Here's a short collection of homecoming truths you can use to debate rationalism, self-actualization, and God's "wholly other" transcendent nature around the dinner table.

- The object of our focus and hope (ourselves, our intellect, or a transcendent God) will eventually dominate our lives. It will ultimately determine *who* we pin our hopes on.

---

62 MacDonald, *Vertical Church*, 48.
63 Chambers, *My Utmost for His Highest*, October 9.

- When we've lost everything, as did the prodigal son, we're often in the best position to find Someone we truly need.

- "It's in our posture of vulnerability and genuine desire that God reveals Himself," says Cameron Strang. "It's there we know He's real… and that we'll never have it all figured out."[64]

- God's transcendence points us to himself. But don't dilly-dally too long without naming him. Come to know the undeniable truth of the God who created the universe, gave us his Son in Christ, and his Spirit to sustain us in life. That will free you from yourself, just like it did for the prodigal.

The Siren Song of Our Culture

A siren jolts our senses, demands our attention, and often sends chills up our spine. If we're driving, we instantly lock our eyes on the approaching emergency vehicle or zero-in on the rearview mirror and scan for red or blue lights.

A *siren* and a *siren song*, however, had a very different and rather bizarre context if you sailed the oceans of the world a few hundred years ago. The mythical sirens back then were provocative and captivating mermaids who lured sailors into the sea with a seductive song and promise of sensual fulfillment. Johnny Depp, as Captain Sparrow, and the bottle-of-rum boys encountered them in the *Pirates of the Caribbean* series. A siren's song was deceptive and deadly. Once the sirens had you in their clutches, you were a dead man. The mermaids were vicious, bloodthirsty creatures bent on evil.

There are some stunning parallels between the ancient siren call of the sea and its modern cultural equivalent. "Come to me," sing the sirens of today. "I'll give you instant gratification, sensual pleasure, and freedom from your constraints." That menu offers everything you want, of course, but nothing you need. It's not unlike what the prodigal son was seeking in a distant land.

---

64 Cameron Strang, "Planning the Unplanned," *Relevant*, January–February 2018, 12.

Today's sirens appeal to the most vulnerable dimension of our existence, mankind's raw human nature and spiritual arrogance. Within that nature lives our pride, independence, rugged pioneering spirit, adoration of heroes, and our inclination to stiff-arm God if he limits our options.

Speaking to our penchant for spiritual smugness before God, Larry Crabb adds an important note. "Nothing more closely masquerades as true [spiritual] vitality than arrogance, and arrogance keeps us from giving ourselves to God in desperate, grateful humility."[65] No doubt, that's why God hates human pride and arrogance. They perpetuate humanity's real issue, the surrender of our will to a transcendent God.

Think about it. Nike's "Just Do It" swoosh is much more than a trendy advertising theme. It's a cultural siren that glorifies limitless boundaries. Not to be upstaged by Americans in trendy running shoes, a French perfume manufacturer bleeps its own siren song: "La vie est plus belle quand on l'ecrit soi'-meme." (Life is best played by your own script).[66] Really?

Our human tendency to suppress truth ebbs and flows with time, but it remains a centerpiece of human existence. The 2016–2017 Bible Study Fellowship's (BSF) worldwide study of the Gospel of John focused on three major themes: Christ Revealed as Eternal God (John 1:1–5), Christ Rejected by the Majority (John 1:6–11), and Christ Received by the Minority (John 1:12–18).[67] The Gospel of John, per scholarly estimates, was written about AD 85–90. In one sense, not much has changed. But in another, our world society has steadily crept toward a level of spiritual arrogance never experienced in history.

From his nineteenth century pulpit, Charles Spurgeon issued his own warning. "The world declares, 'Sure, be spiritual by all means, but don't deny yourself a little worldly fun now and then. After all,

---

65 Crabb, *Finding God*, 88.
66 Guinness, *The Call*, 21.
67 Bible Study Fellowship, "The Prologue: John 1:1–18," BSF Lesson 1- Notes, p.1–4.

what's the point of criticizing something when it is so fashionable and everybody is doing it.'"[68]

"The Siren Song of the Culture" would make a great book title. I'd love to research and write it. But until I do—or someone else does—permit me to leave you with a few cautionary thoughts.

There are many rationalists and self-actualizing flag bearers from the past whose influence still echo in our culture. That's to be expected. But if your kids come home from school with a skewed interest in Friedrich Nietzsche's "God is dead!" mantra, take notice. Nietzsche was a binary thinker. In his math, mankind has only two choices, "Obey yourself... or be commanded."[69] Our society, schools, and colleges are tilting more every day toward choice number one, because if you're led to believe God is dead (or irrelevant in your life), there's no reason to obey commands from a higher Authority.

Rene Descartes is another cultural warrior of the past who is enjoying a present-day renaissance in our schools and colleges. His self-actualizing chant, "I think; therefore, I am," is trumpeted to a new generation of young people, encouraging them to rely solely upon themselves without any spiritual compass in their life. Look around; what is Descartes's message producing?

Finally, be wary if you find your high-school sons or daughters are overly eager to recite the central verse in Richard Henley's *Invictus:* "I am the captain of my soul." Allow their me-centered enthusiasm to prompt you to ask a few questions about their homework assignment—and perhaps to step into their lives before they become victims of the sirens of their time.

A Word on Secular*ism*

It's not possible to talk about the siren song of the culture and ignore the impact of our secular society. A secular society separates religious affairs from civic or public matters. In one sense, we should celebrate

---

68 Reimann, *Morning by Morning,* Day 179.
69 Guinness, *The Call,* 22.

that, because over the centuries, every time government gets into the business of churches—or churches into the business of governments'—it turns out to be an unholy mess.

Secular*ism*, however, over the last thirty to forty years, has cast a wider and troubling net. Its belligerent proponents now pursue an aggressive agenda to marginalize faith in all forms; it's an -*ism* gone awry. Secularism has morphed from the maintenance of healthy civic-religious guardrails to an edgy post-theism platform that attacks God as a tired and outdated idea. It largely categorizes faith-based people as Neanderthals. Aggressive secularism embraces antireligion and antifaith rhetoric and mocks the moral conviction embedded in traditional Judeo-Christian ideals.

Certainly, one of the crowning victories of secularism is its reengineering of the word *tolerance*. For eons, tolerance has stood for a willingness to coexist with opinions or behaviors that one may not necessarily agree with. But today, if you don't affirm and applaud a lifestyle or set of values that don't align with your beliefs, secularism's henchmen will quickly halt the conversation by pinning a label on you. You might be called a religious fanatic, bigot, dogmatist, or hypocrite. The list continues to grow. No longer can faith-based advocates say, "I respect your opinion and even your free choice to go in that direction, but I don't agree with it." If you go that route, you will be -*ismed* out of relevance and made to look reactionary.

The impact of rampant secularism on younger faith-professing adolescents is profound. They are hammered in their schools, civic organizations, and recreational programs with secularism's agenda and bullied as weird ducks when they resist and defend themselves. In one sense, I'm concerned about the future of my grandchildren as they mature in the crescendo of our culture's siren song. But in a greater sense, I'm confident in my sons' and daughters' parenting skills as they equip their kids with a robust faith in God.

As a nation and a people who claim civility and compassion as core values, we seem to have lost our way and forfeited much of our social decorum and foundational faith. No, we were never founded as a strictly Christian nation, but we were imbued with godly values. I don't own a halo, but for twenty years, a Post-it note on the back page of my Bible has helped calibrate my attitude. "Nothing taken for granted, everything received with gratitude, everything passed on with grace."

That wisdom is credited to G. K. Chesterton, a nineteenth-century British writer and poet. I find it much more inspiring than the words of television's foul-mouthed Bart Simpson. When asked to say grace at dinner, he sneers and says, "Dear God, we pay for all this ourselves. So thanks for nothing."[70]

Looking Forward: Coming Home to Truth

I said earlier that we're all self-actualizers to some degree. We also possess some residual genes of the prodigal son. Who doesn't like going their own way on occasion? For many of us, however, coming home to transcendent truth and resisting the siren song of the culture will be a lifelong battle.

Second Corinthians 10:3–4 tells us explicitly that God's people are on a cultural wartime footing. "For though we live in the world, we do not wage war as the world does. The weapons we fight with are not weapons of this world. On the contrary, they have divine power to demolish strongholds." No, we're not at war with those who disagree with us or even those who attack our faith. Rather, the battle is a deeply personal one. It's fought in the hidden places of our hearts and minds that give shelter to habits and behaviors that align with the culture's siren song. The battle rages in the strongholds of our human nature that oppose God's truth.

If you haven't engaged with the God of the universe, the wisdom in Second Corinthians chapter 10 won't help you much, because you possess only the "weapons of this world" and not spiritual weapons with divine power. Therefore, you're at great risk of defeat in the most important battle you will ever fight, the natural-versus-spiritual battleground of life, the battle cry that routs the seductive siren song of the culture and sets you on a pathway that honors God.

---

70 Guinness, *The Call*, 208.

Speaking to the power of God's Spirit, Paul says this: "We demolish arguments and every pretention that sets itself up against the knowledge of God, and we take captive every thought and make it obedient to Christ" (2 Cor. 10:5). You will never find that in a desert vortex; it's only possible in the divine power of "we" that Paul speaks to.

There, strongholds are defeated and a homecoming to truth begins. Paul goes on to celebrate the victory. "In all these things we are more than conquerors... For I am convinced that neither death nor life... neither the present nor the future... nor anything else in creation, will be able to separate us from the love of God that is in Christ Jesus our Lord" (Rom. 8:37–39).

So, if you're looking forward to the joy of coming home to truth in any dimension of your life, reach beyond yourself and the siren song of the culture. God will grab your hand—at any time, in any circumstance—just as the prophet Isaiah described twenty-six centuries ago. "For I am the LORD, your God, who takes hold of your right hand and says to you, 'Do not fear, I will help you'" (Isa. 41:13).

Epilogue

House on Fire

"As surely as I live," says the Lord, "every knee will bow
before me: every tongue will confess to God."
—Romans 14:11

A Life in Good Order

On June 12, 2015, Jan and I traveled to NYC for a few days of fun and memories with my Babylon contingent, John Hemendinger, Jimmy Van Bourgondien, and Kenny Torrey. Our wives, of course, always join the entourage but sometimes deny knowing us when the stories get exaggerated and out of hand. John got us a bargain rate at the famous and opulent Waldorf Astoria—$180 a night! When I checked in, the clerk asked if I was part of the General Electric party under the name of Hemendinger.

"Well, yes and no, ma'am," I answered. "Mr. Hemendinger made the reservations, but I don't know anything about an affiliation with GE."

"No problem, sir. Enjoy your stay," she said, handing me the key.

Later that evening, I approached my friend of fifty-plus years, "John, what's the story on the GE rate? You never worked a day in your life for GE!"

"Well, that's true," he said, "but they offer the best nightly rate!" At that point, I just quit asking questions. I didn't want to know any more.

Shortly after checking in, Jan and I walked two blocks east to Third Avenue and found a trendy Italian restaurant to have lunch. We grabbed an outside table opposite one of NYC's glass and steel architectural miracles. This one housed the headquarters of beauty products producer Avon, Inc.

"Do you smell smoke?" Jan asked.

"Yeah, a hint of it," I replied, more interested in my mozzarella and tomato appetizer. But as my eyes scanned the complex across the street, I could see large numbers of people on the second and third floors moving hurriedly away from their desks toward the exit signs that were clearly visible from our side of the street.

Within minutes, smoke started to billow from the back side of the complex, and I could see that people inside the building were becoming increasingly agitated. Then the sirens started to wail, and in a short NYC minute, three fire trucks converged on the scene. I got up from lunch and made my way to the front of Wollensky's Grill on Forty-Ninth Street to watch the show. Ladders from the fire trucks were quickly launched to upper floors of the building. Some NYC firemen, in all their firefighting regalia, courageously attacked the blaze while others helped the building occupants to safe ground.

And then my eyes were drawn to something that riveted my attention. Emblazoned on the side of the fire truck nearest to me was this: "In Memory of Capt. William F. Burks Jr. 9-11-01." I approached the truck and engaged the fireman tending to the hoses. "Did you know Captain Burks?" I asked him, pointing to the memorial crest.

"No, I didn't," he said. "Burks was before my time, but we lost a lot of good men that day. Look," he said, pointing to another nearby fire truck. "Their names are listed there. Sometimes when you go into a burning building, you don't know if you're gonna get out, so you better have your life in good order."

In Memoriam—Some Don't Make It Out!

Everyone safely exited the Avon building that afternoon, and the fire in the adjoining restaurant was snuffed out. But fourteen years earlier on September 11, as we all know, the story was disturbingly different and chaotic. Firemen went into the World Trade Center, and many didn't come out… and office workers jumped to their death from high above the street rather than submit to the tortuous flames that would have enveloped them.

Is It Well with Your Soul?

While on tour in Israel two years later, we enjoyed a farewell dinner at the iconic American Colony Hotel in Jerusalem. Originally an Ottoman palace, the American Colony has stood in East Jerusalem for over one hundred years. Even today, the hotel entertains heads of state from around the world. Lawrence of Arabia, Winston Churchill, Mikhail Gorbachev, and Tony Blair have been some of its distinguished guests.

Exploring the hotel history in the lobby, I happened upon a display case that contains the original handwritten poem "It is Well with My Soul," penned by Horatio Spafford in 1873. After nearly 150 years, the poem is barely readable, but it's nonetheless authentic. Some years after Spafford wrote it, the poem was put to music by the famous composer Phillip Bliss. The popular hymn is still sung today in churches around the world.

When Spafford wrote the poem, he had lost nearly everything he valued in life—his only son to illness, his business holdings in the Great Chicago Fire of 1871, and his four daughters to a shipping disaster in the Atlantic Ocean. Yet, miraculously, it was well with his soul. That should make one think: what does it take for it to be well with our souls?

I can't fathom the magnitude of Spafford's losses—who can? But when I carefully probe the verses of his poem and not just mindlessly hum the tune of "It Is Well with My Soul," I better understand the depth of Spafford's faith. It rests on the rock-solid foundation of biblical truth. If you examine those truths more deeply, here's what you'll find. I hope you'll ponder it well.

Let's start with *faith*. Hebrews 11:1 tells us that "faith is being sure of what we hope for and certain of what we do not see." Not long after his catastrophic loss, Spafford sailed over the precise latitude and longitude in the Atlantic Ocean where his four daughters had perished. In faith and hope, what was he sure of? And though he could not see it, what was the certainty that he clung to in that devastating reality? If it is to be well with our souls, we need to answer those two questions in our hearts and minds. Let's follow Spafford's thoughts.

> When sorrows like sea billows roll;
> Whatever my lot, Thou has taught me to say,
> It is well, it is well, with my soul.[71]

---

71 I'm taking the verses of *It is Well with My Soul* from a bookmark mailed to me in early 2018 by The Navigators, a ministry organization that has a special heart for American military men and women. The original in the American Colony Hotel was not sufficiently legible to quote.

Spafford apparently had assurance and certainty in what he had been taught—a foundation of faith established well before the catastrophic events that shook his life. Now, in the gale of the current storm, what God had "taught" him to say would be applied in faith to another devastating reality. Jesus's promise—we've encountered it before—no doubt buoyed Spafford's spirit, "In this world you will have trouble. But take heart! I have overcome the world" (John 16:33).

We know, too, that Spafford was certain of his salvation in Christ. His certainty begs the same question for each of us. What is your certainty?

> My sin, not in part but the whole,
> Is nailed to the cross, and I bear it no more,
> Praise the Lord, praise the Lord, O my soul!

Romans 10:9 tells us that when you "confess with your mouth, 'Jesus is Lord' and believe in your heart that God raised him from the dead, you will be saved." That's more powerful certainty and truth! But what exactly does "saved" mean? Consider this:

When you and I profess, "Jesus is Lord" (no matter how we say it), we are acknowledging that in our own strength—and with *all* the dedicated resolve we could ever muster—we're still utterly unable to present ourselves as perfect before the Holy God of the universe. In fact, we're confessing that all the misdeeds and acts of nastiness and corruption that have—and ever will—find their way into our lives have been absorbed by Christ's death on the Cross. "Forgive us our sins…" (Luke 11:4), the words we find in the familiar Lord's Prayer, merge with a faith certainty. Jesus at the cross said, "It is finished" (John 19:30). And with that, he's able to present us as *his* perfect work to our *Abba,* Father.

I often explain the concept of being "saved" with a captivating example. Even with a running start and the lightning speed of Usain Bolt, you will never make the leap across the Grand Canyon. Why even try? Because on the other side sits the sovereign and perfect God of the universe, who invites his children to cross the divide. It's patently impossible to make the grand leap unassisted, but with faith in Christ, you have the certainty that you will float like a butterfly into God's eternal presence on the other side. It's an important truth for all of us, and apparently, Spafford held it close to his heart.

But there's still another hope and certainty of our faith that the poem reveals.

> And Lord, haste the day when my faith shall be sight,
> The clouds be rolled back as a scroll;
> The trump shall resound, and the Lord shall descend.
> Even so, it is well with my soul.

What is Spafford talking about? Ah, nothing less than the assurance and certainty of eternal life in "a new heaven and a new earth" (Rev. 21:1), which is being fashioned in God's timing by the Author of Eternity. There, "the dwelling of God is with men and he will live with them" (Rev. 21:3). Furthermore, heaven's brand of eternity will be a place of peace, not turmoil like we endure here. "He will wipe away every tear from their eyes. There will be no more death or mourning or crying or pain" (Rev. 21:4). Do you desire more great certainty and hope? "He who is seated on the throne said, 'I am making everything new!'" (Rev. 21:5).

Two thousand years ago, Christ came to earth as a servant and savior of mankind (Matt. 20:28; Mark 10:45). But when the heavenly "trump shall resound" (borrowed by Spafford from 1 Thessalonians 4:16), Jesus will return as the triumphant King of kings and Lord of lords (1 Tim. 6:15). In the blink of an eye, evil will be forever eradicated, and Christ will rule in eternity with all his children and followers.

Never forget that heaven is the eternal dwelling place of our *living* Savior. Don't long for billowing clouds and angelic cherubs playing harps. Instead, long for Christ, who will greet you at heaven's gate! Jesus is much more than a ticket *to* eternity; he's the living savior *of* eternity. Sometimes we get that out of order. If you know and believe that, it will be well with your soul.

Let's step back for a moment to the Avon building fire. Is it possible that your house or office could catch fire today and you won't get out? It could happen! But in faith, be assured and certain that if Christ is your savior, your life will be in good order... and it will be well with your soul. You can also take encouragement from Job, the beleaguered Old Testament character. It was just as well with Job's soul as it was with Spafford's. Says Job, "I know that my Redeemer lives, and that in the end he will stand on earth" (Job 19:25).

The *Metamorphyx* Journey—And the Gospel Crescendo

Over the two years that I've labored to write *Metamorphyx*, I've been asked countless times about the book's focus and content. "It's my story of life experience, life change, and my pursuit of life purpose," I tell folks, "but the book also has a Gospel crescendo."

"A *what* crescendo?" is often the response I get, as you might imagine.

The Gospel crescendo is this. For the first thirty years of my life, I knew nothing—or the wrong things—about God's grace, his plan of redemption for me, his Word in the Bible, pursuit of life purpose, or anything related to eternity. But if you follow the chapters of *Metamorphyx* from beginning to end, you will see that God's presence in my life has become increasingly evident; the crescendo of his grace has overwhelmed a pugnacious lad from Babylon. I embraced it, and life changed. Today, it is well with my soul.

So, I ask you, is it well with yours? Do you know in your heart and soul what Horatio Spafford apparently knew, and have you declared it to God?

If not, there will never be a better time than this minute to surrender to the Hound of heaven. Give Christ your heart and soul and let him take you on your own personal *Metamorphyx* journey. It's the most important decision you will ever make. Be forewarned however, it may very well lead you into the most difficult and humbling journey you will ever undertake. But the destination is eternity... and it will be well with your soul.

"'As surely as I live,' says the Lord, 'every knee will bow before me: every tongue will confess to God'" (Rom. 14:11). This is vitally important wisdom for life. Why? Because it prepares us to meet the God of the universe face-to-face. There will be no exceptions; *every* knee will bow before the Lord, one way or the other.

What kneeling posture will you take before God? Will it be in humble submission and worship before the God who sent his Son to reconcile you (and me) to himself? Or will it be one of apprehension because of a decision never made?

"For God so loved the world that he gave his one and only Son, that whoever believes in him shall not perish but have eternal life" (John 3:16). As the fireman at the Avon building reminded me that balmy afternoon in NYC, before you meet the All-Powerful God of the Universe, "have your life in good order."

"May the Lord direct your hearts into God's love and Christ's perseverance" (2 Thess. 3:5).

Bibliography

Barton, Ruth Haley. *Strengthening the Soul of Your Leadership.* Downers Grove: InterVarsity Press, 2008.

Blackaby, Henry T. and Claude V. King. *Experiencing God.* Nashville: Lifeway Press, 1990.

Bonhoeffer, Dietrich. *Life Together.* New York: Harper & Row Publishers, 1954.

Chambers, Oswald. *My Utmost for His Highest.* Nashville: Thomas Nelson, 1992.

Crabb, Larry, Jr. *Finding God.* Grand Rapids: Zondervan Publishing House, 1993.

Dobson, James. *When God Doesn't Make Sense.* Carol Stream: Tyndale Momentum, 1993.

Foster, Richard J. and James Bryan Smith. *Devotional Classics.* New York: HarperCollins Publishers, 1993.

Frankl, Viktor, *Man's Search For Meaning.* New York: Washington Square Press, 1984.

Gibran, Kahlil, *The Prophet.* New York: Alfred A. Knopf, 1966.

Guinness, Os. *The Call.* Nashville: World Publishing: 1998.

C.S. Lewis, *Mere Christianity.* New York: HarperOne, 1952.

_____. *The Problem of Pain.* New York: Macmillan Publishing Company, 1962.

Long, Charles. *Forward Day by Day*, Cincinnati: Forward Movement Publications, November 1993–January 1994.

Mulholland, Robert M. Jr., *Invitation to Journey.* Downers Grove: InterVarsity Press, 1993.

Newton, Carl. "Caroline." Filmed [June 2017]. YouTube video, 20:07. Posted [July 2017]. https://www.youtube.com/watch?-feature=youtu.be&v=bYO_adNuimE&app=desktop.

Newport, Cal. *Deep Work*. New York: Grand Central Publishing, 2016.

Nouwen, Henri J.M. *In the Name of Jesus*. New York: The Crossroad Publishing Company, 1989.

Packer, J.I., *Knowing God*. Downers Grove: InterVarsity Press, 1993.

Piper, John. *Don't Waste Your Life*. Wheaton: Good News Publishers, 2003.

Reimann, Jim. *Morning by Morning*. Grand Rapids: Zondervan, 2008.

Scott, Habeeb. "Tom Brady-There has to be more than this." YouTube video, 1:31. Posted July 2009. https://www.youtube.com/watch?v=4HeLYQaZQW0.

Stanford, Miles J., *The Complete Green Letters*. Grand Rapids: Zondervan, 1983.

Thompson, Francis. *The Hound of Heaven*. New York: Dodd, Mead and Company, 1926

Scripture Index

Introduction

- Romans 12:2
- Acts 9:1
- Isaiah 48:10
- Psalm 119:71
- 1 Timothy 1:18-19

Part I

1 Survival

- Jeremiah 29:11
- Romans 5:1
- Revelation 17:5
- 1 Corinthians 15:10
- 1 Peter 2:17
- Ecclesiastes 5:17
- Isaiah 6:5
- Luke 11:1
- Exodus 20:12

2 Failure to Launch

- Philippians 1:6
- 2 Corinthians 12:9
- Proverbs 16:9

- Isaiah 65:1
- Proverbs 12:15
- Romans 8:28

3 White Hot!

- Isaiah 48:10
- Psalm 22:1
- John 14:6
- John 16:33
- John 9:7
- Luke 6:8-10
- Luke 17:14
- Romans 12:1
- 1 Kings 9:3-15
- Philippians 4:11

4 Fix Your Eyes

- Job 23:10
- Hebrews 12:1
- 2 Corinthians 4:16
- Hebrews 11:1
- Ephesians 2:10
- Job 10:2
- Job 13:15
- Job 23:11
- Job 38:4-5, 12
- Psalm 46:10
- Ecclesiastes 4:12
- Isaiah 61:1
- Exodus 14:11
- Exodus 13-14
- Isaiah 55:9

5 Shepherding Perils

- 1 Peter 5:1-3
- 1 Corinthians 1:10-13
- Romans 12:1

6 A New Country Experience

- Psalm 12:1
- Romans 8:15
- 2 Corinthians 12:9
- John 13:37
- John 18:27
- Psalm 40:2-3
- Isaiah 41:13
- Colossians 2:6-7
- Psalm 121:8
- Romans 8:1
- John 19:30
- 1 Samuel 17:45-46
- Psalm 18:23, 18:2
- Romans 8:6
- 2 Samuel 12:1
- Psalm 51:1
- Proverbs 31:26
- Ephesians 5:25

7 Life Purpose Contemplation

- Psalm 92:12-14
- Matthew 26:39
- Luke 8:31
- John 5:17
- James 2:18, 2:26
- 2 Corinthians 5:20
- 2 Peter 3:18

- Colossians 2:6
- Colossians 1:28
- Ephesians 6:11-12
- 1 Peter 3:15
- Psalm 139:13
- Philippians 3:13-14
- 1 Samuel 13:14
- Acts 13:22
- Psalm 92:12-14
- Psalm 139:14-16

Part II

1 Life Purpose Visioneering

- Joshua 14:12
- Numbers 14:8
- Joshua 14:10-11
- Proverbs 29:18
- Proverbs 16:9
- Matthew 6:19, 21, 33
- 1 Peter 1:13
- 1 Peter 5:8
- John 10:27
- Matthew 6:30
- Colossians 3:23-24
- 1 Peter 5:6-7
- Numbers 11:11
- Job 13:15
- John 16:33
- 1 Peter 4:10
- Philippians 1:6
- Joshua 14:12
- Joshua 14:9
- John 17:4
- John 10:10

- Isaiah 48:2
- Exodus 33;20
- Hebrews 12:29
- 1 Timothy 6:16
- Hebrews 1:3
- Romans 14:8
- 2 Corinthians 5:18-20
- John 3:16, 17

4 Coming Home to Truth

- Luke 15:12-13, 17
- John 1:1-5, 6-11, 12-18
- 2 Corinthians 10:3-4, 5
- Romans 8:37-39
- Isaiah 41:13

Epilogue

- Romans 14:11
- Hebrews 11:1
- John 16:33
- Romans 10:9
- Luke 11:4
- John 19:30
- Revelation 21:1
- Revelation 21:3
- Revelation 21:4
- Revelation 21:5
- Job 19:25
- Romans 14:11
- John 3:16
- 2 Thessalonians 3:5

Author Biography

I kept God at bay for decades, but he burst into my life after the tragic death of my six-year-old daughter, Vanessa. It's bruising theology to believe that a sovereign God loves us so passionately that he's willing to grievously afflict us to get our attention. But with God, there's always a larger life narrative at work.

My life's journey has been exciting, chaotic, filled with great success and liberally seasoned with trials, tragedy, and failure. But God's hand has been in every chapter of it. I grew up in Babylon, NY, a cozy residential village on Long Island's south shore. Babylon is also an inglorious setting in biblical history. My Babylon had its own undertow of social and spiritual upheaval which permeated my adolescence and hardened my adult core—something I would have to deal with in my later years.

In the larger narrative of life, I was an unlikely appointee to the US Naval Academy, a pugnacious wrestler (according to a *Washington Post* writer), commissioned as a US Marine Corps officer after graduation, and won a berth as an alternate on the 1976 Olympic wrestling team. After a stint in corporate America, I cofounded a consulting firm which flourished for twenty-two years. In parallel, I dedicated fifteen years of fulfilling work to the poor in the slums of Nairobi. I then attended Dallas Theological Seminary and served in a pastoral role in a large Atlanta church.

Book writing would follow. Having trouble connecting those dots? That's the story of *Metamorphyx*. Life change is a process, not an event. I've been on the journey for decades. Through the rearview mirror of life, I can clearly see God's hand directing the show. But there were years when I dillydallied in the weeds of life change and life purpose. My pivot point of life, however, is the truth of Romans 12:2, "Do not conform to the patterns of this world, but be transformed by the renewing of your mind." Even more so, that's the story of *Metamorphyx*.

I love investing in people. I feel God's pleasure when I see men and women persevering in the battle of life. My wife, Jan, and I have lived in the northern suburbs of Atlanta for thirty-four years. We have five wonderful children. Vanessa is home with the Lord, but our other children (and two rascally grandchildren) are the joy of our lives.

If I'm not reading more books than I can carry or enjoying time with my family, I'm usually found on the golf range attempting to master my vindictive five iron, taking an ocean-side prayer retreat, or contemplating life alongside the churning rapids of the Chattooga River in North Georgia.

CONNECT ONLINE
www.metamorphyx.com
www.metamorphyx.com/tom-schuler